HOT HANDS, DRAFT HYPE, AND DiMAGGIO'S STREAK

HOT HANDS, DRAFT HYPE, & DiMAGGIO'S STREAK

DEBUNKING AMERICA'S FAVORITE SPORTS MYTHS

Sheldon Hirsch

FOREEDGE

ForeEdge
An imprint of University Press of New England
www.upne.com

Manufactured in the United States of America

Designed by Richard Hendel
Typeset in Arnhem, Aller, and Champion types
by Passumpsic Publishing

For permission to reproduce any of the material in this book,
contact Permissions, University Press of New England,
One Court Street, Suite 250, Lebanon NH 03766;
or visit www.upne.com

Library of Congress Cataloging-in-Publication Data
available upon request

5 4 3 2 1

In memory of

MARTIN HIRSCH:

mathematician, sports fan,

and loving dad

CONTENTS

INTRODUCTION

It was 1962, I was seven years old, and my love affair with sports began. Those were heady times for New York sports fans, with the Mantle/Maris/Ford Yankees regularly going to the World Series and the football Giants reaching the NFL championship game three years running. By the end of the decade, the Amazing Mets, football Jets, and basketball Knicks also had their day; in 1969, all three won their respective titles for a New York Triple Crown.

My dad, a calculus professor, inspired a love of math that manifested in my studying box scores—first thing every morning, every game. My younger brother, Alan, and I habitually played Strat-O-Matic baseball and APBA football board games. I kept score, season standings, and player statistics (calculated with a slide rule), and reported the year-end results in APBA newsletters.

Some early sports memories remain indelible: sitting in a buzzing Dodger Stadium crowd during a summer vacation in 1962, with Maury Wills leading off first base and threatening to steal; Mickey Mantle almost hitting the ball out of Yankee Stadium in 1963; the 1963 Dodgers versus Yankees World Series being piped into classrooms through the PA system (illustrating baseball's grip on America at that time); brooding as Sandy Koufax struck out Yankee after Yankee; Mantle's first-pitch walk-off home run in the 1964 World Series.

In high school, I played baseball and wrestled, and also joined the debate team. My mom coached debate, so I really had no choice, though an inveterate arguer needed little coercion. These interests coalesced later on when I wrote essays that debated sports topics.

After college and medical school, my internship took me to Chicago. Following a thirty-six-hour hospital shift, I sometimes recovered at a White Sox or Bulls game, often buying a cheap seat and walking down to field or court level.

Magic, Kareem, and the most exciting basketball ever played

lured me after medical residency to UCLA for a kidney fellowship selected over other equal or perhaps even more reputable programs. I often took hospital calls from my Los Angeles Lakers season-ticket seat at the "Fabulous Forum." In 1984–85, the Lakers reversed their curse by finally defeating the Celtics for the NBA championship. Nothing in professional sports ever beat that for me.

Eventually, I settled into private practice in nephrology, back on the South Side of Chicago. In the Jordan era, one could no longer walk down to the floor seats at Bulls games, but by now I could afford better seats and continued to go from hospitals to stadiums and sometimes back to the hospital.

Understandably, my sports mania puzzled some of my medical colleagues, but they didn't know that my passion for sports predated my interest in nephrology by twenty years. Nor did they know that I skipped medical school to watch the 1978 Yankees versus Red Sox playoff game and took several days off to attend the 1979 Pirates versus Orioles World Series in Baltimore.

Watching games may have occasionally trumped medical studies, but the academic training influenced my thinking about sports and more. I learned from my scientific research and immersion in clinical medicine the basics of statistics, the weaknesses of various forms of evidence, and about causation, unintended consequences, chaos theory, and how difficult it is to understand complicated systems. I also learned how to apply Occam's razor and Bayes's theorem and about cognitive traps like anchoring and availability.

The scientific and medical papers I wrote were routinely returned for revision before subsequent publication. Every argument had to be supported by the evidence and express no more confidence than the evidence allowed. Reviewers did not tolerate exaggeration, and contrary evidence could not be ignored.

After years of medical writing, I turned my attention back to my first love, sports. Science teaches both skepticism and analytic rigor; from that perspective, I realized that much of what many people (including myself) thought about sports stood on shaky ground. Alan and I cowrote a book, *The Beauty of Short Hops: How Chance and Circumstance Confound the Moneyball Approach to Baseball* (McFarland and Company, 2011) that exposed myths about *Moneyball* and challenged apparent excesses of the sabermetrics approach. As a regular contributor to RealClearSports.com I questioned more so-called truths about baseball and the conventional wisdom in other sports. Many of those essays inspired this book.

I ask, for example, why so many exalt Joe DiMaggio's 56-game hitting streak above other long consecutive-game streaks, sequences of great games, and individual accomplishments? What do "consecutive" and "consistency" mean, and how do they apply to DiMaggio's streak? Should hitting in 56 consecutive games be viewed so differently than hitting in 55 out of 56 games?

Our love of heroes (like DiMaggio) commonly causes us to ignore contrary evidence. Many observers minimized LeBron James's poor shooting in the 2015 NBA Finals in the interests of the comforting story that his was the greatest postseason performance ever. Basketball coaches ask star players to take often failing "hero shots" in the last seconds, rather than continue the more successful team approach.

Frequently, story lines persist for no reason other than people seem wedded to them. Babe Ruth's World Series–ending failed steal remains in baseball lore as a huge blunder even though both basic math and intuition support the attempt. Many claim that the AAU system and the "one-and-done" rule are killing NBA basketball even as NBA shooting keeps improving and American players dominate foreigners in international competition. The three-point shot is thought of as a must-have in the current NBA, even though data say otherwise. We tend to see what we believe.

Our fondness for simple and easy explanations leads many to say that you can't win an NBA championship with a shoot-first point guard or without a superstar. Many claim that small ball is the best way to play basketball but not baseball, that all players tainted by steroid allegations should be kept out of baseball's Hall of Fame, that correct pitching mechanics will end the Tommy John surgery epidemic. None of these commonly held beliefs pass analytic muster.

My questioning perspective led to some odd thoughts, such as touchdowns should be valued at seven points and that Kurt Vonnegut would have disapproved of Miami Heat fans booing LeBron's return to Miami as a Cavalier. Other topics included Adrian Peterson's marijuana charge, Bob Costas's NFL gun concerns, and Chris Paul calling out a female referee.

I argue for alternatives to the mainstream thinking in these areas. Hopefully, these analyses provide "unconventional wisdom." Certainly, the "unconventional" part should not surprise, coming from someone who postponed his wedding to avoid conflict with the NBA Finals. That worked out fine; it may have been the most unconventional wisdom of all.

1. BASEBALL

1 MYTHS

DiMaggio's Hitting Streak Is Overrated

Joe DiMaggio's 56-game hitting streak is widely considered in the realm of epic sports feats that includes Wilt Chamberlain's 100-point game, Bob Beamon's 29-feet-2-inch broad jump, Wayne Gretzky's 92-goal season, and the like. Some sports fans even regard it as the greatest achievement in sports history.

As sacrilegious as this may seem, The Streak does not deserve that sort of veneration. DiMaggio certainly had a terrific 56-game run in 1941 with a .408 batting average and fifteen home runs. However, several players out-hit DiMaggio over 56-game sequences: Rogers Hornsby batted .476 over 56 games in 1924; George Brett hit .480 over 56 games in 1980; and, notably, over the exact time period of DiMaggio's streak, Ted Williams (in 55 games) hit .412 with more than twice as many walks and a higher on-base plus slugging percentage.

History celebrates DiMaggio's 56 games over the superior feats of Hornsby, Brett, and Williams solely by virtue of the consecutive-game hitting. However, The Streak is based on a contrived form of consecutiveness—"at least one hit in every game"—in which the hits are unrelated, separated from each other by many at bats; that is to say, they have zero interactive value. This oxymoronic "interrupted consecutiveness" provides none of the benefit of true consecutiveness, as demonstrated by, for example, successive hits in an inning leading to runs, or planks laid in a row constructing a bridge.

Thus, from the Yankees' perspective, the whole of The Streak was the sum of the many base hits, and nothing more. Hitting safely in all 56 games differed from 55 of 56 by merely one hit in 223 at bats. If

DiMaggio had one hitless game partway through the sequence (leaving consecutive streaks of 28 and 27 games, for example), but had two more hits or one more home run in any other game, the hypothetical non-consecutive 56-game sequence would have helped his team more than the actual 56-consecutive-game hitting streak.[1]

Furthermore, the so-called consecutiveness does not confer the unparalleled consistency that many Streak fans claim. The alleged consistency is also contrived and overstated.

The general understanding of consistency is to obtain similar results over and over again. Streak fans claim consistency by noting that DiMaggio got at least one hit 56 games in a row. However, this is an artificial formulation created by eliminating a single possible result from each game—zero hits for a batter—without leaving a narrow range of allowable performances. Consistency should not be inferred from a batter getting anywhere in the wide range of one to four (or even more) hits in a game. As noted, consistency requires similar results over and over; for example, mostly one hit in a game, and occasionally zero or two.

Another example can illustrate: a grade of B on 56 consecutive exams would clearly demonstrate consistency. A grade of B or B+ on 56 consecutive exams might also be considered consistent. However, a student who received grades scattered from A+ to D− on 56 consecutive tests could say he got "at least a D− on every test" or "no F on any test" but would not be considered consistent. He does not demonstrate the spirit of consistency, as it is commonly understood. (If he wants praise, the student needs better grades.)

We can quantify DiMaggio's consistency in The Streak with the standard deviation (that is, the amount of variation) from his average number of hits per game (1.63). The Streak's standard deviation (+/− .93) denotes considerable variation in game-to-game results, similar to that of Williams's performance over the same time period (1.40 +/− 1.05 hits per game). Thus, basic mathematical analysis does not suggest any dramatic consistency in DiMaggio's performance.

Importantly, the reverence for and mania surrounding "56" stands alone among the many long consecutive streaks. For example, Tom Brady came within one foot of throwing a touchdown pass in 53 consecutive games, a shade short of Drew Brees's all-time record of 54. There's no bigger name in the NFL than Brady and no more prominent team than the Patriots, yet the game in which he neared the all-time record drew little attention (imagine the hullabaloo if a baseball player got a base-hit in 54 consecutive games).

There was also little hoopla when Michael Jordan broke Kareem Abdul-Jabbar's record for consecutive games scoring at least ten points, and continued on to 866 in a row. Or when Gretzky scored a point in 51 consecutive games. Returning to baseball, Orel Hershiser's 59 consecutive scoreless innings in 1988 receives substantially less attention than DiMaggio's streak. The record for most consecutive games getting on base (held by Ted Williams with 84 in 1949) —a streak similar in nature and value to "56"—remains largely unknown. This was understandable in 1949, before the modern emphasis given to on-base percentage (OBP), but it is noteworthy that few noticed when Orlando Cabrera reached base safely in 63 consecutive games in 2006, and Mike Trout in 46 games in 2013.

The absence of great fanfare around the other long consecutive streaks suggests that fans and media intuit the limitations of these streaks. They regard them as excellent performances based on the usual criteria, without undue exaltation.

Why the exception for DiMaggio?

The major reason advanced to separate DiMaggio's streak from other (far less exalted) long consecutive streaks is that his was the least likely to occur; therefore, the most difficult. One can compare the relative odds of different streaks occurring based on the likelihood of each specific result in a game, and the length of the streak (that is, a fraction less than one multiplied to the 56th, 59th, 84th, or 866th power). Several calculations of this sort are possible, yielding different results, but no matter how this type of analysis plays out, it surely misses the point: *All* of these long streaks have a near infinitesimal chance (typically 1 in ~10 or 100 million or even less) of actually occurring.

For all practical purposes, the results are the same: You should not make grandiose claims about the difference in sizes of amoebas. Thus, DiMaggio's streak did not demonstrate unusual consistency, was consecutive only in a contrived, non-beneficial manner, and was not appreciably more difficult than other long consecutive streaks.

Then why the mania?

Perhaps we should look to the context of The Streak and speculate. By 1941 DiMaggio was an MVP winner, admired around the country as the Yankee Clipper, a rags-to-riches son of an immigrant fisherman. At that time baseball reigned in American culture. We are always partial to finding heroes, and America in 1941 may have been particularly ready for one. The Depression was not far in the rearview mirror. World War II raged, Hitler was advancing; six days after DiMaggio's streak started, a German U-boat sunk a United States ship for the first time. Perhaps the situation was ripe for defining a superhero: the right player in the right sport at the right time.

Then the superhero married Marilyn Monroe, and he was celebrated in song ("Where have you gone Joe DiMaggio?"), literature ("the Great DiMaggio" of Hemingway's *The Old Man and the Sea*), and television ("Mister Coffee"). As the DiMaggio aura blossomed, "56" became fixed in the American psyche and grew to transcend sports: the late Harvard professor Stephen Jay Gould called it "the finest of legitimate legends because it embodies the essence of the battle that truly defines our lives . . . he cheated death."

Wow. The Streak reduces even the smartest among us to schmaltz.

More Ado about Zero

DiMaggio's streak is the most well known but not the only example of baseball treating zero as hugely different from one.[2]

Two prominent instances of excessive focus on zero took place in the 2015 season. The first was when pitcher Jon Lester finally threw to first base to hold a baserunner (ending a "zero-throwing-over" streak); the second, when Max Scherzer hit batter Jose Tabata with two outs in the ninth inning, ending his perfect game (zero baserunners allowed) aspirations.

Lester averaged about eighty pickoff throws a year from 2009 to 2011. The lefty precipitously dropped to five and six throws in 2012 and 2013, respectively, but no one seemed to notice until Lester attempted zero in the entire 2014 season. Jon Roegele tweeted about that before the 2014 Oakland versus Kansas City wild-card game. After Lester gave up three stolen bases on Opening Day in 2015, his "zero throws in an entire season" stoked national attention.

The failure to throw over to hold runners close hadn't hurt Lester. He allowed only sixteen stolen bases from more than 200 base runners in 2014, at a success rate similar to the league average. And he made the All-Star team, finishing with a 16–11 record and an admirable 2.46 ERA.

However, the publicity given to his Steve Blass–like angst about throwing to first discomfited him. (Blass was a Pittsburgh Pirate pitcher who won nineteen games in 1972, then abruptly developed a psychological inability—the yips—to control his pitches.) In Lester's first game after the national head-scratching began, having not thrown to first in sixty-six games and almost 400 innings, he twice threw over to hold a runner. His first throw pulled the first baseman several feet off the bag. His second throw sailed over the first basemen's head into right field, illustrating why he'd become averse to throwing to first.

After Lester ended the zero streak with those throws, he returned to his previous modus operandi, yet media interest abruptly ceased. Two throws satisfied everyone (even one would have sufficed). The transient fascination with Lester's phobia had been much ado about zero.[3]

Scherzer's zero streak involved something far more substantial than pickoff attempts: not allowing any baserunners in a game. Still, the postgame media focus on whether umpire Mike Muchlinski should have ruled a hit-by-pitch (Tabata did not attempt to avoid the pitch)[4] diverted attention from a more important point: Scherzer pitched the greatest back-to-back games in Major League Baseball history. His near-perfect game followed a one-hit shutout with zero walks and sixteen strikeouts, a dual performance that surpassed even Johnny Vander Meer's successive no-hitters in 1938 (Vander Meer walked eleven batters in the two games).

Several years ago, Bill James devised a "game score" formula for more comprehensive analysis of pitching performances than simply considering hits and runs allowed. Game score also debits pitchers for walks and, most importantly, credits strikeouts more than batted-ball outs, diminishing the impact of defense and luck (where a ball is hit) in pitcher evaluations (see the related discussion in chapter 3, "Did Bad Luck Cost Clayton Kershaw the Cy Young Award?").

By James's criteria, the two greatest nine-inning games ever pitched (Kerry Wood's one-hit, no-walk, twenty-strikeout effort; Clayton Kershaw's no-hit, no-walk, one-error, fifteen-strikeout game) were not perfect games.

In fact, if Scherzer had retired Tabata, the now-perfect game would still have ranked behind his previous game (the imperfect one-hitter with sixteen strikeouts). That's because for the purposes of evaluating pitcher performance, Tabata's at bat was simply one out of twenty-eight in the game, and barely changed Scherzer's evaluation. Actually, it didn't change it at all, since (as an oversight) game score does not debit for hitting batters, but had the hit batsman been treated as equivalent to a walk, Scherzer would have lost only one point from his game score evaluation of 97—a nonstory from the performance standpoint.

Perfect games and other consecutive streaks satisfy our fondness for discrete distinctions (for example, a perfect game versus a non-perfect game, as two completely different entities) and provide an exciting, persistent drumbeat—every pitch potentially ending a perfect-game possibility, every game potentially ending DiMaggio's streak. These make for great dramas, but in terms of evaluating performances, the difference between one hit or baserunner per game and zero is only one.

But the sports world does have a fascination with records and streaks and, in some instances, oddly considers zero as hugely different from one. The media focused on Lester only when his aversion to throwing to first reached a prolonged zero stage. He threw to first solely to end the zero streak and get the media off his back.

That worked for him, but only addressed his less important zero streak: he had zero base hits in thirty-seven career at bats at the time of the streak-breaking pickoff attempt—the worst hitting performance in major-league history. Lester needed some base hits, and not simply to end the streak before the media attention became nettlesome, nor simply to rid himself of the stigma of a zero-hit career à la Gus Triandos's farcical single stolen base in 1958.[5] Lester is now in the National League, batting regularly, and base hits help his team.

Lester ended up having a curious season, with "sixty-six" an oddly prominent component: he not only threw over to first base to end a sixty-six-game no-throw streak but he finally got a base hit, ending his hitless streak at sixty-six career at bats.

It's So Easy to Find a Goat

Baseball does not lack for myths, dating back to the false attribution of its creation to Abner Doubleday. Many myths are attached to Babe Ruth, most famously his "called shot" home run in the 1932 World Series (at the moment in question Ruth almost certainly pointed in the general direction of the St. Louis Cardinals' dugout rather than to center field, where his subsequent home run traveled). There's also the story of Ruth promising and hitting a home run for a hospitalized boy, the tale of his hitting a ball through a pitcher's legs that then went over the center-field fence, claims of preposterously long home runs, and others, each of which fueled his larger-than-life aura.

Myths exaggerate some events in the opposite direction: we create goats as well as heroes.

BABE RUTH DID NOT BLUNDER

Ruth was thrown out attempting to steal second base with two outs in the ninth inning of game seven of the 1926 World Series, making the St. Louis Cardinals World Champions. This constituted one of the strangest endings ever to a World Series game. Ruth is still unfairly maligned for this play.

Yankees general manager Ed Barrow, Cardinals Hall of Fame pitcher Grover Cleveland Alexander and his teammate, legendary second baseman Rogers Hornsby, all called it a dumb play. Ruth succeeded in only about 51 percent of his steal attempts throughout his career and 55 percent (11–20) in 1926. With .315 hitter Bob Meusel at the plate and the great Lou Gehrig on deck, a stolen-base attempt by a subpar base stealer seemed boneheaded.

Thus, the play entered baseball lore as a monumental blunder, described as such in *Rob Neyer's Big Book of Baseball Blunders: A Complete Guide to the Worst Decisions and Stupidest Moments in Baseball History*, in *Yankees Century: 100 Years of New York Yankees Baseball*, in Ruth biographies, and in myriad articles, Internet sites, and more. Sportswriter Allen Barra called it a "reckless and selfish moment . . . a stunt." A Baseballreport.com analysis called it one of the ten worst moments in Yankees history, and even the Babe Ruth Museum website acknowledges it as a blunder.

History is casting judgment based on the result. This is wrong.

Ruth actually faced the ultimate situation favoring a stolen-base attempt: one run down with two outs in the ninth and a great pitcher, Alexander, on the mound at the top of his game (Alexander had easily retired all six batters he faced prior to walking Ruth). This was similar to when Dave Roberts stole second with the Red Sox trailing by one run against Mariano Rivera in the ninth inning of game four in the 2004 ALCS. The prudent strategy in such situations is to play for one run. Under the circumstances, an attempted steal of second makes good sense (even more for a great base stealer like Roberts than for Ruth).

The two most likely (simplified) scenarios by which the Yankees could score one run were as follows:

Successful stolen base + Meusel hits safely

versus

No steal attempt + Meusel hits safely + Gehrig hits safely

This comparison is straightforward: since "Meusel hits safely" is in both scenarios, the difference in the two comes down to the relative odds of "successful stolen base" versus "Gehrig hits safely." As noted, Ruth's stolen-base percentage in 1926 was 55 percent. Gehrig hit .313 that season, and his chance for a base hit was surely even less against Alexander. The percentages (55 percent versus < 31.3 percent) decisively favor the attempted stolen base. A more complicated calculation, including the small likelihoods of walks, infield hits, run-scoring extra-base hits by Meusel, and so on, also favors Ruth's attempt.

Moreover, Ruth may plausibly have believed his chance of success was even better than usual. He noted in his autobiography that he had the element of surprise in his favor; Alexander admitted that he "forgot all about Ruth" on first. The element of surprise is no small thing: It allowed David Ortiz, the Red Sox' lumbering, thirty-seven-year-old slugger, to succeed on all four stolen-base attempts in 2013, two of third base (one of which did not even draw a throw).

Ruth had little time to think everything through, and certainly did not do any mathematical calculations. Most likely, he had an intuitive sense that the situation called for a stolen base and that his chances were good enough to justify the attempt. At any rate, he got it right. Only the result was bad.

History too often relies on results, so Ruth's smart play went down as a blunder. History can be an ass.

GENE MAUCH: NO HARM, NO FOUL

History did not learn from wrongly labeling Babe Ruth a goat in the 1926 World Series; it made a similar mistake with Philadelphia Phillies manager Gene Mauch in 1964.

Mauch's Phillies blew a 6½-game lead with just 12 games left by losing 10 consecutive games, perhaps the worst collapse in baseball history. During that free fall, Mauch pitched star hurlers Jim Bunning and Chris Short twice each on two days' rest, *rather than their usual three days*—they lost all 4 games, and the Phillies lost the pennant. For allegedly panicking, Mauch became known in baseball lore as the goat, the architect of "The Phold." Local sportswriter Frank Fitzgerald recently noted that Mauch's name remains "a sporting obscenity in Philadelphia."

In the 155th game of the season, Mauch bypassed the struggling Art Mahaffey (ERA 4.58) in favor of Short (ERA 2.14)—on two days' rest—in an attempt to reverse the momentum of four consecutive losses and a dwindling lead. Nothing controversial there. The Phillies appeared rattled by the losing streak, and Mauch had ample precedent for using an ace on two days' rest in an important game. Among other examples, Johnny Sain won eight of ten on two days' rest in 1948; his teammate, Warren Spahn, won two of three; Lew Burdette pitched a shutout to win game seven of the 1957 World Series; both Burdette and Spahn threw solid games in the 1958 World Series; Don Drysdale pitched well on short rest three times in 1962, as did Sandy Koufax in a key game down the stretch in 1963. In fact, Short had thrown a ten-strikeout, complete-game victory on the same limited rest three weeks earlier. And he had pitched only 4.2 innings in his previous start.[6]

Not surprisingly, Short pitched well, going 7.1 innings and giving up only two earned runs; the short rest did not hurt him. The Phillies lost in extra innings, but no reason to blame Mauch.

Mahaffey started game 156 and the Phillies lost, dropping their lead to half a game. With first place now at stake, future Hall of Famer Bunning asked to start on two days' rest in game 157, and Mauch granted the request.

He really had no choice. Mauch's other regular starter, Dennis Bennett, had an increasingly painful shoulder and probably would have been placed on the disabled list if Ray Culp's elbow wasn't just as bad; Culp had been bombed for twenty-nine hits and eighteen earned runs in his previous 15 innings. The Phillies' remaining possibility, nineteen-year-old rookie Rick Wise, had gotten one out in his previous two starts combined. Such was the state of the Phillies rotation.

Philadelphia lost their seventh straight, but Mauch still hadn't done anything remotely unusual (given the successful history of aces on two days' rest). That didn't happen until he started Short and Bunning *again* on two days' rest (making three games in seven days for both) in the 158th and 160th games, respectively.

Philadelphia lost game 158 with Short and 159 with Bennett; the injured Bennett (someone had to pitch!) got only four outs, taxing the bullpen. Perhaps Short would have won game 159 on three days' rest. However, moving Short's start up a game allowed Mauch to pitch him on three days' rest in game 161, rather than start Mahaffey, who hadn't won a game in a month. Short pitched superbly in the 161st game, helping Philadelphia to a one-run win; if Mauch cost the Phillies a game by using Short in game 158 (rather than 159), he probably recouped it a few days later.

The 160th game was a must-win: Philadelphia trailed by 1½ games with only three left to play. Mauch went with his ace, Bunning, on two days' rest. Bunning got bombed, and the season was essentially over.

Perhaps Mauch should have opted for Mahaffey in game 160, but that meant starting—in a critical game—a pitcher who had not lasted three innings in eight different starts during the season (including two in September). Further, Mahaffey had pitched an inning in relief in game 159 (when the game was still winnable). Mauch's reluctance to go in that direction seems understandable. Once again, the reality was that a depleted staff gave Mauch no good options.

Baseball media and Phillies fans subsequently went way overboard with their disdain for Mauch. His pitching selections did not blow the Phillies lead, as proffered by the belittling accounts that took hold. By the time he broke new ground—Short, in game 158 —the Phillies were *already one game behind* in the pennant race and had lost 7 in a row, while their rivals were red-hot (the St. Louis Cardinals had won 6 of their last 7 and the Cincinnati Reds 12 of their previous 13). At that point, the Phillies were decided underdogs. Even from the harshest perspective (ignoring the absence of decent alternatives), Mauch's most controversial moves (games 158 and 160) came after his squad had fallen apart and faced a steep uphill climb, evoking "no harm, no foul."

Almost everyone ignored that, as well as the Phillies schedule— they played 31 games in September without a day off, and simply lacked the health and pitching depth needed to deal with a schedule that unforgiving. Four of their six starting pitchers were either injured or ineffective. Further, during the ten losses, they scored only 3.4 runs per game, committed thirteen errors, had four passed balls, ran the bases poorly, and suffered horrific luck.[7] The entire package unraveled, but Mauch went down with virtually all of the blame.

The unfair judgment plagued Mauch for the rest of his life.

BILL BUCKNER HAD PLENTY OF COMPANY

Fast-forward twenty-two years, and media and Red Sox fans mistreated Bill Buckner in similar fashion. Buckner let a routine ground ball hit by the New York Mets' Mookie Wilson go through his legs in the bottom of the tenth inning, allowing the winning run to score in game six of the 1986 World Series. But singling out Buckner as the reason the Red Sox lost the World Series—you'd have thought his error blew a lead, and came in game seven—was as unfair as blaming Mauch alone for the Phillies' demise.

The Red Sox made poor decisions and many bad plays besides

Buckner's error. Manager John McNamara failed to remove Buckner for a defensive replacement. Relief pitcher Calvin Schiraldi blew a 5–3 lead with two outs and nobody on base in the tenth inning; worse yet, he got two strikes on several batters and couldn't put them away. Then Bob Stanley threw a wild pitch (some considered catcher Rich Gedman at fault) that allowed the tying run to score. Following all that, the Red Sox blew a 3–0 lead to lose game seven: starter Bruce Hurst gave up three runs in the bottom of the sixth, Schiraldi yielded three more in the seventh, and three Red Sox hitters left the tying run on second base in the eighth.

And none of that was the worst of it!

According to McNamara, all-time great pitcher Roger Clemens asked out of the potentially World Series–clinching game six with a 3–2 lead after the seventh inning because of a blister. Bob Gibson pitched to exhaustion in winning game seven in 1964; Jack Morris threw a ten-inning shutout to win the 1991 World Series; the Red Sox' own Curt Schilling pitched in game six of the ALCS in 2004 with a sutured ankle tendon (the "bloody sock" game) and Clemens . . . left with a blister.

Clemens, of course, denied McNamara's brutal accusation, claiming that the manager chose to pinch-hit for him in the top of the eighth. But it really doesn't matter. One of them messed up badly and the other should have screamed bloody murder. Clemens should have been out on the mound for the eighth inning.

Nevertheless, Buckner became the scapegoat. Unruly Red Sox fans vilified Buckner and his family to the extent (there were death threats and physical altercations) that he moved out of Massachusetts to Idaho. To many of those fans, it was a just punishment: forty years in the wilderness.

The Red Sox welcomed Buckner back to throw out the first pitch on Opening Day in 2008. He received a warm ovation, but the damage had been done.

Singling out Buckner for blame, as with Mauch, turned a multifaceted collapse into a more satisfying simple story. By explaining the losses as due to one person's failings, Red Sox and Phillies fans avoided the harsher reality that their beloved teams collectively fell apart.

But those distortions came with a price even beyond mangled lore: Bill Buckner and Gene Mauch suffered needlessly.

Are Today's Players Better Athletes Than Ever?

Mythmaking does not limit its scope to events and players of yore: we also exaggerate the deeds of modern players. Many observers tout Yasiel Puig, Mike Trout, Bryce Harper, and some of their peers as a new breed of athlete—bigger, faster, and more powerful than ever before seen in baseball.

Puig hit three triples and a double in one game during the 2014 season, an impressive demonstration of power and speed. In his first 200 games, he hit 31 home runs, stole 18 bases and made numerous terrific throws from the outfield. Though Puig's production declined significantly after his auspicious start, perhaps only Trout and Harper, among current players, rival Puig in overall athletic ability. Nearing the end of his fifth full season, Trout has already hit 163 home runs and stolen 134 bases. Harper hit 42 home runs in 2015, stole 18 bases in his rookie season, and owns a cannon arm.

MICKEY MANTLE, UNSURPASSED

Puig stands 6 feet 3 and weighs 235 pounds; Trout, 6 feet 2 and 230; Harper 6 feet 3 and 215. In comparison, Mickey Mantle, baseball's traditional standard-bearer of combined speed and power,[8] stood 5 feet 11 and weighed 195 pounds.

The modern guys are certainly bigger than Mantle, but faster and more powerful? Not really.

Comparisons of athletes across generations typically rely on subjective recollections. In this case, however, we have data for objective analysis. The data suggest that even sixty years after his prime, Mantle's power and speed combination remains unsurpassed.

With kudos to author Jane Leavy and "homerunology" savants Alan Nathan and Greg Rybarczyk, we can compare Mantle's longest home runs, as an index of baseball power, to Trout's, Harper's, Puig's and those of other sluggers.

In *The Last Boy*, Leavy detailed her dogged investigation of the famous 565-foot tape-measure home run Mantle hit off Chuck Stobbs in 1953. As it turns out, the home run was neither measured with a tape nor 565 feet. But it was monstrous.

On its path out of Griffith Stadium the ball deflected off a sign 460 feet from home plate, about 60 feet high. Fifty-five years later, Donald Dunaway, who retrieved the ball during the game, showed Leavy where he had found it. The ball landed on the rooftop of a house and bounced into the backyard, where it came to rest. Leavy then enlisted physics professor Nathan for the math. Using the distances of the sign and the house from home plate, the height of the roof, and the potential trajectories from the contact point on the sign to the roof, Nathan calculated that unimpeded, Mantle's shot would have traveled at least 538 feet.[9]

Now turn to Rybarczyk, who developed a mathematical model for the aerodynamics of batted balls and calculated the distances of all home runs hit since 2006.[10] He also analyzed previous notable home runs for which the necessary information was available. It appears that few home runs traveled 500 feet. (Per Rybarczyk, Ted Williams hit a 530-foot homer in 1946, and Reggie Jackson hit a wind-aided 539-foot home run in the 1971 All-Star game.) Over the last ten years, only Adam Dunn's 504-foot shot in 2008 reached the milestone. Trout's longest traveled 489 feet, Harper's 481, and Puig's 452.

Mantle's 538-plus footer, like Jackson's, benefitted from a strong tailwind. But the two home runs he hit (May 29, 1956, against Pedro Ramos and May 22, 1963, against Bill Fischer) that struck the façade hanging from the Yankee Stadium roof in right field did not. Both balls hit the façade about 370 feet from home plate, over 100 feet in the air. Rybarczyk calculated the 1963 smash as en route to 503 feet. (Mantle hit another home run off the facade on May 5, 1956, off Ed Burtschy, but that didn't travel quite as far, striking the overhang closer to the 296-foot foul pole.)

Although Yankee Stadium has been renovated and then completely rebuilt, the right-field dimensions did not significantly change. Thus, the façade provides an objective marker by which other sluggers can measure their power against Mantle's. In the fifty-three years and 100,000-plus left-handed at bats since Mantle's third façade shot, no one has hit a ball over the façade; no one has hit the façade; no one has come close to hitting the façade. (Similarly, a seat in Fenway Park, painted red to commemorate the landing spot of Williams's 530-foot blast, remains undisturbed.)

With many years ahead of them, Trout, Harper, and Puig might hit longer home runs than their current bests. But at the rate of one home run barely over 500 feet in the last ten years for all of Major League Baseball, it seems unlikely that any of them (or anyone else) will surpass Mantle.

What about speed? Sportswriter Lou Miller reported in the *Sporting News* in 1952 that he had timed Mantle (on a drag bunt) from the lefty batter's box to first base in 3.1 seconds. Miller also clocked Mantle on other occasions from 3.2 to 3.4, and at 3.5 from the right side. Thus, 3.1 seconds does not appear unusual for Mantle. (Remarkably, these times came after an unreconstructed ACL injury in 1951.)

The fastest times to first base recorded since then belong to Bo Jackson (another all-time great power-plus-speed package) at 3.2 seconds and Deion Sanders and Billy Hamilton (also on a drag bunt) at 3.3. Hamilton had the fastest time in Major League Baseball in 2015 (on another drag bunt) at 3.52. Trout has been hand-timed from the right side at 3.53, though his best time in 2014 by video was 3.97. A hand-timer clocked Puig in Double-A ball at 4.2.

These are not exactly comparable measurements. Some of the times were obtained by hand, others through video, and no one used a starting block, a starter's gun, or a fixed distance. But even if Miller erred by ten feet on the 3.1 time, Mantle would have clocked 3.4 to 3.5 (as he did on other occasions), still among the fastest times to first base ever recorded.

Mantle hit into five or fewer double plays each of his first seven years—another indication of his terrific speed. Batting lefty, he hit into one double play for every 117 of his batted balls in play over this time period, which compares favorably with lefty-hitting speedsters Ichiro, Lou Brock, and Joe Morgan (each of whom averaged a double-play ball in fewer than 100 batted balls in play), as well as Harper (1 every 37). From the right side, Mantle's double play rate on batted balls in play (1 in 75) was far superior to that of contemporary sluggers Willie Mays (1 every 37) and Hank Aaron (1 every 31) for their first seven years, in addition to Trout and Puig (both around 1 every 50).

These are imperfect comparisons.[11] Nevertheless, Mantle's minuscule double-play rate reinforces his documented speed to first base, placing him among the fastest runners in baseball history.

Mantle's long reign at the top of objective measures is not unique in baseball: no modern pitcher has thrown a fastball clocked faster than those of Bob Feller and Nolan Ryan. The technology used with Feller and Ryan was comparatively unsophisticated, but limiting comparisons to speeds obtained by modern devices reveals a similar stasis: J. R. Richard threw 100 mph in 1976, Rob Dibble 101 in 1992, Mark Wohlers 103 in 1995, and in the twenty-one years since Wohlers, the modern record has been extended only 2 mph by Aroldis Chapman. The fastest pitches in baseball remain clumped around 100 mph.

The phenomenon transcends baseball. Consider representative track and field events (untainted by steroid allegations): The broad jump world record is twenty-five years old and has advanced less than three feet since Jesse Owens eighty-one years ago. The men's 1,500-meter record is eighteen years old and has decreased only seven seconds in almost fifty years. The 800-meter record has decreased less than one second, and the pole-vault record increased only six inches in over thirty years. The men's high jump record is twenty-three years old. This pattern characterizes much of women's track and field and even horse racing. Secretariat still holds the record for all three Triple Crown races, forty-three years later.

We find similar results in basketball. Bill Sharman shot 90-plus percent from the free-throw line sixty years ago; no one can do much better than that.

Julius Erving dunked from roughly the foul line in the slam-dunk contest in 1976. In the forty contests since, no NBA player has dunked from appreciably farther out. No NBA player ever jumped higher than Vince Carter, when he leaped over the seven-foot Frenchman Frederic Weis to dunk in the 2000 Summer Olympics—called "*le dunk de la mort*" ("the dunk of death") by the French media.[12]

Thus, in multiple areas with objective measurements, we find only incremental improvement over time—sometimes seemingly no improvement at all—in the greatest achievements.

Professor Stephen Jay Gould (*Full House*) provides the correct explanation: Once someone has done nearly as well as anyone can do, by definition nobody can do much better. Gould illustrated the gamut of talents within a sport as a bell curve on a graph, the x-axis characterizing increasing ability as it goes from zero out to the right, and the y-axis describing the number of people with different levels of ability. As the overall performance of most athletes improves over time, the bulk of the bell curve moves to the right on the x-axis. However, the improvement at the right-hand tail of the bell curve—the few very greatest athletes—slows down considerably. Eventually, the right tail hits a "right wall," an apparent "outer limit to human capacity."

Objective comparisons of the greatest athletes ever—for example, Mantle, Williams, Bo Jackson, Feller, Ryan, Mike Powell in the long jump, and Dr. J dunking from the foul line—to their modern counterparts suggest that human anatomy and physiology allow only so much speed, leaping ability, and power. Once someone nears the limits of human performance, further advances (without pharmaceuticals or improved equipment) will likely be incremental.

Trout, Harper, and Puig may have found surpassing Mantle's athleticism daunting, but that's only because Mantle approached the right wall. Generations to come will also find it difficult to go farther.

HANK AARON DIDN'T BAT AGAINST BLACK PITCHERS EITHER

When Hank Aaron broke Babe Ruth's career home run record in 1974 a spirited argument broke out over who was the greater player. Ruth supporters cited his many dominant seasons and greater overall hitting performance. To them, Aaron had won a lifetime-achievement award based on longevity and consistency rather than peak brilliance (Aaron won only one MVP and never hit more than forty-four home runs in a season).

Aaron supporters answered with a seemingly compelling argument: Ruth never batted against a black pitcher. Given the influx of talented black players in the 1950s and '60s, Aaron faced tougher pitching than Ruth.

But the pro-Aaron argument had a surprising flaw: Aaron didn't face black pitchers either! That's an exaggeration, of course, but only slight. African American players never took to the mound in significant numbers, accounting for at most 6 percent of pitchers in Major League Baseball at any one time, and almost always less than that. Only three black pitchers (Bob Gibson, Don Newcombe, and Ferguson Jenkins) are among the fifty pitchers Aaron faced most often in his career. One could hardly exalt Aaron above Ruth on that basis.

The initial influx of black players included few pitchers because Negro League teams, for economic reasons, usually kept only sixteen players and did not have pitching coaches. The reason for the paucity of black major-league pitchers later on is less clear.

Whatever the actual reasons for the dearth of black pitchers, the number recently diminished even further, as a subset of the overall decline in black baseball players: only fourteen black pitchers manned major-league rosters on Opening Day in 2016, less than one for every two teams. Mike Trout and Bryce Harper barely face more black pitchers than Ruth did ninety years ago.

Of course, Latino and Asian pitchers now populate major-league teams—there are currently ten times as many Latinos as blacks on the mound—so Trout and Harper fans could make the ethnicity argument far better than Aaron's fans. They could contend that neither Aaron nor Ruth would have done as well as Trout and Harper have against today's broader pitching pool.

On the other hand, we can make objective assessments of Ruth's ability—at least his power—and here, like Mickey Mantle, he stacks up well compared to all the greats who followed, even nearly a hundred years later.

Ruth's contemporaries described gargantuan home runs, several allegedly longer than 600 feet. Some of those accounts were absurd and tainted by hero worship, but like the façade at Yankee Stadium that only Mantle ever hit and the red seat in Fenway Park's right-field bleachers that only Ted Williams reached, Ruth hit balls over and near physical markers that no other hitters matched, and that allow estimates of distance. For example, he hit a home run well over the 467-foot center-field fence of Navin Field (Tiger Stadium) on July 18, 1921, that surely traveled 500 feet or more.

In addition, *Boston Herald* sports writer Burt Whitman wrote that in St. Petersburg, Florida, in 1934, "Babe Ruth socked a pitch . . . far over the right field canvas and almost into the West Coast Inn, where the Braves live between games."[13] St. Pete's writer Pete Norris later noted, "The distance was surveyed and verified in 2008, measuring from the old home plate location at Waterfront Park to the closest part of the now demolished West Coast Inn. An engineer estimated the actual distance in the air as at least 610 feet."

Whatever the exact length, Ruth's home run clearly landed near the inn, a massive blast (like the Navin Field shot), longer than anything Harper or Trout have ever hit.

Like Mantle, Ruth's power—objectively measured—dominated his peers and stood the test of time (as did Mantle's speed). We can only speculate, but there's no good reason to consider these measures anomalies; more likely, the whole of their athletic ability and baseball skills would also have held up, even through demographic changes.

That's characteristic of the few greatest athletes who approached the limits of human ability.

2 MISUNDERSTANDINGS

Media Misses

Sports commentators provide the public equivalent of our own conversations about sports, typically with expert description and analysis. They shine most when they address controversial areas with insightful thought. But sometimes they tee up, swing—and miss.

OLBERMANN STRIKES OUT ON JETER RANT

Derek Jeter mans the shortstop position on anyone's all-time Yankee team. Jeter's prominence and great reputation may explain why Keith Olbermann took pot shots at him in a sad "please look at me" type of exercise.

Olbermann makes a living out of rants. He finds something that bothers him and goes off on a diatribe. Olbermann entertains when he's on the mark, but his attempted knockdown of Jeter completely whiffed.

He began sarcastically, "Contrary to what you've heard, Jeter is not the greatest person in human history," and moved on to the purported insight that Jeter does not rank with Ruth, Gehrig, DiMaggio, and Mantle (and others) on the Yankees' Mount Olympus. Of course, no temperate baseball fan (or anyone outside of a press conference convened to laud Jeter) equates Jeter with those four—a classic strawman argument. On the other hand, Jeter, a certain Hall of Famer, did play twenty mostly outstanding seasons as one of the best shortstops ever.

Olbermann then decried Jeter's farewell tour. For sure, the pregame ceremonies dragged on and derived in part from management obligations and gate promoting. But that's always the case with these affairs—no big deal. Olbermann ignored the important aspect of Jeter adulation: all season long opposing players quietly paid homage to Jeter, even during games.

Jeter's statistics, according to Olbermann, do not justify the hype. However, his comparison of Jeter's numbers to all-time greats at other positions misleads. He ranks eleventh all-time in stolen bases and fifth in home runs among shortstops. Considering hitting and baserunning together as a measure of overall offense, Jeter ranks third all-time among shortstops (behind Honus Wagner and the discredited Alex Rodriguez) by both traditional and newer statistics.

Not surprisingly, Olbermann emphasized Jeter's poor ranking in advanced defensive metrics. However, these are among the least accurate statistics in the sabermetric armament (see "MAKE LOVE, NOT WAR" in chapter 3). In addition, even a subpar fielding shortstop remains more skilled and valuable defensively than most other players on the field.

Moreover, statistics alone don't do justice to Jeter. His hustle, leadership, calmness under pressure, intelligence, consistency, and more, cannot be quantified. See, for example, the flip that nailed Jeremy Giambi at home in a playoff game and saved the Yankees from elimination. Jeter's play differed from, for example, Bill Mazeroski's home run in the 1960 World Series—a great accomplishment without any broader implications for Mazeroski's skills. The intangibles that enabled Jeter's flip play surely manifested at other times as well.

Jeter batted poorly his last season, yet remained at the top of the batting lineup. Olbermann blamed Jeter (rather than manager Joe Girardi) for not dropping lower in the lineup and argued that Jeter's misguided ego may have prevented the Yankees from making the playoffs. Olbermann claimed that in contrast, Gehrig, DiMaggio, and Mantle all retired rather than hurt their teams by continuing to play after they declined.

Gehrig, however, suffered from soon-to-be fatal health problems, not exactly the same thing. Mantle batted .245 (less than Jeter in his final year) in his seventeenth season, yet stuck around for another season in which he did even worse (.237). DiMaggio hit only .263 his last year. Neither of them could run or throw any more. Basically, they all played poorly at the end.

Moreover, optimizing team performance requires more than heeding data. Girardi surely considered whether marginalizing the Yankees' captain and spiritual leader would adversely affect the team psyche. Perhaps that explains why neither Mantle nor DiMaggio dropped in the lineup in their final seasons.

In truth, Jeter did not stray from the norm for great athletes. Greatness typically includes an indomitable spirit and utter confidence. That confidence does not abruptly vanish when skills fade (for example, Muhammad Ali, Johnny Unitas, Willie Mays, among many others). No one should have expected Jeter to ask for a demotion.

Finally, perhaps Olbermann's worst error: he stressed that while Jeter led the Yankees to five World Series titles, only one came in his last fourteen seasons. Multiple World Series titles apparently do not impress Olbermann unless they come with some sort of mathematical regularity. Great players may complete entire careers without winning a World Series—twenty years or more—as was the case with Ted Williams, Ken Griffey Jr., Gaylord Perry, to name a few. Yet Olbermann diminished Jeter's five championships because they weren't spaced properly!

Olbermann's rants only succeed when he picks on the right guy for the right reasons. Not this time.

LE BATARD WHIFFS ON STEROIDS AND THE HALL OF FAME

Jeter will easily be inducted into the Hall of Fame on the first ballot (no matter what Olbermann says), but more commonly, the voting stirs up ample controversy. First, I'll examine the biggest dilemma of recent votes—steroid use—and then propose my own broadly applicable inclusion criteria.

The Baseball Writers' Association of America (BBWAA) made another strong statement against steroids in the 2014 Hall of Fame balloting. No player known or widely believed (Barry Bonds, Roger Clemens, Mark McGwire, Sammy Sosa, and Rafael Palmeiro) or even simply suspected (Mike Piazza and Jeff Bagwell) of steroid use was inducted. In anticipation of this result, Dan Le Batard gave his ballot to *Deadspin* to protest the "sanctimonious" anti-steroid crusade. In turn, he received a scathing response from his peers, along with loss of his balloting privileges and suspension from the BBWAA.

Kudos to Le Batard for standing up for his convictions, but in this case, neither he nor the BBWAA got this right.

An anti-steroids stance need not involve controversial moral judgments, much less sanctimony. Users risk major health problems and even death. If steroids were allowed, all players would be confronted with the choice of taking life-threatening substances or losing competitive ground (perhaps not even having a major-league career). This situation would be intolerable.

The serious health risks distinguish regular anabolic-steroid use (and growth hormone, which, in excess, causes acromegaly) from pregame-only amphetamines (as opposed to regular amphetamine use), plasma or platelet infusions, creatine, protein or other supplements, and the like—steroid use cannot be justified as being no different from other means athletes have used to enhance performance. Nor should we excuse steroid use prior to baseball's formal testing and penalties. Federal law proscribed nonprescription use of anabolic steroids in 1991. Baseball does not need a formal penal code that specifically lists all banned behavior. It should be obvious that illegal activity is unacceptable.

We do not want a baseball culture that condones illegal substances, and we do not want to commemorate performances that required them.

But while this principle should be unobjectionable, particular cases present difficulties. We don't always know for sure which players used steroids or for how long. Because of that uncertainty, some argue that no one should be penalized in the balloting. Others argue the opposite: all suspected steroid users from this era should be denied induction. Neither extreme is justified.

The demand for certainty and direct evidence belies the world around us. Civil law cases are decided by the "preponderance of the evidence"—something must only be more likely than not. Circumstantial evidence is accepted in all courts and puts many criminals behind bars. We all make important decisions based on uncertain evidence: whom to marry, what job to take, where to live, and so on. We do the best we can based on the evidence at hand and accept that errors are inevitable. There is no reason that Hall of Fame voting should be held to a standard of certainty not required with other important decisions. We can and should assess Hall of Fame candidates via the available evidence.

McGwire, Sosa, and Palmeiro are fairly easy cases. The evidence suggests that they lack a steroid-unaided body of work worthy of induction. Bonds and Clemens are different. Their late-career statistical surges, along with obvious changes in their physiques, indicate that they began using steroids after they had already amassed careers that easily established their Hall of Fame credentials.

Inducting Bonds and Clemens would not condone their steroid use. Rather, we can commemorate the steroid-free part of their careers but not the later steroid-fueled parts. Their plaques should avoid mentioning career totals or the MVPs, Cy Young Awards, and other achievements that were aided by steroids. Bonds's plaque, for example, should make no mention of his record-breaking seventy-three-home-run season. (Hall of Fame plaques are not intended as a complete history of the player; for that, we have biographies and other Hall exhibits.)

Of course, voters should be mindful of the presumption of innocence. According to the oft-cited maxim in criminal law, it is better to acquit many guilty people than to convict any who are innocent. While excluding someone from the Hall of Fame is not the same as convicting him of a crime, some asymmetry between false positives and false negatives makes sense in the Hall of Fame context. Inducting a few players who were actually users would hardly be catastrophic, but excluding players who were entirely innocent would be a grave injustice. Accordingly, writers should resolve doubts about steroids in favor of players. Bagwell should get in, as there is no specific evidence against him (he just missed in 2016 with 72 percent of the vote; a 2017 induction seems likely).

In addition, the presumption of innocence probably justifies Piazza's 2016 election, though not to the extent it supports Bagwell. Piazza's back acne, scoffed at by some, matters. Physicians consider de novo adult acne as a symptom of androgen excess that might prompt an evaluation for various diseases. In Piazza's context, a physician would consider it as suggesting exogenous steroid use, supporting Hall of Fame voters who deemed him a likely user. Nevertheless, this situation was murky enough to understand Piazza getting the benefit of the doubt.

Looking forward, Alex Rodriguez, Gary Sheffield, and Manny Ramirez should be excluded, as each of them either reportedly failed a drug test in 2003 and/or were admitted users (Rodriguez as of 2001, Sheffield as of 2002). Unlike Bonds and Clemens, they lack a clear Hall of Fame record prior to the onset of steroid use (particularly since use might have antedated their failed test or self-admission). David Ortiz and Ivan Rodriguez seem like Piazza —some incriminating evidence (for Ortiz, a single allegedly failed test that remains disputed; for Rodriguez, marked waxing and waning musculature corresponding to vacillations in performance) but perhaps not enough to overcome the presumption of innocence. Albert Pujols is more like Bagwell—no evidence of steroid use—and should be inducted.

It is regrettable that voters must assess possible steroid use, as it adds an unnecessary layer of complexity to an already subjective and difficult process. Readers will, of course, disagree with some of the assessments above. But we add some clarity, with regard to steroids, by noting that informed judgments on a case-by-case basis using the available evidence beat an all-or-nothing approach.

Fortunately, with stricter testing now in place and steroid use declining, steroids should eventually fade as a Hall of Fame dilemma. But the voting will remain controversial, even without the steroid issue. Why do fans so often disagree about player qualifications and what can be done about this?

One core problem is that baseball fans may reasonably prefer different induction standards. Should the Hall of Fame include only the truly greatest players ever? The top 1 percent? The top 5 percent?

The first Hall of Fame class in 1936 included the five greatest players in baseball history to that point: Ty Cobb, Babe Ruth, Honus Wagner, Walter Johnson, and Christy Mathewson. The quality of inductees had to decrease from there, but (with some exceptions) the Hall of Fame continued as a shrine for the very finest.

However, the 1984 induction of pitcher Don Drysdale seemed to signify an evolution of the induction standard. Drysdale won twenty games only twice, with an unexceptional .557 lifetime winning percentage despite playing on many outstanding Dodgers teams. His record fell below the standard set by Johnson, Mathewson, and other Hall of Fame pitchers, including Bob Feller, Sandy Koufax, Warren Spahn, Bob Gibson, and Juan Marichal.

The Drysdale precedent paved the way for Jim Bunning, Phil Niekro, Burt Blyleven, and Don Sutton. There's nothing intrinsically wrong with any of these fine pitchers being in the Hall of Fame. The point is that the standards are not only arbitrary but they change over time—a ripe recipe for disagreements among fans.

I do wish that the Hall of Fame had remained more restrictive, celebrating only dominant players (a "dominant-player standard"). At neighborhood pick-up basketball games where the winning team keeps the court, we revere the elite player who makes the difference between winning and losing. No one player in baseball assures victory, but there are players who stand apart, head and shoulders above the crowd in rarefied air. In Major League Baseball, in my youth, this group included Mickey Mantle, Willie Mays, Hank Aaron, and Frank Robinson; for pitchers, Koufax, Marichal, Gibson, and Tom Seaver. Not Drysdale and his ilk.

Fealty to the dominant-player standard favors exalting peak performance over longevity, with Hall of Famers Koufax and Dizzy Dean, who had only five or six outstanding seasons, as prime examples. In that spirit, my Hall of Fame would include Dwight Gooden and Ron Guidry for the sheer brilliance of their peak periods. Although they were both most celebrated for one season of epic dominance, they were not one-hit wonders. Gooden compiled a 132–53 won-lost record for his first eight seasons (for comparison, Dean was 133–75 in his six quality seasons). Guidry won 154 games with only 68 losses over his first full nine years.

In addition, I'd include Nomar Garciaparra and Don Mattingly. They dominated, and in my book, for long enough. Nomar hit over .300 (including back-to-back seasons of .357 and .372) with more than twenty home runs seven times—superb for a shortstop. Donnie Baseball had six consecutive great seasons before he declined because of injury. During much of that time, he may have been the best hitter in baseball, and he also won nine Gold Glove Awards.

In contrast, longevity and big career numbers might not always be quite what they seem. For example, after fifteen seasons, Blyleven compiled a 195–167 won-lost record. Had he retired then, he would not have been inducted. Instead, Blyleven pitched seven more seasons averaging only 13 wins a year, barely above .500 in winning percentage. He retired with 287 wins, deemed worthy of the Hall of Fame by the voters, but achieved by adding a mediocre seven-season coda to a non–Hall of Fame body of work.

Blyleven and other Hall of Famers with similar career arcs deserve credit for persevering. They also had some great individual seasons; domination versus longevity is not an either-or proposition. But I would choose Gooden and Guidry—more dominant—over Drysdale, Bunning, Blyleven, Sutton, Niekro, and other Hall of Fame pitchers. I certainly would not exclude Gooden and Guidry (or Mattingly and Garciaparra) solely on the basis of lesser career totals.

Thurman Munson's career further illustrates the point. His tragic death limited him to eleven seasons, but during that time contemporaries considered him the equal of rival catcher Carlton Fisk. Fisk, to his credit, played fourteen more seasons after Munson's death, but many of them were quite ordinary. Fisk in the Hall and Munson not, based on longevity, seems a poor distinction.

Middle infielders provide another difficult problem—it's very hard to compare them to other players. Perhaps only Honus Wagner and Rogers Hornsby dominated like Mantle, Mays, or Aaron. Conceivably, the dominant-player standard underestimates middle infielders. If so, advanced statistics do the same. For example, by the career wins above replacement (WAR) standard, Jeter ranks only 88th. Twelve Hall of Fame middle infielders rank from 150th (Lou Boudreau) to 604th (Bill Mazeroski). Some Hall of Fame middle infielders do not rank in the top 1,000 hitters of all time by modern measures. The induction of many second basemen and shortstops with comparatively modest hitting records suggests that middle-infield defense is valued higher by Hall voters than by either the dominant-player standard or sabermetrics—but nobody knows who's right.

Considering these ambiguities—different induction standards, different valuations of prime performance versus longevity, and dif-

ficulty in measuring defense and various intangibles—it's no wonder that Hall of Fame elections routinely engender controversy.
That's not likely ever to end.

There's no right answer to a number of relevant Hall of Fame questions, but if there is an approach that deserves consensus, I think it
should be the dominant-player standard. That would make the Hall
of Fame more uniform, and more importantly, more meaningful.

Baseball's Exaggerated Demise

Rob Manfred's appointment in August 2014 as the new commissioner fueled a discussion of baseball's state of affairs: What
problems should Mr. Manfred address? Fortunately, baseball's commissioner no longer had to discuss steroid and other performance-
enhancing drug use.

Instead, Anthony Rendon of the Washington Nationals identified
the major issue as "I don't watch baseball—it's too long and boring." Commentators routinely lamented that youngsters do not embrace three-hour games. Obviously, no business should move in an
opposite direction from its consumer base.

Many observers attributed the slowed pace to batters taking more
pitches (the average number of pitches per game increased 9 percent since 1988). This trend presumably derived from the insight
into the undervaluation of walks.

Longer games might be an acceptable price to pay (at least for
batters) for improved offensive performance, but the walk-seeking
strategy did not lead to offensive success, or even more walks. In
2014, MLB had the fewest walks since 1968, the lowest batting average since 1972, and the fewest runs scored since 1981. All followed
downward trends. Thus, Rendon's one-two punch, "too long and
boring" (emphasis mine)—the additional game time contains little
action, much of it filled with strikeouts (the most ever in 2014, then
again in 2015 and 2016).

Why didn't the insight into drawing walks and the Oakland A's alleged success implementing it translate broadly into more offense?

One reason is that a single change often does not significantly affect a complex system. For most of its modern history baseball main-
tained a narrow equilibrium between offense and defense. In over

90 percent of seasons from 1940 to 2015, teams averaged between four and five runs a game. Over that same seventy-six-year period, except for the low-scoring era from 1963 to 1972, the mean batting average stayed between .250 and .271 every season—essentially .260 +/- .01. Deviations routinely regressed toward the mean.

The equilibrium is partly explained by countermoves that develop in response to any change. In this instance, when batters take more pitches, pitchers throw more strikes. Bob Gibson predicted that the walk-seeking strategy would not favor hitters. Referring to the huge drop in batting average when batters fall behind in the count, Gibson stated, "I'd love to pitch today, because you hear a lot of these guys talk about getting deep into the count. I think I would eat 'em alive." Reggie Jackson responded to Gibson, agreeing, "Because it's going to be oh and two" (in *Sixty Feet, Six Inches* by Gibson, Jackson, and Lonnie Wheeler). In fact, the percentage of first-pitch strikes increased 7 percent from 1988 to 2012.

However, there was more to declining offense than batters taking pitches. Lower strike zones and defensive shifts also contributed. In addition, pitching depth increased; almost all teams now have hard-throwing closers and eighth-inning setup men and even seventh inning setup relievers. Nowadays, just six decent innings makes for a quality start. Starters do not pace themselves, and forcing a starter out of the game no longer yields the benefit of facing a weaker relief pitcher.

What did this mean for Manfred? A few modest changes in the off-season (for example, introducing a countdown clock for breaks between innings; making batters keep one foot in the batter's box) decreased average game time in 2015 by about six minutes (even more, earlier in the season). Complaints about excessive length ceased. That was the easy part.

As for reversing declining offense, baseball history advised patience. First, the matter had not reached the tipping point: both runs scored and batting average per team in 2014 still fell within (though barely) the usual historical range, and baseball remained popular. Baseball still had time before it hit the anomalous nadir of 1968 (3.4 runs scored per team, .237 batting average) that prompted lowering the mound.

Second, baseball tends to self-correct. Fans and media should have considered that batters might cut back on taking first strikes, or respond to defensive shifts by bunting or hitting to the opposite field. General managers might devalue pure pull hitters diminished by shifts; umpires might tighten the strike zone; more foreign sluggers might be signed; baseball's recent investment in American urban areas might provide more hitters; some combination of these and other factors could stem the tide without any intervention from the top.

The clamor for action neglected baseball's history and propensity for homeostasis.

All that suggested that Manfred should have resisted the noise (and calls for lowering the mound again!) coming from all corners and follow the prescription for patience. Whether from inertia or insight, that's exactly what he did. Kudos to the commissioner.

Without any formal changes, simply allowing the regression to the mean that characterizes most of baseball history, home runs increased 18 percent in 2015, and mean batting average (.251 to .254) and runs per team per game (4.07 to 4.25) also rose. These three statistics increased again in the 2016 season (as of late August): home runs (1.16 per game) to the highest rate since 2000; batting average to .256; runs scored per game (4.49) to the most since 2009.

Thus, we're no longer fussing over baseball's problems. Quite the opposite: the spirit around baseball now seems strong and rising.

There's reason for that. For one thing, a bevy of young superstars emerged, and not much fuels fan enthusiasm more than great players. Bryce Harper and Mike Trout provide baseball with arguably the finest duo of youngsters since Mickey Mantle and Willie Mays entered the majors over sixty years ago. Harper won the National League MVP in 2015 at age twenty-two with a .330 batting average and forty-two home runs. He was the youngest unanimous MVP winner in baseball history. Trout, twenty-four years old, won one MVP (2014) and finished runner-up three times in his first four full seasons, perhaps the greatest start ever to a career. In 2015, he hit .299 with forty-one home runs.

They might not ever capture the same national attention as the Hall of Fame duo of yore: neither Trout nor Harper enjoy the New

York limelight like Mantle and Mays did; nor do they have the charisma of the cap flying off, basket-catching, say-hey Mays; nor the Oklahoma mines upbringing, fear of early death, and valor-in-the-face-of-injury pathos of Mantle. Nobody knows how the careers of today's youngsters will play out, and the Mantle and Mays combo presents an incredibly high standard to meet. However, the on-field play of youngsters Harper and Trout recalls the glorious early Mantle and Mays period.

Add to the mix Miami's twenty-six-year-old Giancarlo Stanton, who threatened a sixty-home-run season in 2015 prior to injury, perhaps en route to the all-time career record. Kris Bryant of the Chicago Cubs may win the MVP in 2016 in only his second season, and twenty-three-year-old Manny Machado of the Baltimore Orioles is on his way to consecutive thirty-five-home-run seasons. Two rookie shortstops—Colorado's Trevor Story and the Dodgers' Corey Seager hit over twenty home runs. And twenty-three-year-old catcher Gary Sanchez elated Yankees fans with a .403 batting average and ten home runs in his first twenty games after a midseason call-up.

Hitters have no patent on youthful brilliance in today's game. Baseball has evolved so that pitchers no longer amass huge numbers of innings or wins, but that actually reflects improvement in baseball's overall performance rather than a decline in pitching skills (pitchers can no longer relax at the bottom of lineups owing to the larger number of good hitters; an increased pool of qualified pitchers allows managers to remove starters earlier without losing anything).

Even without pitching as many innings as their predecessors, several current pitchers have dominated. Washington's Max Scherzer completed the greatest three-game pitching sequence in history (and threw two no-hitters) during the 2015 season, yet was outshone in June by Chris Sale of the Chicago White Sox. Sale held batters to a ridiculous .219 on-base percentage and struck out seventy-five in forty-four innings pitched in the month. Only twenty-seven years old, Sale began 2016 with a 9–0 record and a 1.58 ERA.

In addition, the Dodgers' Clayton Kershaw's first nine seasons draws appropriate comparison to Sandy Koufax, and Kershaw is only twenty-eight years old. The Giants' Madison Bumgarner, only twenty-six, has not equaled Kershaw's regular-season success but his postseason performance (0.25 ERA in thirty-six World Series innings) rivals any in history. The Cubs' Jake Arrieta finished 2015 on a Bob Gibson–like streak that continued through the beginning of the 2016 season without skipping a beat.

There's still more to baseball's resurgence. Recent emphasis on defense, defensive shifts, and baserunning added strategic nuances and put athleticism on greater display. The steroid influence waned, lifting suspicion from every good accomplishment.

Finally, competitive balance has never been better. Small-market teams like Houston, Kansas City, and St. Louis led or won their respective divisions in 2015, with Kansas City winning the World Series for the first time in thirty years. In addition, Houston and Pittsburgh made the playoffs, and Minnesota returned to winning ways.

In 2014, Manfred fretted over a list of issues when he addressed the "State of Baseball." In 2015, the conversation centered on Pete Rose, a peripheral off-field issue. Manfred's 2016 "State of Baseball" report did not put forth any major concerns. That's a big advance for baseball in just a short time and portends more good times ahead.

Imagine the excitement if the surging Cubs, with an ongoing 100-plus year championship drought, play in a World Series. Better yet, what if they face the Boston Red Sox, another team with national allure on the upswing?[1]

Too Much Tommy John in Baseball

Major League Baseball's return to good times is tempered by the epidemic of pitchers injuring the ulnar collateral ligament (UCL) of the elbow and undergoing Tommy John surgery to repair it. Approximately 25 percent of active pitchers have had this operation. More MLB players underwent Tommy John surgery in 2014 than in the entire decade of the 1990s, and the incidence shows no sign of abating.

WHY TOMMY JOHN SURGERY IS HERE TO STAY

Most analysts have ascribed the epidemic (beyond improved diagnostic imaging) to excessive pitching and/or improper pitching mechanics. However, neither adequately explains the surge in UCL injury.

First, consider the purported role of throwing too many pitches: In baseball's earlier days, pitchers threw many more pitches than they do today, yet suffered far fewer injuries. As two illustrative examples, in the 1960s Warren Spahn completed a twenty-one-year, 5,243-inning career, and Juan Marichal began a run of ten consecutive winning seasons averaging twenty-one complete games and 280 innings. Neither suffered a significant arm injury. The two made a mockery of the modern pitch limits on July 2, 1963, in a magnificent sixteen-inning dual complete-game 1–0 victory for Marichal over Spahn. Marichal threw 227 pitches and Spann 201 (reviewed in Jim Kaplan's *The Greatest Game Ever Pitched*). After the marathon session, Marichal proceeded on to a 25–8, 321-inning season. Spahn, forty-two years old, completed nine of his next ten starts and finished the season with 260 innings pitched, 23 wins and only 7 losses.

The huge dissociation between numbers of pitches and UCL injuries continues to this day. Pitchers in Japan's professional league throw more pitches per game than their counterparts in MLB, yet suffer comparatively fewer UCL injuries. Moreover, MLB's pitch limits have failed to even blunt the increasing incidence of injury.

The American Sports Medicine Institute suggests that many UCL injuries begin with overuse at a young age, and surely that's a valid point. However, this also fails as an adequate explanation for the UCL injury epidemic in MLB: Latin major-league pitchers aren't known to pitch as many innings as American youngsters at the same ages yet appear to suffer UCL injury at a similar rate. Japanese youngsters often throw far more pitches than their US counterparts yet appear to suffer fewer injuries as professionals.

Clearly, more is involved than just pitch counts.

Many of those who've analyzed pitching motions with advanced video technology cite flawed pitching mechanics as the reason for UCL injury. Back in 2006, Will Carroll wrote (in *Saving the Pitcher*) of the former Cy Young Award winner Dr. Mike Marshall: "If pitchers would just do things the way he teaches them, he could eliminate pitcher injuries." Carroll notes, "There is an absolute, an ideal pitching delivery." Further, that "The single most damaging and common flaw is inwardly rotating the upper arm." "Pulling the arm across the body" and "the forearm flyout" also damage the UCL.

Major-league consultant Ron Wolforth concurs with improper mechanics as the cause of UCL injury, but sees faulty "arm deceleration" and "the elevated distal humerus" as the major culprits.

This focus on pitching mechanics follows a medical paradigm best seen in infectious diseases: a specific etiology causes a disease that may be prevented or cured by eradicating the offending agent. However, this linear paradigm does not appear to apply to pitching injuries.

First, it implies (without evidence) that a significant, harmful change in pitching technique occurred in the 1990s, after which the incidence of Tommy John surgery abruptly skyrocketed. Second, as noted, Wolforth and Marshall (and other well-regarded analysts) disagree about the so-called optimal pitching form and the reasons for UCL injury, which makes a discrete biomechanical cause of injury less likely. Finally, after more than fifteen years of careful study of pitching technique, we lack a single well-known instance of a team following a new training/technique program designed to reduce UCL injury and reporting clearly beneficial results.

Perhaps that's because a different medical paradigm more aptly explains the persistence of the UCL epidemic in the face of sophisticated biomechanical study: lower back pain. Low back pain remains common despite improvements in physical therapy and major medical and technological advances, including microsurgical techniques and precise pharmacologic injections. The human spine and its ancillary structures simply never evolved to adequately support (without suffering damage) an erect posture and the superimposed stresses of running, jumping, lifting, and the like. Even advanced medicine cannot change that.

Similarly, the biomechanics of the human arm are poorly suited to support throwing overhand at high speed and with powerful torques (in comparison, competitive underhand softball pitchers suffer relatively few arm injuries). The overhand pitch has always been an accident waiting to happen.

Yet something additional had to have taken place to explain the recent increased incidence of UCL injury. One possibility is that pitching evolved in a variety of ways that, taken together, place even more stress on the UCL, now often beyond what it can endure.

Among these, pitchers commonly throw harder than previously; their breaking pitches break more; they throw new pitches (cutters, split-fingers, and others); they can no longer throw easier to batters at the bottom of the lineup.[2] The totality of modern pitching stress may be more important than any individual component in damaging the UCL.

Interestingly, the evolution in pitching that may have prompted the UCL injury epidemic probably developed as part of the overall improvement in baseball performance. For the last seventy-five years (with the brief exception of the late 1960s, when pitching dominated), hitters and pitchers have competed within a reasonable equilibrium; as noted, the mean batting average for Major League Baseball has straddled .260.

Hitting improved significantly during that time, particularly in the depth of good hitters. Racial tolerance and globalization dramatically increased recruiting grounds. Hitters got bigger and stronger. Technique improved through better coaching and video study.[3]

Pitchers also evolved, benefiting from a similarly larger talent pool of bigger, stronger players, advanced coaching, and refined techniques. The greater speed and movement of today's pitches are required to compete with modern-day hitters (even at younger levels). Pitchers threw almost twice as many balls 95 miles per hour or more in 2015 than they did eight years prior. Any changes in pitching technique probably served the purpose of faster and/or sharper-breaking pitches.

The parallel improvements in hitting and pitching abilities that kept baseball in equilibrium differed in one huge way: swinging a bat is a relatively natural motion that does not put undue stress on any joints. More powerful swings seem no more injurious. However, as noted, overhand pitching is unnatural and inherently joint endangering, and the changes in modern pitching associated with improved performance took pitching beyond a tipping point of sustainable elbow health.

With that in mind, what to do?

The UCL undergoes some healing during rest periods in between starts (explaining why partial tears sometimes completely heal with prolonged rest). The optimal balance between risking damage in the service of a pitcher's job and allowing self-repair remains unknown. Increasing the healing period between starts may be more important than limiting the number of pitches thrown in a game. Notably, starting pitchers in the Japanese professional league pitch only once a week and appear to suffer less UCL damage than major-league pitchers in the United States who throw fewer pitches in a game, but pitch more frequently.

The failure of pitch counts and kinesiologists to affect the UCL injury epidemic, as well as the more favorable Japanese experience, prompted the New York Mets to implement a six-man pitching rotation during the 2015 season. If that doesn't reduce UCL injury, a seven-man rotation should be considered. We don't know that more rest will solve the problem but it makes sense, with the Japanese experience as a basis, and the time has come to try something new.

Team rosters would have to expand to allow additional pitchers. Fortunately, globalization and other factors provide an increasing talent source. It should not be difficult for teams to find another one or two end-of-the rotation pitchers to throw six innings once a week. Many teams already employ additional pitchers over the course of a season to replace those lost to injury.

As the increase in talented hitters may have contributed to UCL injuries in pitchers, the expanded pool of qualified pitchers allows a potential solution: the once-a-week starter.

SCOTT BORAS, TOMMY JOHN, AND THE ILLUSION OF EXPERTISE

New York Mets pitcher Matt Harvey's previous Tommy John surgery contributed to quite an uproar at the end of the 2015 season.

Harvey's agent, Scott Boras, suggested that the Mets shut Harvey down prior to the postseason. This was Harvey's first season pitching after undergoing surgery and Boras claimed that Harvey's surgeon, Dr. James Andrews, recommended a strict 180-inning limit. Harvey had already thrown 166 innings at the time, so Andrews's decree, if followed, would have ended Harvey's season before the playoffs, echoing the Washington National's refusal to pitch Stephen Strasburg in the 2012 postseason.

Assuming Boras cited Andrews correctly (the Mets insisted otherwise), he and Andrews fell prey to the fallacy illuminated by the

Nobel Prize–winning psychologist Daniel Kahneman—the false notion ("the illusions of punditry") that expertise in a field tends to yield predictive power. As political scientist Philip Tetlock put it, experts in many fields predict events no more accurately "than the average daily reader of the *New York Times*" or even a "dart-throwing chimp."

No one should question Andrews's ability to diagnose or repair arm injuries. However, his 180-inning recommendation was not based on science, but on the observation that Harvey had never pitched more than 178 innings in a season, and the inference that surpassing his previous maximum carried risk to his surgically repaired elbow. That was at most an educated guess, and a 180-inning limit no more reasonable than keeping Harvey within 10 percent (196 innings) or 20 percent (214 innings) of his previous maximum.

Any number would be arbitrary, and the entire enterprise of limiting Harvey's innings was questionable. As Major League Baseball has increasingly emphasized pitch and innings restrictions, the incidence of Tommy John injury and reinjury has increased rather than decreased. These restrictions appear ineffective.

Moreover, any precise innings limit creates an unjustified aura of certitude; a limit of exactly 180, as opposed to "around 180" implies more knowledge than exists. It falsely suggests that the putative increased risk of injury occurs abruptly with Harvey's 181st inning. In fact, if the risk of injury increases with more innings, it surely does so along a very gradual continuum. The difference in risk between 180 and 181 innings asymptotically approaches zero. The increase in risk from 180 innings to 200 or 220 must be small. A recommendation of "around 180 innings" would still be arbitrary, but would at least mitigate the pretense to knowledge. Less intellectually arrogant and more flexible suggestions like "around 180 innings" leave room for judgment, including consideration of the stakes involved.

Concern for a player's long-term health is laudable, but every situation must be evaluated on its own merits based on a reasonable risk-versus-benefit assessment. It may have been foolish, for example, for Kevin McHale to play on a broken foot in the 1987 NBA Finals, probably shortening his career. It is surely foolish for a concussed football player to return to a game and risk permanent neurologic damage. Harvey's situation was completely different. He was healthy, and an extra 30 or so postseason innings increased the chance of injury only slightly, if at all.

And *postseason* innings mean much more. While playing in and ideally winning the World Series is not a player's only goal, it is crucial to most players. The postseason trumps the regular season. Try to imagine an NBA or NFL player going through the regular season but sitting out the postseason due to a previous ACL injury and a games limit. Why should baseball be different?

When the Nationals kept Stephen Strasburg out of the postseason in 2012, they were looking ahead to future postseasons. A young and talented Nats team would have many opportunities to win the World Series. Better to preserve Strasburg's health for the long term.

That decision didn't turn out so well: the Nats lost the 2012 National League Division Series to St. Louis by only three games to two; Strasburg might have changed the result. Then Strasburg became injury-prone anyway and the Nats missed the playoffs in both 2013 and 2015. Given the inherent uncertainty in any pitcher's health or team's long-term prospects, depriving a *healthy* pitcher of postseason participation based on an arbitrary innings limit seems absurd.

The Mets did choose to limit Harvey's innings, but at the sensible time—the regular season—by spotting his starts at the end. They wisely allowed him to pitch in the postseason and he contributed significantly to their success. Harvey won two playoff games and pitched eight strong no-decision innings in game five of the World Series. He finished with a total of 216 innings.

So far, so good, for Harvey's elbow (though he suffered an unrelated shoulder injury in 2016), and the positive vibes the Mets generated from pitching Harvey contrasted nicely with the bad taste left when the Nationals sat Strasburg.

Boras surely meant well in advocating for his client, but the faux appeal of expert precision threw him off course. He treated Andrews's opinion as gospel even though it was not based on science or even convincing observations. A layman with common sense and a decent understanding of the basic issues could have given better advice: don't keep a healthy pitcher out of the postseason.

Causation versus Luck

Prior to their 2015 World Series loss to Kansas City, Harvey and the Mets put an epic whipping on the Chicago Cubs in the NLCS, sweeping the four-game series without ever trailing.

The Mets' four star pitchers (Harvey, Jacob deGrom, Noah Syndergaard, and Steven Matz) dominated the Cubs stars (Anthony Rizzo, Kyle Schwarber, and Kris Bryant), who hit a combined .190. Overall, Mets pitchers held the Cubs to a paltry eight runs in the four games, recalling the greatest performances in postseason history.[4]

Yet looking ahead, I'd pick the thrashed Cubs over the dominant Mets, and the Cubs core over the Mets core.

COIN FLIPS, BUTTERFLY WINGS, AND THE CUBS' REVENGE

How can one prefer the vanquished to the victors?

Because comparing the teams' prospects for the future takes on a different light when we dismiss the false notion that the sweep owed to the Mets' intrinsic superiority. That notion came only from post hoc analysis and hindsight bias (the Cubs were pre-series favorites). One team must win in every series, and, in retrospect, the winner appears the better team and the loser has weaknesses exposed. That's particularly true for the many people who see order in the universe and cause-and-effect all around them.

However, even a sweep does not mean that the winners were certain to win, ought to have won, or will win again in the future. In reality, best-of-seven postseason series are mostly coin flips. By the time baseball whittles down the field to the few best teams, one is rarely far superior to another. Randomness typically predominates in a short series between two reasonably competitive teams. Over the first one hundred World Series in which the competing teams had nonidentical regular-season records, the team with the better record won fifty.[5]

Sometimes randomness manifests in a bizarre key play late in a series: catcher Hank Gowdy stepping on his mask and missing a pop foul in game seven of the 1924 World Series; a routine grounder to short hitting a pebble and bouncing off Tony Kubek's throat (1960 World Series); umpire Don Denkinger missing an easy call at first base (1985 World Series). Or it manifests in never-to-be-repeated performances like Bobby Richardson driving home twelve runs in the 1960 World Series after an entire season with just twenty-six RBIs and Daniel Murphy (career high fourteen home runs) hitting homers in six consecutive postseason games in 2015.

But often, and more interestingly, random results owe to seemingly innocuous things that happen earlier, a phenomenon termed the butterfly effect by meteorologist Edward Lorenz. Lorenz found that the flapping of a butterfly's wings in Brazil could set off a tornado in Texas. That might seem hyperbolic, but the general idea is not: tiny changes in initial conditions can mushroom and lead to unexpected results.[6]

A sweep in a sports series gives the false appearance of a fixed, linear pathway. But owing to butterfly effects and other random twists, events in complex systems like baseball commonly unfold unpredictably in a bush-like pattern with many possible end points. Barely noticed early events—a 3–2 pitch called one way and not another; a ball that lands an inch fair and not foul; a runner who stumbles rounding a base; a fielder double-clutching a ball—may have profound consequences. One team takes an early lead rather than the other. That may change the psychological dynamics, the pitching rotations, batting lineups, pinch hitters, and relievers, and a host of other things we can't even think of, each of which in turn sets off a new cascade of events and moves a series along in unanticipated fashion.

Even the Mets pitching was not certain to dominate. After the series, we heard a lot of the cliché "good pitching beats good hitting." It's something that's said whenever a pitching staff dominates—another example of hindsight bias—and is ignored whenever a great staff doesn't. The Atlanta Braves had three Hall of Fame pitchers in their prime for nine seasons and won only one World Series. In a short series, randomness often holds its own against great pitchers: Steve Carlton, Greg Maddux, Randy Johnson, Clayton Kershaw, and David Price lost forty-two of a combined seventy postseason decisions.[7]

The Mets deserve all the credit they've been given for their accomplishment. We reward performance, not theory. But that shouldn't prompt us to over-interpret victories. Sometimes things just happen without revealing essential truths about the contestants. Events could easily have proceeded in many other directions.

As for 2016 and beyond, the Cubs have been helped by several off-season acquisitions. Moreover, another point favors the Cubs: their core four field players (including Addison Russell, who missed the NLCS due to injury) are more likely to remain healthy than the Mets' core four pitchers.

In fact, Harvey, deGrom, and Matz have already undergone Tommy John surgeries to repair career-threatening torn ulnar collateral elbow ligaments. In the modern era, major elbow injury (and reinjury) is nearing the rule, rather than the exception, and no preventative strategy has proven effective. Predicting the continued health of the Mets' stars nearly boils down to another coin flip.

In contrast, the Cubs' core players are all on the upward arc of predictably outstanding careers. Bryant, Schwarber, and Russell were rookies in 2015, and although none of them played full seasons they combined with the twenty-six-year-old Rizzo to hit eighty-six home runs. (Schwarber hit sixteen home runs in only 69 games.) That's merely a baseline, and certain to rise as these youngsters, as well as Javier Baez and Jorge Soler, develop.

On that basis, the Cubs' budding stars are more likely than the Mets' fragile pitching studs to take their team into the coin-flip stages of seasons to come.

THE GOOD (AND BAD) LUCK TWINS

The 2015 Cubs versus Mets NLCS, and many others before it, demonstrate the randomness of a short postseason series. What about the regular season? Here, randomness and luck play smaller roles than in the postseason. Over 162 games, teams have more time to recover from various problems, and luck often evens out. Nevertheless, even in the regular season we tend to underestimate the role of luck. Many teams have succumbed to injury or ill fortune in key spots during the course of a season, courtesy of merciless baseball gods. Conversely, others are blessed with various unforeseen good breaks.

Consider the Minnesota Twins, a financial have-not team with an inexplicably successful decade from 2001 to 2010. They actually outperformed the more publicized Oakland Athletics as the leading small-market, low-budget success story of the era. The Twins had more wins per dollar than Oakland, suffered only one losing season, and won their division six times over the decade.

Their success did not owe to following the Oakland model. Twins manager Rob Gardenhire and Assistant General Manager Rob Anthony both explicitly expressed disinterest in advanced analysis. They typically ignored Billy Beane's alleged insights. For example, Minnesota's starting lineup in 2010 featured five players drafted out of high school (contra Beane's policy), including superstars Joe Mauer and Justin Morneau.

How did the Twins succeed despite paltry resources? Hard to say. No unifying motif can be identified, even in retrospect. Their ranking in various categories—runs scored, stolen bases, batting average, ERA, and so forth—fluctuated widely from year to year, sometimes at or near the top of the league and sometimes at or near the bottom.

There was one exception: walks allowed. The Twins pitching staff, oddly, despite complete roster turnovers, distinguished itself from the mid-1980s on by allowing very few walks. We can't attribute a decade of success to this single modest accomplishment (the Twins struggled in the 1990s despite giving up similarly few walks) but there it is, steady as a metronome, idiosyncratic as can be.

We do know the Twins enjoyed one piece of supergood luck during this time, ironically stemming from their cash-strapped status. The Twins had the first overall pick in the 2001 draft. Everyone had pitcher Mark Prior as the top prospect, but the Twins knew he wanted more money than they could afford. For that reason only, they chose catcher Joe Mauer instead. Prior, of course, succumbed to repetitive arm injuries while Mauer became one of the best players in baseball—for the Twins, great fortune born out of poverty.

A second dose of good luck followed. Mauer became a free agent after his 2009 MVP season and could have signed elsewhere—as the best players on cash-strapped teams typically do—and in his case, for near-unprecedented money. However, he opted to stay with the Twins and gave them a hometown discount. For sure, his eight-year, $184-million contract was considerable, but he could have gotten more elsewhere, outside the Twins' ability to match.

The Twins' good run abruptly hit a wall after 2010 with four consecutive seasons winning 70 games or less. One reason for the precipitous decline: bad luck. Both Mauer and Morneau suffered injuries in 2011 and neither came back the same as before. It's hard to overcome the diminution of your two best players, particularly without the resources for replacements.

The Twins rebounded in 2015, winning 83 games and almost making the playoffs. How? No obvious important reason, perhaps more happenstance than anything else. But their staff, as always, gave up few walks — the second fewest in the American League.

The Twins' good luck came and went over the years, and their success or lack of it followed, but through it all they continued a thirty-year run of pitchers with great control. We like to seek discrete causes of everything, but there's no good explanation for that three-decade run — not good luck, not old statistics and traditional baseball thinking, not new statistics and modern baseball thinking. More just a quirk of nature.

3 ANALYTICS

Evaluating Baseball Statistics

As baseball is intrinsically numerical, its mathematical study began in the sport's infancy, progressed continuously, and mirrored trends in other fields. Though Bill James and Billy Beane publicized and accelerated the development of sabermetrics, they followed many like-minded thinkers. For example, writer F. C. Lane criticized batting average in the 1920s, Allan Roth provided numerical analysis (including emphasis on on-base percentage) for the Brooklyn Dodgers in the 1940s, and Earnshaw Cook considered many statistical issues in *Percentage Baseball* in 1964.

Thus, sabermetrics is not brand-new, and the issue is not whether to accept or discard it, but how best to apply its findings.

Many excellent sabermetric contributions are widely accepted: noting the limitations of traditional statistics; emphasizing on-base percentage and defense-independent pitching; providing insights into bunting, stealing bases, batted-ball patterns, and defensive shifts; and more broadly, fueling open-mindedness and the quest for more knowledge about the game.

But that does not mean that everything offered advances understanding, particularly as baseball analysis evolved from simpler data and ideas to complicated formulas and approaches that address nuanced issues like defense. Baseball media and fans do not always respect the limitations of newer advanced analytics. These are worth discussing, particularly as we have simple measures that suggest which statistical analyses are more useful than others.

First, we should acknowledge the difficulty in assessing any statistical formulation or baseball strategy. Baseball cannot perform the prospective, randomized testing that science (and social science) demands before drawing confident conclusions. In fact, assessments and strategies in baseball—how to rate players, when to steal or bunt, whom to play, where to position fielders, and so on —are based on retrospective observations that can only generate hypotheses.

Baseball's inability to formally test these hypotheses is important. Even seemingly powerful observations often cannot detect variables that lead to unanticipated results when those observations are put to use, as described by the law of unintended consequences.[1]

In the absence of formal study, baseball strategy proceeds as educated guesses, utilizing tenuous presumptions about cause-and-effect—a recipe for uncertainty, whether in science, baseball, or our personal lives. This contributes to wide fluxes in baseball thinking, for instance, from favoring aggressive baserunning to criticizing it and then backing off the critique; from extolling defense to diminishing its importance and then returning to the initial emphasis.

Thus, we should approach these kinds of retrospective-based formulations with healthy skepticism. As mathematician John Allen Paulos wrote (*A Mathematician Reads the Newspaper*), "nonlinear systems demonstrate a complex unpredictability," and we should be "wary of . . . precise assertions" in these areas.

However, while skepticism is warranted, it should not apply equally to all proposals. We have, as noted, quantitative ways to analyze statistical formulations for characteristics   reliability and precision—that should bestow more (or less) respect for the conclusions the data suggest.

Reliability measures how much a statistic measures a true attribute of a player versus chance. The reliability of many baseball statistics may be assessed by their year-to-year reproducibility (autocorrelation), as quantified by their correlation coefficient. Notably, some older statistics like batting average and ERA have low correlation coefficients, meaning that the results randomly fluctuate from year to year well beyond the effect of evolving player abilities. Consequently, sabermetricians hold these traditional statistics in lesser regard.

Moreover, statistics should come with a mathematical expression of their precision (or lack of it)—confidence intervals, standard errors, or similar measures. For example, a wins above replacement (WAR) value (a composite measure of hitting, running and fielding; see next section) of 5.0 for one player and 4.0 for another, with a standard deviation of 0.1, would indicate a major difference between the two players (5.0 +/– 0.1 versus 4.0 +/– 0.1). However, with a standard deviation of 1.0, the same WAR values essentially overlap (5.0 +/– 1.0 versus 4.0 +/– 1.0) without any significant difference between them.

To summarize, statistics should be reliable (as measured by reproducibility) and precise (as measured by small margins of error).

We can illustrate the use and value of reliability and precision measures by assessing the WAR statistic, which is widely cited by the media and by fans, often without apparent recognition of its limitations.

We'll take some big whacks at WAR but need to keep in mind that the foibles of WAR do not impugn all of sabermetrics. As noted, there have been many significant contributions of advanced analytics, and we'll move on in this section to discuss some of them, including the emphasis on on-base percentage (OBP) and on-base plus slugging percentage (OPS); the development of batting average on balls in play (BABIP) and defense-independent pitching (DIP) and how they might be used; several of the managers who (variably) use them; insights into clutch hitting and pitcher-versus-hitter matchups; and end by speculating about the future of analytics.

MAKE LOVE, NOT WAR

The search for a single number to assess a player's overall performance and/or ability appeals to the desire for clarity and addresses one of baseball's central and most difficult questions: Who's better? Cobb or Ruth? DiMaggio or Williams? Mantle or Mays? Kershaw, Greinke, or Arrieta? Player-value assessments inform award selections, Hall of Fame votes, free-agent signings, and trades. They make up a basic currency of baseball.

Historically, these determinations have been subjective and the questions often unsolvable. WAR addresses these frequently intractable problems by combining separate assessments of hitting, baserunning, and defense (with additional adjustments, and with separate evaluation of pitching) into a single number. Each of the three components is expressed in the common unit of runs (added or lost). These are added together to yield a final run value. Runs are converted into wins, and wins are compared with a hypothetical minimum salary "replacement" player. Thus, the final term: wins above replacement (player).

WAR came to public attention during the 2012 season. Miguel Cabrera won the Triple Crown and was widely known as the league's best hitter. However, Mike Trout was a superior base runner and defensive player, giving him the higher WAR value. Who deserved MVP, the Triple Crown winner or the WAR winner?

The WAR-based case for Trout relied on WAR's accuracy. How good a statistic is it? For WAR to provide an actionable assessment of player performance, each WAR component must be accurate (putting aside the issue of intangibles—leadership, hustle, and other factors that elevate players like Pete Rose and Derek Jeter beyond their statistics).

As it turns out, each of the three WAR components has weaknesses that belie the accuracy of, and hype given to, the cumulative WAR value and, therefore, the case for Trout as MVP.

Let's look at the WAR components, beginning with defense.

HOW WELL CAN WE MEASURE BASEBALL DEFENSE?

The value of defense has fluctuated in the minds of baseball analysts over time. Historically, baseball revered many of its greatest players, including Willie Mays, Joe DiMaggio, Roberto Clemente, and Johnny Bench, for their defensive prowess almost as much as their offense. Hall of Fame voters elected Ozzie Smith and Bill Mazeroski primarily based on their field play. The defense of Brooks Robinson, Mark Belanger, and Paul Blair was considered crucial to the success of the Baltimore Orioles in the 1960s and '70s, and Graig Nettles's acrobatics at third base helped swing the 1978 World Series to the Yankees.

But as sabermetricians gave thought to defense, they became skeptical of its importance. For example, in *The Hidden Game of Baseball*, John Thorn and Pete Palmer asserted that fielding amounts to just 6 percent of baseball. More famously, Billy Beane considered defense overrated, and felt that he could get more value by replacing defense-oriented players with similarly priced alternatives who produced more runs.

It was hard to know how to value defense when the available data —errors, putouts, and assists—had obvious flaws. Sabermetricians logically responded by seeking better data, a journey that led to Mitchel Lichtman's ultimate zone rating (UZR), the best known of the modern defense-measuring systems used in WAR calculations.

UZR and related systems reflect an ambitious and creative attempt to introduce scientific reasoning (for the first time) into baseball analysis. UZR evaluates a fielder on every play by comparing the result of the play to historical results of other players on similar or, ideally, exactly alike batted balls—that is, a certain kind of ball (velocity, trajectory, and so on) hit to a specific area on the field (one of sixty-four zones) in specific situations (outs, baserunners, types of pitchers, and so on). The cumulative results of all the batted balls hit to a fielder, as compared with the historical norms of similar balls, translates into the number of runs that a fielder saves or gives up per season.

Thus, UZR deals with the myriad characteristics that distinguish one batted ball and its fate from another by eliminating them as factors, except for the one variable of most interest—the fielder's performance. If you control for all other variables, the fate of a batted ball (caught or not caught) depends only on the fielder.

UZR is a terrific idea, carefully considered, and meticulously calculated. But how well does it work?

Unfortunately, we cannot test it against a gold standard or by prospective study. But UZR's difficulties go beyond that. Most importantly, it is not particularly reliable: the year-to-year correlation coefficient is modest, reported as low as 0.35–0.45 by sabermetrician Benjamin Baumer and sports economist Andrew Zimbalist (*The Sabermetric Revolution: Assessing the Growth of Analytics in Baseball*) and 0.5 by Lichtman.[2]

These values are similar to or even worse than the year-to-year correlation coefficients of ERA and batting average—statistics that, as noted, baseball analysts consider excessively random.

UZR's modest reproducibility derives from the inability to eliminate the many variables that complicate defensive analysis. Notably, UZR does not account for where a fielder stood as a pitch was delivered, nor whether the fielder or a manager or coach from the bench directed that positioning, that is, it does not assess positioning as a skill. And many of the details of the batted balls are decided by the *subjective* judgments of observers called "stringers," belying the precision sought for by the basic idea of UZR.

To his credit, Lichtman acknowledges that "we don't know precisely where a ball is hit, we don't know exactly how long the ball was airborne or on the ground before it lands, is touched, or passes a fielder, and we don't know exactly where the fielders were positioned." Those are just some of the variables UZR doesn't account for.

Lichtman does not publicly report confidence intervals, standard deviations, or similar indices of the data's precision, but the inability to capture so many variables does not inspire confidence. In fact, Baumer and Zimbalist note that UZR's margin of error is large enough that "among all players from 2002 to 2011, almost 92 percent had a performance (UZR value) that was not distinguishable from zero at their position."

These problems manifest in some odd and illustrative results. Derek Jeter typically had poor UZR values until 2009, when his UZR abruptly soared, only to revert to usual in subsequent seasons. Alfonso Soriano, widely regarded as a poor outfielder, turned in the single best defensive season (in 2007) of any player from 2002 to 2012. Yet two years before his unprecedented great defensive season, Soriano had a terrible UZR. In 2012, at age thirty-six and virtually immobile, he bounced back for a strong rating. Examples like these abound.

With its modest reliability and its imprecision, one-year measurements of UZR (and, therefore, WAR) are not accurate enough to make confident real-time decisions about awards,[3] all-star teams, and personnel. Lichtman acknowledges the problems with one-year data, and notes that increasing the sample size to three years yields better results. Unfortunately, three years of data do not help MVP voters.[4]

Of course, these systems are works in progress, and Lichtman and others strive to improve them. One hope is that more specific data (for example, from computers and ballpark cameras) will reduce variability and allow comparisons of more nearly identical batted balls.

However, the UZR approach has intrinsic, insurmountable limitations. The problem involves the trade-off between sample size and precision. If we determine that a batted ball traveled at exactly x miles per hour, at an arc of y degrees, and landed within a four-square-foot area in right field, on a sunny, ninety-degree day, and we know the right fielder began the play at another four-square-foot area, then we will have controlled for many more variables, yielding greater accuracy when comparing the result of the play with other plays sharing those precise characteristics.

Unfortunately, we will find very few plays with all those exact characteristics. What we gain in precision we lose in sample size, and smaller sample size increases the chances of error. We can increase the sample size by easing the precision—say, by enlarging the zones on the field to sixteen square feet. But every relaxation of precision increases the extent to which we are comparing unlike batted balls, thereby decreasing the usefulness of the comparison. This trade-off cannot be eliminated, which suggests that acquiring more specific data with improved technology will not lead to a significant increase in knowledge. Smaller sample sizes will introduce new errors that replace those of larger sample sizes containing more dissimilar batted balls.

BASERUNNING AND BALLPARK EFFECTS

The problems with measuring defense troubles the WAR statistic. The same can be said for baserunning and for the same reasons. Sabermetricians have devised complex systems (for example, "equivalent baserunning runs," or EqBRR) to measure baserunning along the same creative principle as UZR: comparing a runner's result on a given play to an expected result based on historical norms. But the effort to capture countless variables in order to isolate a runner's performance is as daunting as the attempt to isolate a fielder's performance. For example, to evaluate a runner's progress on a base hit (for example, did he go from first to third on a single?) you should consider exactly where the ball landed, its velocity and geometric course, how the fielder caught it (backhand, coming in, going out), who the fielder was or what kind of throw he made, the game context (the score and inning determine the runner's and fielder's aggressiveness), and much more. The difficulty in capturing baserunning variables explains why the year-to-year correlation coefficient for "ultimate baserunning" (FanGraphs baserunning WAR component) is also only about 0.5.

That's two independent statistics of questionable reliability that contribute to the final WAR result—a double whammy.

How about the third component—batting? Here, measurements are more straightforward and accurate. A simple statistic like OPS (combining on-base and slugging percentages) correlates well with runs scored. But even batting statistics may be problematic—after all, batters hit in different-sized parks and cities with varying weather. These factors surely affect batting statistics without reflecting player skills.

Returning to the Trout versus Cabrera 2012 MVP argument, sabermetricians actually supported Trout not only for his fielding and running superiority, but for his hitting superiority too! Although Cabrera won the Triple Crown and also led the league in on-base percentage and slugging percentage—an impressive batting résumé—Detroit's Comerica Park is considered a more hitter-friendly park than Angel Stadium. After adjustment for the different parks with sabermetric "park factors," Trout outhit Cabrera as measured, for example, by Baseball-Reference's adjusted on-base plus slugging percentage. This gave Trout his own triple crown—outdoing Cabrera in baserunning, fielding, and hitting—and suggested to some an easy decision for MVP (nevertheless, the Baseball Writer's Association of America awarded Cabrera the MVP award in both 2012 and 2013).

However, FanGraphs describes ballpark adjustments as "more problematic than one might think." Consequently, FanGraphs' park rankings differ significantly from ESPN's ranking and others. When qualified sabermetricians provide very different answers to the same problem, the results do not inspire confidence in any of them.

The problem with unreliable park factors deepens when we apply them to player comparisons such as Trout versus Cabrera. Adjusting for Comerica Park and Angel Stadium alone does not suffice to address the problem. Trout and Cabrera played different eighty-one-game away schedules. Cabrera played in five parks in 2012 that Trout did not; Trout played in three that Cabrera did not; and they played different numbers of games in other parks. The final park adjustment for the two players involves perhaps twenty-one different parks with twenty-one imprecise measures. A calculation that combines so many imprecise components yields an untrustworthy result.

Thus, even the hitting component of WAR is problematic, making it a clean sweep: All three components—defense, baserunning, and (to a lesser extent) hitting—leave something to be desired. Combining three troubled components yields an even worse composite result.

With all these problems, why did WAR gain prominence in baseball conversation? First, the baseball public tends to accept sabermetric proclamations, particularly complex formulations, as gospel. But also because some people aware of the problems still insist that WAR remains useful as the best available measure of player performance. To those, I ask, how do you know that WAR improves on the traditional approach of combining simpler statistics, observation, general knowledge, and intuition? Why assume that? Although we have good reasons to question traditional player evaluation, adding numbers to and increasing the sophistication of analysis does not automatically bring progress. Sometimes it does, and sometimes it doesn't.

An informed fan did not need UZR or EqBRR to understand Trout's defense and baserunning superiority over Cabrera, nor to tout Trout for MVP based on superior all-around play. But an informed fan (like the majority of MVP voters) might still reasonably argue for Cabrera on the basis that his incredible hitting overrode Trout's obvious defensive and running superiority.

WAR is not good enough to solve the Trout versus Cabrera dilemma. It isn't good enough to solve any of the difficult player choices going back to Ruth versus Cobb. No matter how often media members cite WAR, it isn't good enough to solve anything.

Let's not go to WAR.

Reevaluating Players from a Modern Perspective

Modern statistical-based thinking does provide insights in areas outside of WAR, leading to surprising findings in player evaluation.

MANTLE BETTER THAN MAYS

Terry Cashman's 1981 song "Willie, Mickey and the Duke" reminded baseball fans of the 1950s controversy over which New York center fielder—Mays, Mantle, or Snider—reigned supreme. Snider faded from the debate early on, but the Mantle versus Mays question continues to this day.

The upper hand fluctuated during their playing careers: Mays grabbed the initial edge with monster seasons in 1954 and 1955; Mantle surpassed him with a Triple Crown (for both leagues) in 1956, was equally outstanding in 1957, hit fifty-four home runs in 1961, and won the MVP award in 1962. Mays answered with a string of outstanding seasons culminating in a fifty-two-home-run MVP year in 1965. Mantle slowed down first, retiring after the 1968 season, while Mays continued playing through 1973.

Mays's more sustained excellence resulted in greater career numbers in traditional measurements (base hits, runs, RBIS, home runs). As the final numbers came in, the comparison of the players turned clearly in Mays's favor, and Mays's higher ranking persisted for decades.

Mays drew stronger support for his Hall of Fame induction (Mantle, in 1974, 88 percent of votes; Mays, in 1979, 95 percent) and by 1999, prominent end-of-the-century player rankings all favored Mays, generally by significant margins: the *Sporting News* (Mays 2nd, Mantle 17th); the Society for American Baseball Research (Mays 8th, Mantle 12th), the Major League Baseball All-Century Team (fan vote: Mays 1,115,896; Mantle 988,168); and ESPN Sport Century (Mays 8th, Mantle 37th, of all athletes).

But in 2012, ESPN's "MLB Hall of 100" rated Mantle higher (9th, with Mays 2nd) than previous polls, and in two recent well-received books, Jane Leavy's *The Last Boy* and Allen Barra's *Mickey and Willie*, the authors argued for Mantle's supremacy over Mays. After all this time, how was Mantle improving?

Leavy's and Barra's endorsements of Mantle over Mays largely derived from recent statistical insights; most importantly, the increased valuation of avoiding outs. Mantle's greater ability to draw walks and reach base safely was probably the single largest distinction between the two players. Mantle had a lifetime on-base percentage of .421, Mays .384. This translated into a higher career OPS (on-base plus slugging percentage) and superior "linear weights" assessments of overall offensive performance (linear-weights formulas include relative valuations of walks, different base hits, and other plays). Mantle's superiority in these measures increases as we select out smaller prime periods (for instance, ten best years, five best years).

The simplest way to illustrate Mantle's advantage is to count the outs from at bats. Mays averaged thirty-four more outs per season (adjusted for plate appearances) than Mantle. During their five best seasons, Mays averaged fifty-four more outs per year (adjusted for plate appearances)—the equivalent of about twelve games of failed at bats each year. (The difference in the number of outs increases if double plays are included—Mantle, as previously discussed, hit into remarkably few: 113 versus Mays's 251).

Of course, Mays was greater on the bases and, especially, in the field. However, these aspects of the game, as noted, are difficult to measure accurately even with advanced statistics. Mays's baserunning advantage was probably small, as Mantle was widely known as the fastest runner in baseball early in his career and was a terrific base stealer (80 percent career success rate, Mays 77 percent—though the Yankees called upon Mantle to steal less often).

Frank Crosetti, the longtime Yankees coach, commented that "Mantle could see better than his coaches exactly when to move from first to third or to score from second on a single, or to stretch doubles into triples. He had a kind of perfect baseball sense."[5] In addition, his contemporaries considered Mantle a good outfielder; he won a Gold Glove Award in 1962. Bill James estimated that Mays's defense saved only five to six runs per year (translating into winning one game every two years) as compared with Mantle's.

Mays conceivably equalled or surpassed Mantle as an all-around player, but the argument for Mays requires his vaguer baserunning and defensive superiority to counter Mantle's demonstrably superior performance at the plate. It is especially difficult to claim Mays's overall superiority when comparing peak performances. James argues that "Mickey Mantle was, at his peak in 1956–57 and again in 1961–62 clearly a greater player than Willie Mays—and it is not a close or difficult decision."

Player evaluations logically change as statistics accumulate and their interpretations evolve. But there may be more to Mantle's initial postretirement decline (relative to Mays and others) than just numbers, rooted in something that should not be relevant: the public unveiling of his sordid off-the-field life.

For most of his career, Mantle symbolized greatness. In the 1960s, he was probably American sports' most venerated figure, "the Last Hero" as described by biographer David Faulkner; he was the only athlete of his era to regularly receive standing ovations in visiting ballparks.

One important aspect of his popularity was his valor in the face of injury. Mantle essentially played his career on one leg (according to Leavy, Mantle's torn ACL and MCL in 1951 were never reconstructed); for the latter half, with only one good arm as well (according to Barra, he never recovered from a 1957 shoulder injury), and even though no one knew these details at the time, the manner in which Mantle persevered in pain seemed epic.

But the details of Mantle's alcoholism and boorish behavior that emerged postretirement tainted his public image. As we learned that he preferred drinking to rehabilitation and training, Mantle's playing with injuries seemed less epic and more self-perpetuated. To many, he was no longer a hero or even a decent person.

The alcohol saga (superimposed on the injuries) also fueled a "what might have been" meme, in part energized by Mantle's public lamenting that he had wasted his immense talent. Mantle's name became associated as much with failure as success. It would not be surprising if this increasingly critical perspective—Mantle's own perspective—affected the evaluation of his play.

That would be unfortunate. Alcohol and what might have been are important to the Mantle biography, but they are not relevant to judging what actually happened on the field. The record is the record, whether generated sober or not, injury-free or not, with maximal or minimal rehabilitation, with or without other impediments. And Mantle's record looks better than ever when reevaluated with modern insights.

As the late Professor Gould wrote in pointed response (and without the flamboyant hyperbole of his DiMaggio Streak analysis) to those preoccupied with alternative histories: "To hell with what might have been. . . . What happened is all we have. By this absolute and irrefragable standard, Mantle was the greatest ballplayer of his time."

ICHIRO, THE ANTI-MANTLE

If modern statistics like OBP and OPS smile on Mickey Mantle, they frown on Ichiro Suzuki, Mantle's opposite, who had few walks, few home runs, and made a lot of outs.

In fact, modern metrics call into question Ichiro's previously certain Hall of Fame induction; under the sabermetric eye, Ichiro becomes a borderline Hall of Famer.

How could that be? Ichiro is a ten-time all-star, ten-time Gold Glove winner, the all-time record holder for hits in a season (a ridiculously high 262 in 2004), and has a sparkling .314 career batting average. He surpassed 3,000 career hits. That surely seems enough for induction.

Modern analytics, however, show a completely different picture on the offensive side: Ichiro ranks 756th lifetime in career on-base percentage plus slugging percentage (OPS) and 1,464th (over the last 100 years) in FanGraphs weighted on-base average (WOBA is a derivative of OPS that applies fractional valuations to walks and every type of base hit). That bears repeating: in a revealing sabermetric batting valuation, Ichiro ranks 1,464th.

His best seasons weren't much better by the newer criteria; his highest single-season OPS is not close to the top 500 of all time.

The challenge to Ichiro's Hall of Fame credentials may seem absurd to his many fans, but OPS is widely accepted as a valid statistic, and WOBA just tweaks it. These statistics suggest that hitters with high batting averages but limited power and few bases on balls (such as Hall of Famers Rod Carew and Tony Gwynn, as well as Pete

Rose) have been overrated. These players best illustrate the difference between traditional (emphasizing base hits and batting average) and modern thinking (emphasizing reaching base safely and on-base percentage) about batting, with almost all observers agreeing on the merits of the modern approach.

But there's more to baseball than hitting. Like Mays, Ichiro excelled on the bases and in the field.

WAR is an imprecise measure of overall performance (including defense and baserunning), but in this instance it tracks OPS. Ichiro ranked in the top 10 in baseball in WAR for a season (4th in 2004) only once. His career WAR value ranks only around 130th for position players. This is much better than 756th or 1,464th, but there are more than thirty players ahead of Ichiro in career WAR who have fared poorly in Hall of Fame voting and have no significant support for induction (for example, Willie Randolph, Willie Davis, Sal Bando, Reggie Smith, and Buddy Bell). Thus, a discrepancy remains between traditional and sabermetric evaluations of Ichiro.

While discussing Ichiro's Hall of Fame merits, we should consider factors in Hall of Fame evaluations emphasized by Bill James: performances in pennant races and postseason play; comparisons with other Hall of Famers or candidates; MVP and All-Star voting; significant intangibles; and notable contributions to the game.

Some of these criteria do not advance Ichiro's candidacy. His rookie season MVP marked his only year in the top five, and he made the top ten in MVP voting only four times—overall, an unspectacular MVP record. In addition, his postseason record was brief (only two seasons and no World Series games) and lacks any memorable moments.

Jacoby Ellsbury and Kenny Lofton compare reasonably well in major aspects of play to Ichiro, and neither merit serious Hall of Fame consideration (Lofton received only 3.2 percent of the Hall of Fame votes in 2013 and fell off the ballot). In their primes, they were as fast and as accomplished base stealers as Ichiro in his, and although Ichiro had a stronger throwing arm, both Lofton and Ellsbury fielded well and played center field, a more important position than Ichiro's right field. Both Lofton and Ellsbury rank above Ichiro in defensive WAR. As hitters, they have similar career slugging percentages, on-base percentages, and OPS (Lofton .794, Ellsbury and Ichiro tied, as of mid-August, at .762). Ellsbury has a superior postseason record, including outstanding performances in the 2007 World Series and in the 2013 ALDS. All things considered, not enough separates the three players to advance Ichiro's case.

Other considerations do support Ichiro. His unique style as a slap hitter and his grace and élan captivated many fans. His courage in leaving Japan and his success in MLB accelerated the movement of talented players like Yu Darvish, Masahiro Tanaka, and more to come. He was an ambassador for the game. Perhaps he should also receive credit for his play in Japan.

All of these factors, alas, do not seem definitive in either direction. In contrast, breaking the seemingly unassailable, all-time single-season hit record seems the stuff of legend, the sort of rare accomplishment and contribution to the game's history that should make a Hall of Famer out of a borderline candidate.

But not so fast—from the sabermetric perspective, the same reservations that pertain to Ichiro's entire career hold for the record-breaking 2004 season: few extra base hits (37; only 8 home runs) and few walks (68) in 762 plate appearances, and a large number of outs (464). Getting 262 hits in a season undoubtedly impresses, but had it occurred a decade later when sabermetrics was more entrenched, it would have seemed less significant in the eyes of many.

Thus, Ichiro's evaluation returns us to an elementary issue raised by sabermetricians: Were singles (81 percent of Ichiro's career base hits) and batting average traditionally overrated? Most analysts believe so.

The Baseball Writers' Association of America (BBWAA), which votes on the Hall of Fame, clearly embraces traditional thinking, having twice voted Miguel Cabrera MVP over the sabermetric-favored Mike Trout. That suggests the writers will not pay heed to the reevaluation of Ichiro's numerous singles and few walks, and will induct him into the Hall.

I hope that's the case. I believe that modern statistics underrate his defense and baserunning. The Hall of Fame–level regard held for him by his contemporaries supports Ichiro's all-around brilliance. It would feel wrong if retrospective reevaluation of his too-few walks and homers overrode the career-long reverence most everyone felt for Ichiro.

Therefore, I'd induct Ichiro, but I'd do so understanding that we now know him as an overrated batter.

THE CURIOUS CASE OF RICKEY HENDERSON

Throughout Rickey Henderson's historic career, he rarely was considered one of the very best players in baseball, at least not by MVP voters, who ranked Henderson in the top eight in the American League only three times in twenty-five seasons.

Yet in 1999, near the end of his playing days, the *Sporting News*, the Society for American Baseball Research, and an expert panel representing Major League Baseball all ranked Henderson around fiftieth to sixtieth among all players in baseball history. Four years later, Bill James ranked Henderson twenty-sixth, and in 2012, another panel of thirty experts chosen by ESPN.com placed him fourteenth all-time. Henderson's legacy seemed to improve as time passed.

How can that be explained?

Henderson's Methuselah-like stamina—twenty-five years in MLB, ending up fourth all time in games played and plate appearances—surely helped as his career proceeded, enabling huge career numbers, including the top totals in runs scored, walks, and stolen bases. Extraordinarily long careers that boosted totals in important categories also helped Carl Yastrzemski and Pete Rose in their all-time rankings. Yet neither Yaz (fortieth) nor Rose (thirty-eighth) came close to number fourteen. Other outstanding players with large cumulative statistical totals, including Robin Yount, Paul Molitor, and Eddie Murray, did not crack the top fifty.

We need more than career numbers—which were apparent before he retired—to explain Henderson's ascension, particularly to the fourteenth spot years later. Could Henderson's late-career and postretirement ascension (like Mickey Mantle's) derive from a sabermetric-based reevaluation?

Henderson drew a ton of walks, which were undervalued during his playing days. They received greater emphasis later on as more comprehensive assessments of batting gained traction, but with a .279 lifetime batting average and modest power (compared with other great outfielders), Henderson still ranks only 306th lifetime in OPS and 301st in its sophisticated relative, WOBA. Even with his walks properly credited by sabermetricians, Henderson does not rank as an all-time great for his work in the batter's box.[6]

Nor does consideration of defense help him. Though contemporary fans and media considered him a very good outfielder (despite a weak arm), analytics did not: Henderson's career defensive WAR value actually places him below the standard replacement player.

Which brings us to the most important aspect of Henderson's career: stolen bases. Any consideration of Henderson's talents immediately brings to mind base stealing, as he holds both the single-season and career records.

But here's where things get puzzling: his stock rose *after* sabermetricians declared stolen bases and baserunning *overrated*. That notion derived from properly recognizing the harm accrued from an out on the bases. For example, during Henderson's record breaking 130-stolen-base season, he was thrown out forty-two times; according to James Click (*Baseball Between the Numbers*), the net benefit of Henderson's stolen bases was trivial.

Largely due to sabermetrics, the incidence of stolen-base attempts in MLB dwindled to a forty-three-year low in the 2015 season. Baseball now views stolen-base attempts as more valuable in selected situations than as a broad strategy. Only a few high-volume stealers remain, none of whom approach Henderson.

The same pertains to baserunning overall: overrated. Click concluded, from mathematical studies of other areas of baserunning besides stealing, that the best base runners add only one additional win a year. Henderson's 1982 masterpiece of baserunning generated only four extra runs for his team.

That included secondary benefits great base runners might provide. My coauthor on *The Beauty of Short Hops*, Alan Hirsch, described a "Hendy effect" when he watched Henderson play for the Yankees in the 1980s. When Henderson reached first base, the entire game changed. The pitcher threw over to first (sometimes time and time again); he varied the timing of his deliveries to the plate; he shortened his stride; he threw more fastballs; he looked frazzled. Alan believed that the batters behind Henderson benefitted from the distraction induced by the threat of a steal. That rang true.[7]

However, when sabermetricians such as Tom Tango (*The Book: Playing the Percentages in Baseball*) studied this hypothesis, they found it lacking. Batters' statistics did not improve with "disruptive runners" (including Henderson) on base.[8]

The modern thinking about Henderson seems paradoxical: He ended his career ranked by analytics around 300th for his work in the batter's box; analysis of his defense did not help him, and his baserunning, especially his base stealing—the skill that separated him from everyone else—was eventually devalued. Yet as his main attribute lost stature, his reputation soared.

Rickey Henderson sometimes puzzled observers with odd behavior and syntax. Turns out, his entire career was a puzzle.

Additional Modern Insights

The run-up to the 2015 National League Cy Young Award voting included discussion of two relatively new statistics (BABIP and DIPS) and one old idea (bad luck). The new statistics and the old idea did not end up changing the expected result (nor should they have), but the discussion served the purpose of bringing these insights to light.

The Chicago Cubs' Jake Arrieta (22–6 won-loss record, 1.77 ERA) won the award over the Los Angeles Dodgers' Zack Greinke (19–3, 1.66) and Clayton Kershaw (16–7, 2.13).

Arrieta and Greinke sported nearly indistinguishable statistics. The major distinction between the two was that Greinke dominated the first half of the season and Arrieta the second. Thus, Arrieta's selection reflected voters' psychology: more voters were influenced by recent, easily remembered events (from Arrieta's finish) than were anchored to initial impressions (from Greinke's start).

DID BAD LUCK COST CLAYTON KERSHAW THE CY YOUNG AWARD?

Some statistical-savvy observers supported the third-place finisher Kershaw for the award, despite his less impressive won-lost record and ERA. They argued that Kershaw actually outpitched his two rivals, but fell victim to bad luck.

Can we really measure bad luck? Perhaps—surprisingly—yes, at least to some extent. The newer statistics—batting average on balls in play (BABIP) and defense independent pitching statistics (DIPS)—suggested Kershaw's bad luck and supported his claim to the award.

BABIP measures the fate of batted balls that remain in play (that is, it excludes home runs)—whether they drop in for base hits or are caught (hits divided by total number of batted balls in play). Historically, baseball observers believed that the best pitchers induce weaker-hit balls that are more commonly caught. However, around fifteen years ago statistician Voros McCracken came to the startling conclusion that "There is little if any difference among major league pitchers in their ability to prevent hits on balls hit into the field of play." This counterintuitive idea is supported by (among other things) the wide year-to-year variations of a pitcher's BABIP, and it garnered widespread acceptance in baseball.

This means that the variable results of (non–home run) balls hit off different pitchers are explained by luck (bloop hits, line drives hit right at fielders, and so on), defense, and ballpark configurations. Pitchers should not be credited or debited for deviations of their BABIP from the league average since these deviations do not reflect a pitcher's skill. A pitcher's ERA should be evaluated with consideration as to whether his BABIP suggested unusually good (or bad) luck, or the other factors. This constitutes a significant contribution to baseball thinking.

Greinke and Arrieta had lower ERAs than Kershaw in 2015 but only because they had lower BABIPs. Therefore, per McCracken's observation, Greinke and Arrieta's superior ERAs do not suggest better pitching than Kershaw. Batted balls were more commonly caught against Greinke than his teammate Kershaw solely due to better luck, and against Arrieta (relative to Kershaw) for some combination of better luck, defense, or a different home ballpark.

DIPS suggests what a pitcher's ERA would have been without the vagaries of defense and luck by measuring outcomes pitchers mostly control—walks, hit-by-pitches, strikeouts, and home runs allowed. If we eliminate the roles of luck and defense in catching batted balls, Kershaw's ERA (as predicted from his DIPS) would have been the lowest of the three pitchers. He performed the best at those tasks a pitcher can regulate. This argues for Kershaw as the Cy Young winner.

But not conclusively: McCracken's claim ("little if any . . .")—based on relatively short-term data—exaggerated the lack of a pitcher's effect on the fate of a batted ball. Great pitchers do often shine by inducing, to a significant extent, weaker contact and batted balls that are more often caught.

Over a long period of time, defense and (especially) luck tend to even out, and the pitcher's effect on the fate of batted balls in play becomes clear. For example, Sandy Koufax has a career BABIP twenty points below league average and well below that of contemporary Dodger pitchers Don Drysdale and Johnny Podres.[9] Mariano Rivera has a career BABIP approximately thirty points below league average, and almost fifty points better than his Yankee contemporary Andy Pettitte. All those broken bats and weakly hit balls off Rivera were not a mirage.

Almost all of the last nineteen modern-day pitchers elected to the Hall of Fame had a career BABIP less than the league average, often ten or more points below.

Thus, for the purposes of 2015's Cy Young Award we must ask: Do Greinke's and Arrieta's extremely low BABIPs, far below their usual values and Kershaw's value, derive from great defense and/or luck, Rivera-like weakly hit balls, or a combination? Does Kershaw's higher BABIP suggest bad luck? In general, how should we apply BABIP and DIPS to Cy Young Award considerations?

There's no exact answer, but we can make sensible judgments. For example, discordance between a pitcher's BABIP and his DIPS suggests unusually good or bad luck, particularly if he has not changed teams/ballparks. If a pitcher strikes out more batters and gives up fewer home runs than usual (that is, improved DIPS suggesting better pitching) it's hard to conclude that an increased BABIP (more batted balls falling in for base hits) derives from harder hit balls (from worse pitching) rather than bad luck or defensive ineptitude. Though not dramatically different, in 2015 Kershaw had his highest BABIP since his rookie year in 2008, despite a major-league leading DIPS and obvious brilliance (including 301 strikeouts, the most in major league baseball in thirteen years)—clearly he suffered some bad luck.

On the other hand, when *all* measures of a pitcher's ability improve—luck/defense-dependent and independent—without a change in teams/ballparks, it's more likely that balls hit off those pitchers were caught more frequently because they were hit more weakly than before. In this situation, we ought to credit a pitcher for the batted balls being caught more often (that is, the pitchers were good, not lucky). This holds for Greinke's and Arrieta's 2015 seasons, particularly given their incredible overall performances.

More broadly, awards like the Cy Young should be based on performance. What actually happened trumps what might or what one thinks should have happened. Removing a pitcher's BABIP from his assessment (to yield DIPS) informs general managers and fantasy-league players about likely future performance (since DIPS does not typically undergo wide year-to-year fluctuations)—potentially very helpful—but it does not change what already took place. The BABIP adjustment serves best to predict the future; the award serves to reward the past.

Fielders caught the balls hit against Greinke and Arrieta in 2015 more frequently than those hit against Kershaw. For the purposes of the Cy Young Award, Greinke and Arrieta should be commended for this, not penalized. Arrieta or Greinke deserved the award.

CLUTCH HITTERS AND "OWNING" PITCHERS

Baseball analytics deserves its greatest kudos when it overturns dogma and/or creates new insights. DIPS provides one example. As another example, analysts debunked the widely held belief that some hitters come through in the clutch—Mr. October Reggie Jackson, Captain Clutch Derek Jeter, David Ortiz, and others have been considered clutch hitters who summon up additional character or skill to excel in important situations. Yet batting statistics for almost all hitters (including Jeter, Jackson, and Ortiz) with runners in scoring position (RISP) roughly track their overall performance.[10] The same holds for "high leverage" and "late and close" situations, as well as postseason play. Small sample sizes and statistical randomness explain the outliers with better clutch-hitting data than expected. It turns out that so-called clutch hitters are simply really good hitters performing as usual.

Bill James summed it up: "Many athletes truly believe that they are successful at what they do not because God made them strong and fast and agile, but because *they're better people than the rest of us*. . . . That's where all the bullshit about clutch ability comes from."

Consider another so-called baseball truism: that a player may "own" an opponent. As Jeter once put it, "There are always situations like that in baseball, where guys own certain pitchers." For example, Mike Redmond, a lifetime .285 hitter, batted .438 in forty-eight at bats against Hall of Fame pitcher Tom Glavine. TV announcers routinely cite statistics like this for batter-pitcher matchups. In fact, this information misleads. Individual batter-pitcher matchups, including Redmond versus Glavine, never reach statistical significance owing to the small number of at bats involved.

However, in contrast to the relatively solid conclusion about the absence of truly clutch hitters, we should be wary about denying that hitters may own pitchers, or vice versa.

If Redmond batted .438 against Glavine in over 1,000 at bats, that would have been statistically significant and predictive of continued success. No batter gets anywhere near 1,000 at bats against one pitcher, but if a batter *would* hit .438 in 1,000 at bats against a pitcher, he'd likely hit approximately .438 in the first 48 at bats. We just cannot distinguish (at the 48-at-bat juncture) hitters who might truly "own" pitchers from the many more whose extraordinary early success reflects the random variation inherent in small sample sizes. But that does not mean that a hitter never "owns" a certain pitcher; we just can't prove it.

This issue came to public attention before game three of the 2003 American League Championship Series between the New York Yankees and the Boston Red Sox. Yankees backup third baseman Enrique Wilson had hit .500 over 20 at bats, including seven for eight in the 2003 regular season, against Red Sox starting pitcher Pedro Martinez. Here, Jeter's certainty about hitters owning pitchers came face-to-face with the finding that statistical randomness explained Wilson's success against Martinez.

Yankee manager Joe Torre played it right: he put Wilson in the lineup, perhaps intuiting that Wilson possibly "owned" Martinez even though statistical analysis said otherwise (did Torre understand sample-size problems?). And in this instance, he substituted Wilson for Aaron Boone, a mediocre hitter. Torre had little to lose if it turned out Wilson's previous success derived from randomness. Presumably, Torre would not have substituted Wilson for Jeter or Alex Rodriguez and risked losing their big bats for nothing.

The statisticians turned out to be correct: Wilson did not really "own" Martinez. He got only one hit in 7 at bats against Martinez in the series and ended up twelve for thirty-two lifetime against the recent Hall of Fame inductee.

However, small-sample-size limitations do not allow us to state categorically that hitters never "own" pitchers. Although the phenomenon of "owning" pitchers is surely exaggerated, there may still be instances in which Derek Jeter had it right.

Modern Statistics: Different Perspectives

Sabermetrics is now firmly entrenched in modern baseball thinking and culture, yet variations remain in the manner and extent to which managers and executives apply its findings.

BILLY BEANE, THE SAVANT

The Oakland Athletics lost a wild-card playoff game to the Kansas City Royals in 2014, their eighth loss in nine postseason series since 2000. Esteemed general manager Billy Beane had explained previous postseason failures: "my [stuff] doesn't work in the playoffs."

Actually, nobody has [stuff] that works in the playoffs. Nate Silver (in *Baseball Between the Numbers*) found that nothing in the regular season correlates highly with postseason victories. No particular style or emphasis predicts or prevents success. Even regular season winning percentage does not correlate well with postseason success.

The postseason, as noted with regard to the 2015 Cubs versus Mets series, resembles a crapshoot. A seven-game series is too short for the better team predictably to win.

Beane should not be embarrassed by the postseason losses. Sometimes a coin flip comes up on the same side in eight of nine flips (see chapter 4, "Did the NBA Really Fix the Lakers-Kings Game?").

Moreover, the Athletics have lost for weird reasons: Jeremy Giambi didn't slide, Terrence Long lost a fly ball in the sun, Eric Byrnes didn't realize he'd missed home plate, catcher Geovany Soto and center fielder Coco Crisp suffered inopportune injuries.

A case in point is the 2014 playoff-game loss to Kansas City. Beane put the A's in good position to win the wild-card game with the acquisition of three-time All-Star pitcher Jon Lester. They started the one-and-done playoff game with Lester, one of baseball's top pitchers on the mound. Brandon Moss hit two home runs, and the A's went into the eighth inning with a 7–3 lead, Lester pitching, and an excellent closer in reserve. All seemed rosy; Beane had done his job. Then, as is often the case in sports, [stuff] happened (including Crisp's pulled hamstring)—nobody's fault.

Curiously, Kansas City's victory showcased the small-ball approach (bunting and stealing bases) that Beane famously eschewed in Michael Lewis's *Moneyball*. In truth, Lewis hyperbolized the success of Beane's reliance on statistics (his "[stuff]"). Both *The Beauty of Short Hops* and *The Sabermetric Revolution* identify many important errors in *Moneyball*. Briefly, the David-beats-Goliath, nerd-outsmarts-bully tale did not explain the A's success.[11] Instead, they had three great starting pitchers, two MVPs in the field, and other good players whom Lewis barely mentioned because they were highly valued by traditional measures and did not support the Beane-as-genius theme. Not surprisingly, the A's floundered when these players left. From 2007 to 2011 they averaged only seventy-six wins per season.

Then the A's rebounded. From 2012 to 2014 they averaged ninety-three wins despite their usual financial limitations. Notably, this time they succeeded without great players—no MVPs or Cy Young candidates and a roster only a fantasy-league participant could remember.

What did Beane do to account for the second wave of success? The only basic statistic that jumps out is that the A's consistently excelled on the mound (as they did a decade earlier), ranking second in the league in ERA from 2012 to 2014 despite significant turnover in personnel. Beane obviously has a talent for finding good pitchers.

He also succeeded at "cashing in" expensive (or soon to become expensive) players and finding cheaper but equivalent talent. For example, the 2011 A's came in third in the league in ERA, yet Beane traded five pitchers (Craig Breslow, Trevor Cahill, Andrew Bailey, Gio Gonzalez, and Guillermo Moscoso). After the trades, the staff actually improved—as noted, it was second in ERA for the next three seasons. The 2014 pitching staff included draft picks Sonny Gray and Sean Doolittle, Jesse Chavez (purchased from Toronto), and, before he was traded, Tommy Milnone (obtained in the Gonzalez deal): Beane paid these four good pitchers less than $2.5 million combined!

But overall, no specific strategy explains Beane's success from 2012 to 2014. The truth seems banal: Billy Beane is a really smart guy and an excellent judge of talent, especially pitching. He makes good baseball decisions over a broad range of issues. He adapts to changing circumstances. His use of statistics probably helps. Thus, the Athletics generally do well, particularly relative to their limited resources.

Though not always: If the Athletics had a disappointing end to a fine season in 2014, the bottom fell out in 2015 when they had the worst record in the American League. This time, Beane did mess up. He traded star player (and eventual 2015 MVP winner) Josh Donaldson after the 2014 season and got comparatively little in return. It seems that he outsmarted himself, unnecessarily following his template of trading his best players before they became free agents. In this case, Donaldson was underpaid and signed until the 2019 season—the kind of player Beane usually acquires rather than trades away. Since Lester left as a free agent after the 2014 season, it turned out that Beane lost his two best hitters—Donaldson and Yoenis Cespedes (previously traded for Lester)—for almost nothing; no wonder the Athletics plummeted in 2015, and spent most of the 2016 season near or in the American League West cellar.

Yet Beane has not come under fire. He has enough of a good track record and reputation as a savant to deservedly withstand yet another postseason defeat, a bad trade and two horrendous seasons.

NED YOST, THE BUMBLING IDIOT (WHO WON THE WORLD SERIES)

If Beane's prior record and high regard allows him to survive down times unscathed, manager Ned Yost is his opposite: Yost gets pummeled in the press even when his Kansas City Royals win, including the 2015 World Series. And he gets pummeled for allegedly not following Beane's approach to the game.

This dates back at least to the 2014 postseason. During the Royals' eight-game sweep to win the American League pennant, fans and media commonly suggested that they won in spite of Yost. Doug Padilla at ESPN wrote, "Everything unconventional that Yost tried, his team overcame." Paul Sullivan of the *Chicago Tribune* harshly described him as a "very bad manager" and a "bumbling idiot" who would be played by Steve Carrell if anyone made a movie of the 2014 Royals.

Much of the Yost criticism attacked his old-school, analytics-adverse style that emphasizes sacrifice bunts and stolen bases. That aspect of the criticism seems unfair.

To state the obvious, a successful steal always helps. Sabermetricians never suggested that teams refrain from stealing bases. They did emphasize the previously underestimated harm that comes from being thrown out stealing. Depending on the overall level of offense for the league, they found that teams must steal successfully around 65 to 70 percent of the time to break even in terms of the overall result.

Kansas City led Major League Baseball in steals in 2014 and had a success rate of about 81 percent during both the regular season and the postseason. That's all good, above break-even rate. No problem there for Yost.

Yost has been criticized even more for sacrifice bunting, with four against Oakland in the 2014 wild-card game, and a first-inning bunt against Baltimore in game four of the ALCS. Jonah Keri of *Grantland* wrote of the latter, "When a team's first two batters of the game reach base, it doesn't want its number three batter sacrificing. Not unless it's 1968, at least. But (Lorenzo) Cain gave himself up anyway, advancing the runners to second and third while giving up a precious out . . . a senseless bunt." Keri's analysis reflects the knowledge that, on average, giving up an out—a valuable entity—via a sacrifice bunt decreases the number of runs expected (mostly by decreasing multi-run innings). Thus, sacrificing recently fell out of favor (an all-time low incidence in 2014, again in 2015, and fewer yet in 2016).

However, those Royal bunts in the 2014 postseason were actually anomalies. Kansas City only sacrificed thirty-three times in 2014, which ranked seventh in the American League. Again, not a problem for Yost.

Moreover, Keri's comments actually provide the basis on which one may defend the allegedly senseless first-inning bunt. They also suggest a broader point: mathematical analysis of baseball is at its best when it studies large databases and mean values and provides general recommendations. It is much less capable of assessing specific game situations. Every situation has unique characteristics that differ from "average" and has variables that are often difficult to quantify.

For example, outs may typically be "precious" but they do not have a fixed value. Their value is contingent, varying inversely with the importance of scoring a single run (or two, in the case of Cain bunting two men over) versus the chances of successive hits and a multi-run inning.

Situations develop in which scoring one run becomes more important than usual (and the value of a multi-run inning declines) and a team might justifiably risk an out stealing or voluntarily give up an out with a sacrifice bunt. As Keri implies, when scoring is more difficult (as in the modern-day nadir of 1968), the value of every run increases and the preciousness of an out decreases.

The values of runs and outs not only change over years (as offense goes through cycles) but also from game to game and even inning to inning. Any time multiple hits seem less likely—a poor-hitting team, a great pitcher—a single run increases in value. The value of a single run also increases late in close games, particularly against great pitchers.

Many observers, as previously discussed (chapter 1, "Babe Ruth Did Not Blunder"), lambasted Babe Ruth when he was thrown out stealing second with two outs in the ninth inning of the seventh game of the 1926 World Series. Yet in that specific situation, down one run so late, facing the Hall of Fame pitcher Grover Cleveland Alexander, the math actually favored a steal attempt.

There are specific circumstances (akin to Ruth's ninth-inning stolen-base attempt) in which a sacrifice bunt makes mathematical sense even though it typically does not.

Could two men on, nobody out in the first inning possibly be one of those circumstances that warrants a bunt? Actually, yes. According to James Click in *Baseball Prospectus*, the chances of scoring at least one run with runners on second and third and one out exceeds that with runners on first and second and nobody out.

That said, one should maintain skepticism with regard to those types of mathematical calculations. As noted, each potential bunting situation contains variables that can only be estimated—most importantly, the anticipated success of the batters who follow. When one anticipates greater subsequent hitting success, hitting away becomes more favored. Plug in lower success rates for the subsequent hitters and bunting is more favored.

Which values to plug in? Season batting average? Lifetime? Last two weeks? Career against the specific pitcher? This year against the specific pitcher? How to enter the pitcher into the calculation? The weather and field conditions? Any mathematical analysis here will suffer from these guesses.

It's possible, as Sullivan implies, that all of this escaped Ned Yost as he considered the first-inning bunt. He surely didn't do any math in his head. But he probably sensed a low-scoring tight game on the way, that multiple successive hits were unlikely, and that a sacrifice bunt, a single base hit, a two-run lead, and a lights-out bullpen would decide the game.

If that's what Yost intuited, no mathematical calculation could be precise enough to prove him wrong. As noted, the available math actually supported him. Yost stood on solid ground by both old-fashioned intuition and modern metrics.

Giants manager Bruce Bochy—a two-time World Series champion—also sacrificed with two men on and no one out in the fourth inning of game one of the World Series, but without eliciting any furor.

Bochy and the Giants defeated the Royals for their third title, but the Royals remained undaunted. Even without any great players, they won their second consecutive American League pennant and the

World Series in the following season. Yost continued to use a leadoff hitter with a low on-base percentage and emphasize old-fashioned aggressive baserunning, stealing, defense, and contact hitting. The Royals' batters (last in the American League in pitches per plate appearance and bases on balls) eschewed the current dogma advising taking pitches to get deep into counts. The Royals echoed the Minnesota Twins of a decade earlier: winning more than Billy Beane, with limited resources and without following *Moneyball* paradigms.

For those wedded to a narrow view of baseball strategy, Yost remains a bumbling idiot, World Series victory notwithstanding. They think his eventual gravestone ought to read "Here lies Ned Yost: the Royals won despite him." People more tolerant of different approaches to baseball disagree.

JOE MADDON, THE NUTTY PROFESSOR

Then there's the endearing Chicago Cubs manager Joe Maddon: If Beane is a baseball professor and Yost (to some) a nut, then Maddon, combining analytics and eccentricity, is the nutty professor.

For example, in the 2015 season, Maddon routinely batted his pitcher eighth in the lineup. What's that about? The pitcher bats ninth for the other National League teams, and did so for most teams in baseball history,[12] because he's the worst hitter in the lineup and the ninth spot gives him as few plate appearances as possible.

Maddon explained his heresy almost as a whim: "I just like the idea of a hitter in front of the 1-2-3 in the order." But it wasn't purely whim. The batting lineup is a continuous loop, so the pitcher (as ninth hitter) immediately precedes the team's best hitters and typically saddles them with an out. Maddon aimed for another runner on base when his better hitters came to bat, even if the eighth position gave the pitcher more plate appearances over the course of the season.

Maddon knows that Tom Tango, Mitchel Lichtman, and Andrew Dolphin carefully studied these competing strategies (reported in *The Book: Playing the Percentages in Baseball*) and concluded that batting the pitcher eighth would provide an additional 1.94 runs for a team over an entire season.

Thus, Maddon has mathematical backing for his strategy, but obviously, not much, and even that tiny amount (1.94 runs per season) may overstate the case. Complex baseball analyses with multiple components often yield imprecise results, with different investigators reporting different answers (for example, ballpark effects on hitting). We don't know the variability of the statistic put forward by Tango et al.—the spread and likelihood of alternate results above and below 1.94. In fact, 1.94 is so close to zero that the difference might be statistically insignificant, that is, no difference between the pitcher batting eighth and batting ninth.

Moreover, the study presumes that nothing else changes when you move the pitcher from ninth to eighth. That's unlikely. For example, what effect does the pitcher batting eighth have on the kinds of pitches thrown to the seventh hitter and his performance? What effect does it have on the confidence of the batter hitting ninth, behind even the pitcher? Does batting the pitcher eighth lead to other counterresponses and/or unintended consequences? Thus, we really don't know whether the pitcher hitting eighth or ninth makes any difference at all.

No matter, Maddon bats the pitcher eighth in a specific context: the Cubs had a bad century. Their last World Series victory came in 1908. After another ninety-loss, near-last-place finish in 2011, they hired Boy Wonder Theo Epstein as president of baseball operations. Epstein had presided over the Boston Red Sox when they ended a similar drought and won two World Series. He came to the Cubs as a new-age analytics maven; someone who brought talents that the Cubs had never had.

In Epstein's first three seasons the Cubs continued to play poorly, averaging ninety-five losses per season. However, he preached patience as he accumulated talented, young prospects, and Cub fans sensed an intelligent design promising better results ahead.

Epstein fueled further optimism prior to the 2015 season by adding the esteemed Maddon to manage the promising mix. Maddon came from Tampa Bay, an organization run by ex–Wall Street employees (as described by Jonah Keri in *The Extra 2%*). Like Epstein's Red Sox, Tampa Bay emphasized and succeeded with a modern analytic approach to baseball. In that environment, Maddon generated a well-deserved reputation for nontraditional thinking. He walked batters with the bases loaded, eschewed the closer role, used starters as relievers, ignored standard conventions about righty and lefty matchups, and more.

Maddon quickly displayed his creativity in Chicago, particularly with his lineups (even beyond batting the pitcher eighth).[13] He moved a struggling Jorge Soler to the leadoff spot for a game ("Maybe he'll do better without the pressure of having to drive in runs"). He routinely batted slugging rookie Kris Bryant second ("Maybe he'll see better pitches to hit") and lighter-hitting shortstop Starlin Castro cleanup. Subsequently, he moved Anthony Rizzo from the traditional (for the team's best hitter) third spot to second in the lineup. In seven games, for no obvious reason, he put the 6-feet-5, 215-pound third-baseman Bryant in center field. At times, he used a closer-by-committee strategy. In one game, he played three different pitchers in left field ("I went out to the mound and did all this stuff and the guys are giggling. It really piques their interest, they're like kids all over again.")

The Cubs turned the corner in Maddon's first season as their manager: Epstein's bumper crop of potential stars made the major-league roster and did well. Bryant, Soler, Kyle Schwarber, and Addison Russell joined Rizzo and Castro and led the Cubs to the NLCS.

Maddon ran out of magic in the postseason against the Mets, but he still had one shining moment. He benched Soler—who seemed perturbed by the cold weather in New York—in game two, but reinserted him for the seventy-three-degree game three in Chicago, in what Maddon called his "Fahrenheit lineup." He explained pregame, "Soler is in the lineup because in this ballpark, under these conditions, there is a decent opportunity he could put the ball over the wall." Soler then homered.

Maddon surely knows these changes, including batting the pitcher eighth, don't make much difference in either direction. First, because that's what studies demonstrate. More broadly, because the Tampa Bay hierarchy viewed their analytic efforts with humility. The "extra 2 percent" in the title of Keri's book reflected the entire advantage that Tampa Bay thought it might gain through increased efficiency in every area of operation, on the field and off. As owner Stuart Sternberg said, "We've worked hard to get that extra

2 percent, that 52–48 edge." If they gained only 2 percent in total, many of the strategic ploys aimed to add a few runs each must have yielded no extra runs at all.

Nevertheless, the process remains worthwhile: nothing ventured, nothing gained. If Maddon's wise tweaking gains just a run here and there, that's better than nothing. A season's success may hinge on a single game or even one at bat.

Further, Maddon's creative tinkering enhances the meme started by Epstein's hiring: that the Cubs are onto something, their management knows things, and they have an edge. If that's overstated: not a problem. If the Cubs' players feel that Maddon's iconoclasm provides them an edge, it can only help their performance. After a game in which he removed his erstwhile closer in the ninth inning, Maddon described it as an effort to get his players to "think differently," to have them believe he is "playing with the ring in mind."

The placebo effect might work in baseball too.

The Future of Baseball Analytics

What's next for sabermetrics?

Analytics has contributed new statistics (DIPS and BABIP), different emphases (OBP, avoiding outs), insights into player evaluation (Mantle and Ichiro) and other areas of the game (clutch hitting, batter-versus-pitcher matchups, defensive positioning, and more). Billy Beane and Joe Maddon (among others) use these ideas to some advantage, if not to the hyperbolized extent of Michael Lewis's *Moneyball* tale. Every team now uses analytics and seems pleased with the input.

However, despite this extensive analysis, much about baseball remains fuzzy, including measuring defense, baserunning, and overall player talent, and determining optimal workloads for starting pitchers. How much more can advanced analytics add?

Perhaps it's only a matter of time before statistics mavens solve these and other problems. To denizens of an information-technology-based world, greater input—more cameras in the ballparks, more data—results in more sophisticated, improved output. Fueled by knowledge, the future inexorably advances from the present.

But there's an alternative, less optimistic possibility: that baseball might follow other complex systems that behave in mysterious ways and resist explanation (for example, the stock market, long-range weather patterns, psychology, and political science).

The Nobel Prize–winning psychologist Daniel Kahneman discusses these limitations in *Thinking Fast and Slow*. He notes that in the social sciences, more effort, sophistication, and data often do not enhance early findings. In particular, psychologist Robyn Dawes found that complex multiple-regression formulas[14] frequently add little or nothing to simpler data.

In this regard, Dawes demonstrated that marital stability is predicted by this simple formula: frequency of lovemaking minus frequency of quarrels.

More complicated analyses fail to improve on that simple calculation. In fact, Kahneman concludes from various studies that an algorithm constructed on the back of an envelope typically competes with more complicated formulas.[15]

That's the social sciences, but what about hard sciences? In these areas, we usually think that over time, with enough effort, we find precise answers. Of course, science and medicine have many fantastic accomplishments to their credit, and laws of physics and other realms are essentially inviolate. Still, the sciences involve more ambiguity than typically suspected; as political psychologist Philip Tetlock wrote in *Superforecasting*, "In one of history's great ironies, scientists today know vastly more than their colleagues a century ago, and possess vastly more data-crunching power, but they are less confident in the prospects for perfect predictability . . . uncertainty is an ineradicable element of reality."

For example, the basis of the universe's physical structure—our subatomic underpinnings—is characterized by imprecision. Heisenberg's uncertainty principle states that we cannot simultaneously know the position and momentum of an atomic particle. The more we learn about one, the less we know about the other. No matter how hard we try, the sum of knowledge in this area remains the same. Further, physicists describe the locations of electrons with probabilities; exact locations are unknowable.

Much of what we think we know in medicine soon proves wrong.

For all the talent and technology that modern medicine brings to bear, treatments for common conditions like headaches, low back pain, and colds often fail. Doctors can't agree on which women should get mammograms and which men should get PSA blood tests to screen for prostate cancer. And expanding the database by sequencing the human genome proved "remarkably unhelpful" in treating diseases, according to double-helix Nobelist James Watson. Forty-five years after President Nixon's "war on cancer," oncologist Siddhartha Mukherjee describes cancer treatments—despite all we've learned—as still often "charging ahead with our best guess. . . . Chemo by hunch" (*New York Times Magazine*, May 15, 2016).

We'll eventually learn whether increasingly sophisticated data mining (for example, the spin velocity of pitches and the exit velocity of batted balls) adds much more to understanding baseball —hopefully, it will— but it's worth noting that Bill James, in *Solid Fool's Gold*, describes the history of baseball analytics in Sisyphean terms: "Nothing has changed at all; all we have done is to take a few buckets of water out of the ocean of ignorance and moved them into the small pond of real knowledge. In reality, the ocean of ignorance is larger than it ever was, as it expands on its own." James also notes "We are all so desperate to understand the world that we manufacture misunderstandings by the yard. . . . The reality is that we're not capable of understanding the world, because the world is vastly more complicated than the human mind."

Several years later, James added (*Fools Rush Inn*), "It is important for (sabermetricians) not to be trapped by the progression of the argument into thinking that we understand the issues better than we do." That's the father of modern baseball analytics stressing its limitations and implying that further progress in understanding the remaining complicated issues may be less than many assume.

II. BASKETBALL

ANSWERING BASKETBALL'S CRITICS

Many commentators report on the disastrous state of American basketball. Young players are poorly trained, the college game is boring, and the players turn pro too early. The ones who make the NBA lack good fundamentals and play in games that are badly refereed and sometimes even fixed. The sky is falling on American basketball—only, in truth, it's not.

Prodigies, AAU Ball, and "One and Done"

University of Arizona freshman Allonzo Trier averaged 14.8 points per game in 2015–16, a solid season that fueled speculation he would enter the NBA as a "one-and-done" player. Trier had previously started on the USA's undefeated 2014 U-18 basketball team and played in the 2015 McDonald's High School All-American Game. That sounds like a success story, but to many, Trier's unusual upbringing and the opportunity to join the NBA after only one college season demonstrate the ills of youth basketball in this country.

I find those concerns misplaced, specifically for Trier, and more broadly with regard to the one-and-done rule.

Trier first came to public attention in March 2009 as a sixth-grader, when Michael Sokolove profiled him in the *New York Times Magazine*.[1] At that time, Trier ranked number one in the country for his age group. Someone ranks at the top every year in every age group (even sixth-graders!), but Trier's devotion to basketball at that age seemed newsworthy. He practiced seven days a week, sometimes for nearly seven hours a day. He shot every morning until he made 450 baskets without hitting the rim. Allonzo also trained with a private tutor and played with various AAU teams, often flying around the country to compete in different events.

Anticipating a backlash to Trier's early-life monomania, Sokolove noted that Trier's training did not really differ in nature from that of Michael Phelps or Tiger Woods as children. He described Trier as self-motivated, simply pursuing his dream, and praised him as a good kid, curious about the world around him, with people skills and "a sweetness and a concern for others." Even on the AAU circuit, Trier resisted the pressures that drove many other elite young players to shot-crazed styles. Instead, he passed the ball willingly and showed a sophisticated feel for the game.

Allonzo continued on this path, subsequently traveling the country in an Ahabian pursuit of basketball excellence.[2] He played for four high schools in four years, far from his Seattle home, transferring from one basketball factory in Maryland (Montrose Christian) to another in Nevada (Findley Prep) for his senior season.

His freshman year at Arizona made it a new coach, team, and home for five consecutive seasons. Though he seems on the way to an NBA career, in the process he'll have given short shrift to friendships, continuity, education, and any semblance of a normal childhood. Many people cringe at the thought of a young basketball player giving up things we hold dear, and deem parents, agents, coaches, and the like, responsible for this craziness.

But in Trier's case, his decisions seem to have worked out both on and off the court. He excels with his dribbling and shooting skills, not his size (6 feet 4, 195 pounds) or athleticism. For example, he shot 94 percent from the free-throw line during his junior year in high school, and a writer observed him making thirty-one consecutive three-point shots in practice. In other words, all those thousands of hours of practice paid off; he's the opposite of the clichéd skill-less AAU player so many people (like Kobe Bryant, see "Kobe's Wrong. US Basketball Is Just Fine" later in this chapter) complain about.

Moreover, Trier was a B student in high school and comes across in interviews as quick, articulate, and grounded. Arizona coach Sean Miller said of Trier, "I have not been around a player that works harder at the game or loves it more than he does. It's this passion to be great that has all of us excited about our future together." His childhood practice schedule, AAU involvement, school and team hopping do not seem to have stunted his personal growth.

Nobody knows whether he'll be an NBA star or journeyman or even make the league. But if Trier fails in the NBA, he probably won't wither away. With his goal-setting ability, work ethic, and inner drive, he'll more likely move on to something else. He'll set another goal and work incessantly at achieving it.

Perhaps we shouldn't be so quick to disapprove when basketball prodigies ignore the so-called collective wisdom in pursuit of their dreams. In other fields—tennis, golf, swimming and other sports, chess, the performing arts, and more—we sing songs and write poems about prodigies who eschew the typical educational path and childhood experiences in pursuit of a singular excellence. Why should anyone view basketball prodigies differently?

Trier's mother Marcie paraphrased Sinatra: "Me and 'Zo . . . We did it our way instead of doing what everybody else told us to do."

Allonzo and Marcie did it right.

THE NBA'S "ONE AND DONE" IS ONE TOO MANY

Trier opted to return to Arizona for his sophomore season, but LSU star Ben Simmons, Duke star Brandon Ingram, and other top college freshmen declared for the NBA draft. To many commentators and fans, the one-and-done rule poisons both college and professional basketball.

These folks argue that players who jump quickly to the NBA (after one year, or previously, directly from high school) often do not fare well on or off the court. To basketball doomsayers, leaving school early follows poor AAU training as a one-two blow to player development. Thus, many observers advise that athletes be required to stay in college longer, to aid their development into better players (and people).

However, leaving college early may have nothing to do with any subsequent poor play and/or poor behavior. The players might do no better, or even worse, if they stayed in school for four years.

To establish whether remaining in college helps basketball prodigies, ideally we would randomly allow some qualified players to enter the NBA after one year in college, keep an equal number of similar players in college, and compare the results of the two groups. While we obviously can't do that, we can at least analyze the major differences between the two pathways in terms of developing basketball skills:

A college coaching staff versus an NBA coaching staff

Ancillary staff: nutritionists, fitness trainers, and doctors

Competition: college teammates (in practice) and opponents versus NBA teammates and opponents

Proximal role models: older, more experienced NBA players versus fellow callow collegians

Game experience: a roughly thirty-five-game seasons versus eighty-two (or more, with playoffs)

Practice time: NCAA off-season restrictions versus unfettered NBA access

Consider the specific choice one representative player faced. After completing his freshman year in college, Karl-Anthony Towns could have stayed at Kentucky and practiced daily against Kentucky's backup center and other teenagers or against all-time great Kevin Garnett and the more mature Minnesota Timberwolves. He could have honed his skills in games versus college players or NBA players. He could have chosen to play a shorter season with NCAA restrictions on practice time, or a much longer season with unlimited practice time and supervised summer training. The Timberwolves would provide a professional coach to guide Towns's development on a one-on-one basis, and Garnett would mentor him as well. All of these factors favored Towns choosing the NBA, as he did.

Of course, variation exists among college and NBA teams. There are good college coaches and poor NBA coaches. Some players in particularly good programs, or for other idiosyncratic reasons, might prosper by remaining in school. But as a general rule, there is no reason why basketball should differ from tennis, golf, gymnastics, soccer, figure skating, chess, music, singing, or acting. Prodigies commonly leave the standard school system early for superior professional training, and eventually the professional circuit. Nor is there any good reason why we complain about early-entry American basketball players but not foreign-born athletes: Latvia's Kristaps

Porzingis joined the NBA at twenty years old with zero college experience, yet no one seemed concerned.

Towns did well by joining the Timberwolves sooner rather than later. He won the Rookie of the Year Award. His eventual success (or lack of) in the NBA will depend on his talent and work ethic, not the duration of his college experience. And he's earning $11 million over his first two pro seasons, while no longer risking loss of those millions as a result of college injury.

That's in basketball terms. But what about the argument that leaving college early contributes to immaturity or bad judgment? We do know that college serves many students well. But the more one group differs from another group, the more extrapolating results from one to the other fails. Students who benefit from college are typically those who enter voluntarily and are prepared for and interested in academic study. By contrast, one-and-done players who never return to school are a self-selected group less (or not) interested in academics, different in many ways from the typical student. The idea that they will benefit from staying in college against their will involves a wild and unjustified extrapolation. College is not for everyone.

There is no good reason to legislate college as a paternalistic "one size fits all" mandate, rather than to allow all players, with input from their families, advisors, college coaches, and NBA scouts, to make their own decisions.

In reality, the one-and-done rule has little to do with the players. It was a sop from the NBA to pacify college powerbrokers concerned that players skipping college completely hurt the college game, particularly economically.[3] This alleged effect was exaggerated (college basketball did fine before one and done when players could join the NBA from high school) but, more importantly, the solution involved the tail wagging the dog. College athletics should serve the athletes, not vice versa. We should not sacrifice athletes at the altar of NCAA coffers.

Freedom of opportunity should govern unless trumped by some compelling purpose. There is no compelling reason to require players like LeBron James and Garnett to remain in poverty (and risk an injury that would prevent them from ever playing in the NBA) for one or more years. There is no compelling reason why young adults should cede their autonomy in this matter.

The notion that college provides better basketball training and instills wisdom into those held captive is a rhetorical air ball.

HOW WELL DOES COACH K PREPARE PLAYERS FOR THE NBA?

In January 2015, the New Orleans Pelicans traded backup guard Austin Rivers to the Los Angeles Clippers. Rivers made the McDonald's All-American Team in high school, had a solid freshman season at Duke (third-team All-America), joined the NBA and floundered. His failings in the NBA prompted Sam Smith, a Hall of Fame NBA writer, to cite Rivers as a classic example of a player who should not have left college as a one-and-done player. Smith suggested that Rivers would have become a better player if he had stayed under the tutelage of the all-time winningest college coach, Mike Krzyzewski. That seemed obvious and many agreed.

However, Rivers's struggles as a pro should not have been taken as evidence that he'd have done any better staying in college. On the contrary, the example cited (additional coaching by Krzyzewski) to illustrate the benefits of staying in school evokes "how soon we forget."

In fact, basketball fans once wondered why Krzyzewski's Duke players underachieved in the NBA, quite the opposite point from Smith's. For example, Josh Levin at Slate.com (April 2, 2010), "Why are so many Blue Devils awesome in college and awful in the pros?"

This question began early in Krzyzewski's career when successive Duke All-Americans Johnny Dawkins, Mark Alarie, Danny Ferry, and Christian Laettner all achieved less in the NBA than predicted. By 2010, only four Duke players in Krzyzewski's thirty years had played on an NBA All-Star team.

Krzyzewski's 2010 NCAA championship team followed suit. The starting five—Jon Scheyer, Kyle Singler, Nolan Smith, Lance Thomas, and George Zoubek—scored every point in the finals win against Butler. Scheyer, Singler, and Smith all earned All-America honors. All five players stayed four seasons with Krzyzewski. Yet the group as a whole fared poorly afterward. Scheyer and Zoubek went undrafted and never played in the NBA. Smith, the only first-round pick of the five, was released when his guaranteed rookie contract expired and is out of the NBA. After four years with Krzyzewski, Singler still felt unready for the NBA, went abroad for a year and returned as a journeyman. Thomas, undrafted, has been a marginal NBA player.

The basketball world once raised the same issue with Bobby Knight, one of Krzyzewski's few rivals for the honor of greatest college coach ever. In fact, only one alumnus (Isiah Thomas) of Knight's thirty years at Indiana made an NBA All-Star team, and Thomas only played two seasons for Knight. None of the five starters on Indiana's undefeated 1976 NCAA championship team shined in the NBA (although to be fair, injury truncated Scott May's NBA career.)

Nobody should think that this indicts either Krzyzewski or Knight. In fact, quite the opposite: the players' modest success in the NBA reflected their relatively limited athletic abilities and skills. Krzyzewski and Knight won huge numbers of games and several NCAA titles each with players who lacked major NBA ability; that's as good an endorsement of their coaching skills as any.

Nevertheless, the modest NBA careers of so many players who played for two of the greatest college coaches ever should make one pause before exhorting college basketball as a superior training ground for the pro game.

We actually don't know (and can never know) whether players improve more under Krzyzewski's tutelage or with NBA coaching (for example, the widely respected Monte Williams, who guided Rivers at New Orleans). I've already noted several reasons favoring turning pro. In looking back at recent college seasons, we can add another: The college game is much slower than the faster, more athletic NBA game (see below, "Don't Worry, College Basketball Will Survive").

In fact, the same writer who espoused players staying in college to improve their game wrote in a subsequent column about college basketball, "The game is awful, endless timeouts, virtually no flow, a long clock to limit action, over-coaching with players in robotic situations running side to side like the coach in *Hoosiers* demanding five passes before looking at the basket, players so poorly trained and coached so they are lacking basic fundamentals of the game."[4]

Not much of an endorsement for staying in school!

Kobe Bryant criticizes the entirety of US basketball, from the early training of players to NBA ball.

Bryant stated midway through the 2014–15 NBA season that European basketball players are "way more skillful" than American players and that American AAU basketball is "horrible, terrible . . . stupid. It doesn't teach our kids how to play the game at all. . . ." Bryant sounded an ominous note, "It's something we really have to fix." Many fans and other observers agree.

Kobe merely resurrected an old idea originally inspired by losses the US national team suffered at the 2002 FIBA World Championship tournament and the 2004 Olympics. European excellence at fundamentals, combined with American lack of the same, supposedly had ushered in a new basketball era with Europe (or more broadly, foreigners) assuming the historical American position of dominance.

In other words, the doomsday prediction for US basketball has already been proposed and tested for over a decade.

It turned out completely wrong.

In retrospect, the US losses derived from a subpar selection and training process, and not lack of skills. US basketball returned to dominance after revising those strategies. By the time of Kobe's comments, the United States, under director Jerry Colangelo and Coach Krzyzewski, had won seventy-two of its last seventy-three games (the single loss took place in the 2006 FIBA semifinals) including the previous two Olympics and the previous two World Championships.

At the 2014 FIBA World Cup the United States won nine consecutive games by an average of thirty-three points, defeating Serbia in the final by thirty-seven points. And the Americans ran up those scores without most of their best players. Bryant, Lebron James, Kevin Durant, Carmelo Anthony, Russell Westbrook, Dwight Howard, Dwyane Wade, and Chris Paul all sat it out. The US second team —the second team!—dominated the world.

Kobe's comments came at an odd time, given these international results and the parallel decline of foreign excellence in the NBA. The entire world outside of the United States contributed just two players (Marc and Pau Gasol), both from the same family, to the three All-NBA teams of 2015. Only five foreign players ranked in the top fifty in scoring in the NBA in 2014–15 (the Gasols, Dirk Nowitzke, Nikola Vucevic, and Goran Dragic). No foreigner ranked in the top twenty in assists per game or three-point shots made (supposedly a European forte).

There were just four elite players (the Gasols, Tony Parker, and Nowitzke) in the NBA from all of Europe, all of them over thirty years old. No current player from the old Soviet Union and former Yugoslavia equals the success achieved by old-timers Arvidas Sabonis, Sarunas Marciulionis, Drazen Petrovich, Vlade Divac, and Toni Kukoc. Argentina's outstanding national team has aged, without equivalent replacements in sight. They appear a one-generation wonder.

Foreign players constitute only about 25 percent of all players in the NBA, even twenty-four years after the Dream Team sparked worldwide basketball interest. And about 40 percent of the NBA's foreign players are centers, which speaks only to the role of height and the greater prevalence of near seven-footers in the entire world as compared to one country (the United States) alone (although the United States also dominates in young big men, with Anthony Davis, DeMarcus Cousins, Andre Drummond, Karl-Anthony Towns, and Jahlil Okafor).

Foreign perimeter players collectively make little impact. Only about twelve non-center foreigners consistently started in the NBA in the 2014–15 season. Perhaps only three of those starters (Nowitzke, Luol Deng, and Jose Calderon) fit the stereotype of a foreign player owing his success to fundamental skills out of proportion to modest athletic ability.

The United States also dominates internationally at the U-17 to U-19 levels. The future looks like the present: the USA's.

Foreigners ought to be asking, "What happened?"

Presuming that Kobe was not just tooting his own horn (he grew up in Italy), how did he (and others) make such an obvious error? The doomsayers seem to have engaged in what psychologists call "anchoring." Once an idea takes root in our minds—in this case, over ten years ago—we have a tendency to bend new information to fit what we "know" to be true. Sometimes we ignore data that belie the initial "truth." In those cases, we're "anchored"—stuck to an old idea even in the face of contrary evidence.

Kobe attempted to bolster his hypothesis by noting that San Antonio won the 2014 title with mostly foreign players. True enough, but he misunderstood the observation. To begin with, he ignored previous titles won by the entirely American Miami Heat (and other teams) and the several American-rich teams that outperformed the Spurs in the following season.

More importantly, having foreign players does not mean that the Spurs won in 2014–15 because of those players, or that they had excellent training abroad. Two Spurs starters (Kawhi Leonard and Danny Green) were American, and a third, Tim Duncan, pretty much so (Duncan comes from the US Virgin Islands and really learned to play in college at Wake Forest.) Leonard and Duncan were the Spurs' best players in the 2014 NBA Finals, and Leonard's injuries helped explain the Spurs' lesser performance the following season.

Moreover, the Spurs' most important foreign players on the title team did not bring outstanding youth-taught fundamentals to the United States. No one should draw any conclusion from modestly talented starting center Tiago Splitter. Parker came from France with great speed but a poor outside shot and an undisciplined style. Similarly, Manu Ginobili came to the NBA from Argentina and the Euroleague with a one-on-one, frenetic style replete with fancy shots and dangerous passes.

Had Ginobili and Parker been American, when they entered the NBA they'd have been criticized (by those who believe in Bryant's generalizations) as characteristic AAU players. They only developed into more fundamentally sound players under Coach Gregg Popovich's tutelage.

The Spurs do, of course, play beautiful team basketball—all of them, from wherever they come: Europe, South America, Australia, Canada, and the United States. Popovich provides the link for these disparate players. He's the major reason for their selflessness.

Many Europeans do have good fundamental skills. They have to —they generally lack the athletic ability of the better American players. But if European fundamentals trump American athletic ability (as Kobe suggests), then American dominance means that Americans must also be fundamentally sound.

That should be obvious. No one can miss the shooting ability of

Stephen Curry, Klay Thompson, Kyle Korver, Durant, and Anthony, or the passing of James, Paul, Rajon Rondo, and others. No big man from abroad is smoother than Anthony Davis, Al Jefferson, Chris Bosh, LaMarcus Aldridge, Towns, or Okafor. The predominance and success of less-renowned Americans on NBA rosters means that they also have sufficient skills.

Whether the AAU system provides better fundamentals training than commonly thought, or (more likely) American players simply receive enough of it elsewhere, they don't seem to be lacking in anything.

Let's not repeat discredited ideas simply because we once believed them.

College Coaches: Saints or Sinners?

Sports Illustrated once named Kentucky basketball coach John Calipari among the most disliked people in sports. Calipari animus resurfaced when *Boston Globe* columnist Dan Shaughnessy absurdly referred to alleged serial rapist Bill Cosby in a diatribe against Calipari.

WHY ALL THE HATE FOR JOHN CALIPARI?

Calipari, whose Kentucky team was undefeated before losing to Wisconsin in the 2015 Final Four, rubs some people the wrong way: for his appearance, his mien, his arrogance, his success (his teams routinely beat ours), and similar reasons.

That's not the entire story. *Sports Illustrated* cited concrete criticisms of the Kentucky coach: His "trail of NCAA violations" and his "position at the forefront of college basketball's 'one-and-done' era."

Unfortunately, many who dislike Calipari's personality twist the facts of his alleged missteps to fit their own bias and feed their anger: verdict first, then trial. The hyperbolized "trail of violations" actually consists of only two discrete incidents over ten years apart. First, Calipari's University of Massachusetts team lost its NCAA designation as a 1996 Final Four participant and returned its tournament revenue because center Marcus Camby accepted money from an agent. Then the NCAA similarly sanctioned Calipari's 2007–8

University of Memphis team when they found that someone took Derrick Rose's SAT for him.

However, no one, including the NCAA, alleged that Calipari knew anything about Camby's behavior or Rose's high school SAT exam. Nor did the NCAA allege lack of institutional control of the basketball program in either case. These were isolated instances of young athletes misbehaving. The Camby incident is now twenty years old, did not involve Calipari, and UMass recently put it to rest by announcing plans to retire a jersey in Calipari's honor.

The more recent Rose affair is no more incriminating. In fact, the official NCAA Public Infractions Report[5] on the Memphis case puts the entire incident in a completely different light than Calipari's critics suggest.

Allegations of impropriety around Rose's SAT score started in October of Rose's freshman year. He denied everything to Memphis authorities and the matter properly went to the Educational Testing Service (ETS), the administrator of the SAT, for an independent inquiry. At that point, there was nothing for Memphis officials to do (imagine the due-process outcry and the lawsuit they'd have faced if they suspended Rose based only on allegation). Eventually, on May 5 of the following year, *after the season had ended*, the ETS notified Rose and Memphis that his SAT scores had been canceled. The NCAA enforcement staff then conducted their own investigation, culminating in sanctions against Memphis for using an ineligible player.

The NCAA infractions report contains an illuminating excerpt from their proceedings:

> Memphis legal counsel: "The University was not aware at the time he was ineligible."
>
> NCAA committee member: "I didn't suggest that they were. . . . *I am not saying that they cheated* [emphasis mine]. I am saying the young man was not eligible to participate."

It's worth emphasizing: the NCAA sanctioned Memphis on the basis of a legal nicety termed "strict liability," which held Memphis responsible without being culpable. The NCAA chooses not to abide ineligible players under any circumstances. It didn't matter that

Memphis did not cheat or even that it couldn't do anything about the situation. As noted, the ETS did not invalidate the SAT, and the NCAA did not declare Rose ineligible until after the season.

The simple truth is that Rose cheated, Rose got caught, Memphis suffered, and Calipari had nothing to do with any of it. (The report also cited Memphis for Rose's brother receiving "occasional free transportation . . . and free lodging." Since that amounted to only $1,700 it would not have merited more than a tsk tsk as a stand-alone item.)

In fact, reading the NCAA Public Infractions Report leads a neutral observer to wonder why Memphis capitulated to the penalties.

The answer probably lies in another surprising aspect of the report: The Rose investigation was only a secondary feature. It piggybacked on a far more substantive indictment of the women's golf team, which directly involved the coach and led to more significant sanctions. Memphis had also previously been put on probation for violations by several other teams. Thus, you can imagine the university not wanting to keep all that (non-basketball) dirty laundry in the public eye. The trivial basketball sanctions—a whitewashing of the record and a fine; no suspensions or loss of scholarships—were well worth Memphis accepting to rid itself of the entire mess as soon as possible.

The many anti-Calipari diatribes ignore these inconvenient truths and paint an opposite picture. Haters concede that nobody found Calipari guilty of anything, but argue that "we know better"—he got off scot-free only because, as Shaughnessy wrote (without providing any examples), "he lied to everyone on his way out of town." They actually use the non-findings in the Camby and Rose cases to suggest widespread Calipari malfeasance—the "where there's smoke, there's fire" thesis. Yet the NCAA has surely kept Kentucky under a magnifying glass ever since they hired Calipari, still without any findings against him.

His critics also distort Calipari's purported role as the evil "one-and-done" coach.

Yes, he has had more one-and-done players in the last decade than anyone else. That infuriates people who dislike the rule, but it's not Calipari's rule; he simply functions under the rule given to him.

In fact, he dislikes it too, having publicly called for a change of the rule to require two years of college for players to enter the NBA draft.

Calipari's much criticized volume of one-and-done players merely reflects his considerable recruiting and coaching skills. Every major Division I basketball coach recruits from the same group of players: the two dozen McDonald's High School All-Americans (all of them potential one-and-done players) and the players ranked just below them. College coaches need players of this caliber to routinely compete for NCAA titles. The top coaches all go after them, as many as they can (unless they make a tactical decision to keep some veteran leadership). Over the last five years about four McDonald's All-Americans per year have gone to Kentucky, two or three to Duke and North Carolina (both of whom have also had as many as four in a year), and the rest scattered among the other top D-I programs. Calipari simply out-recruits his competitors.

His players then do well, and many of them become NBA first-round draft picks, often after only one collegiate season (this helps explain his recruiting success). Their success derives in part from their considerable talent, but also from Calipari's coaching. He emphasizes defense, passing, and teamwork—the "right way to play," which speeds their development and eases their NBA transition.

Rival coach Rick Pitino called the 2014–15 Kentucky squad "the best defensive team I've seen in the last 20 years,"[6] no small coaching feat given that most of the players came in as hotshot scorers. Calipari subjugated their egos remarkably well. None of Kentucky's nine McDonald's All-Americans played over thirty minutes a game, and no one complained or gave less than outstanding effort.

Importantly, the players make the decisions about leaving—not Calipari, who only advises. More Kentucky players leave after one year than those at other schools (though Duke is catching up) because more Kentucky players are deemed first-round worthy at that stage. Likely first-round picks at other schools also frequently opt for the NBA.

That shouldn't surprise. These athletes have long dreamed to play in the NBA. When they get that opportunity and are likely to receive the guaranteed huge money that goes to a first-round draft pick, one can understand why they turn pro rather than stay in college and risk blowing it all with an injury (the real idiocy of the one-and-done rule lies in the NCAA's refusal to allow athletes to return to school if they are not drafted in the first round).

Calipari's players (whether they stay one year or more) routinely shine in the NBA and have no regrets about leaving school early. The 2016 NBA All-Star game featured three Calipari alums (DeMarcus Cousins, John Wall, and Anthony Davis). Eric Bledsoe, Brandon Knight, and ex-MVP Rose also played well during the season. In addition, Tyreke Evans, Patrick Patterson, Michael Kidd-Gilchrist, and Terrence Jones are solid NBA players. Karl-Anthony Towns won the Rookie of the Year Award and Nerlens Noel showed potential. We may soon see an NBA All-Star game with six or seven Calipari proteges.

They all seem grateful for Calipari's efforts. For example, Rose said, "Calipari was great for me (at Memphis). If he was at Kentucky, there's a good chance I would have gone to Kentucky." Wall followed in kind, crediting Calipari for getting the most out of his talent: "His demeanor, how he treats players on the court and off the court, he's going to push you to be your best every night. . . . He does a lot of stuff to make sure that you're together, bonding together and getting along."

In other words, Calipari delivers what his kids want and deserve: Great coaching, winning teams, and a path to NBA success.

CALIPARI'S PEERS ARE NOT ROLE MODELS

Shortly after Shaughnessy's ill-conceived rant against Calipari, *Sports Illustrated* (March 18, 2015) coincidently published a pair of disturbing articles about two esteemed universities, Duke and North Carolina.

Writer Emily Kaplan discussed alleged rape charges against Duke basketball player Rasheed Sulaimon, noting that Coach Mike Krzyzewski had refused to speak about the situation. To be fair, she indicated that privacy issues restricted Coach K's comments, but merely by citing his silence she implied possible impropriety.

More alarmingly, S. L. Price reviewed the academic scandal at North Carolina, characterized by athletes (and other students) getting credit for bogus classes in order to maintain their eligibility. In addition, admissions standards at UNC declined to the point where one admissions committee member said "we were admitting [athletes] who had a lot of trouble reading and writing, and they were taking classes like Arts and Crafts for Elementary School Teachers." Most of this occurred during the reign of current coach Roy Williams, but the malfeasance also tainted the previous coach, the late Dean Smith.

Williams maintains an excellent reputation and Smith was held in even higher regard. In fact, Smith and John Wooden of UCLA are widely considered the icons of high character for college coaches. Smith not only preached unselfishness on the court but social awareness off it, and he did more than his share of fighting racism and speaking out against the Vietnam War and other injustices. He received the Presidential Medal of Freedom in 2013. Smith's death evoked an unusual outpouring of praise of his character, even more than of his basketball victories.

Price reluctantly writes, "That Williams—or the detail-demon Dean Smith, for that matter—didn't suspect something awry in the . . . classes seems impossible." Moreover, a UNC professor wrote a book in which he argued that Smith's basketball program provided the impetus for the fake courses.

Perhaps that shouldn't shock us. After all, even Wooden turned the other way when a rogue booster named Sam Gilbert ran amok at UCLA, giving players money, gifts, and apparently even paying for abortions for their girlfriends.

The *Sports Illustrated* articles followed the suspension of Syracuse's Jim Boeheim for over a decade of alleged misdeeds. Several years ago, Connecticut coach Jim Calhoun suffered the same fate. Both Boeheim and Calhoun, like Wooden, Smith, and Williams, won NCAA championships and were generally held in high regard.

What's the lesson to be learned from this purging and smearing of the college head-coaching ranks, including some of the apparent finest? Surely not that universities predominantly hire bad people. When fine folks like Wooden and Smith turn their heads at rampant rule breaking or other illicit conduct, perhaps it says something about the absurdity of the rules. Or perhaps we simply underestimate the forces and pressures of high-level D-I basketball that lead otherwise honorable people to this.

It also makes me think again about Calipari, and how his indiscretions (if any) pale next to the far greater misdeeds of some of his peers.

More Problems with the College Game?

Dan Gavitt, an NCAA men's basketball vice president, said of the college game "I have great concerns. The trends are long-term and unhealthy. I think some people understand the urgency of it." Iona coach Tim Cluess agreed, "The product stinks. . . . We've accepted mediocrity." *Sports Illustrated*'s (March 2, 2015) Seth Davis wrote, "College basketball is facing a crisis . . . it stinks. It's time for an extreme makeover."

Men's college basketball had become a punching bag. And this time, the critics didn't even fuss over one-and-done or allegedly unethical coaches. Instead, they cited a plodding pace, lower scoring (67.1 points per team per game in 2014–15, down 10 points from 1972), and seven consecutive years of decreased Division I attendance.

DON'T WORRY, COLLEGE BASKETBALL WILL SURVIVE

No one can dispute those basic facts. Nevertheless, as Aaron Rodgers said in response to the 2014 early-season angst of Green Bay Packer fans: "R-E-L-A-X." College basketball merely followed a course previously taken (and ultimately reversed) by other major sports: higher scoring early in the sport's history, then a significant decline.

In Major League Baseball, the mean batting average dropped from .296 in 1930 to .237 in 1968, with a concomitant decrease in runs scored from 11.1 to 6.8 per game. Similarly, points per game in the NBA dropped from 118.6 in the 1961–62 season to 91.6 in 1998–99. Points per game in the NFL dropped from 47.2 in 1948 to 34.4 in 1977. Scoring also decreased over time in the National Hockey League and World Cup soccer.

Each sport has its own reasons for declining offense, but some share themes influenced by the mantra "defense wins championships." Talented defenders receive playing time at the expense of scorers. Practice time and other preparations may be disproportionally allotted to defense. The guideline also affects game strategy. For example, many basketball coaches emphasize getting back on defense over offensive rebounding.

Coaches in basketball and football developed more effective defensive concepts, advancing from a simple "guard your man" approach to sophisticated team strategies; "help defense" entered the vernacular. In the early 1960s, NBA teams often single-covered Wilt Chamberlain in the low post. Defenders today would double-team Wilt, with players coming from different areas on the floor and at different times in the shot clock.

Basketball also applied "help defense" to thwart penetrating dribblers. The classic 1985 NCAA championship game between Villanova and defensive stalwart Georgetown did not have a single charge/block play. That might shock today's fans, because defenders now commonly jump into the lane to draw charges.

Basketball's current defensive sophistication goes far beyond drawing charges and doubling the post. Today's college and pro teams routinely employ comprehensive strategies—for example, some variation of ex–Chicago Bulls coach Tom Thibodeau's "five men on a string" approach—that makes older defenses look primitive. These teams hinder driving by overloading the strong side. They react to ball movement with coordinated team actions, moving defenders to important areas on the court. Done well, this makes scoring a challenge.

Pro football also evolved from its basic 4-3 man-to-man defense. Tom Landry introduced the "flex" in the 1960s; the 3-4 front followed in the '70s and the 46 defense in the '80s. Zone blitzes and the Tampa 2 and a whole variety of nuances also entered the fray.

At the other end of the spectrum, football and basketball found value in brute force, in the form of extra-physical defense. This dates back at least to the 1970s when NFL defensive backs began manhandling wide receivers coming off the line of scrimmage.

Luke Winn described in *Sports Illustrated* how Bobby Knight brought that style to college basketball. After UCLA played Indiana in 1975, a Bruins coach described Indiana's defense as "They've got five guys fouling at the same time, and it's hard for the officials to pick out one man." John Thompson did the same at Georgetown, and Knight's many disciples dispersed the strategy around the country. Chuck Daly's 1980s Detroit Pistons and Pat Riley's 1990s New York Knicks took physical defense to and sometimes past the limit of the rules, at times bringing NBA scoring to its knees.

Field-goal and three-point shooting percentages in college basketball both fell 4 percent from 1988 to 2015. Davis noted that foul-shooting percentage remained the same, suggesting that the lower live-action shooting percentages reflect better defense rather than inferior shooting skills. Improved defenses and slower pace combined to reduce scoring.

But, contrary to what the doomsayers preached—not to worry.

Whenever low scoring reached a tipping point in the major professional sports, relevant authorities responded. MLB lowered the pitching mound in 1968. The NBA changed rules about handchecking, isolations, zone defenses, and more. The NFL enacted a series of rules restricting defenses, including the five-yard chuck rule in 1978 that limited defensive backs' contact with wide receivers. In each case, scoring increased to more usual levels following the rule changes. Pro football has been particularly proactive, making changes to maintain or increase scoring in the face of increasingly sophisticated defenses.

These precedents should have suggested that new rules would save college basketball. In fact, Davis provided several promising ideas: A thirty-second shot clock, extending the arc under the basket, a wider lane, a deeper three-point line (to spread out the defense), and fewer timeouts. A return to the offense-favored block/charge interpretation of 2013 would also help scoring.

Nevertheless, Davis and others remained pessimistic, doubting that favorable rule changes in college basketball would be enacted. Davis noted that many coaches prefer the slower, rougher game because it favors their less talented teams, and they are reluctant to make changes that reduce their own influence. In addition, the major D-I conferences have long-term, lucrative television contracts, which blunt coaches' concerns over immediate problems.

The gloomy outlook seemed unwarranted, if for no other reason than that the dollar eventually prevails. The TV contracts do come up for renegotiation, and lower ratings prompt networks to reduce fees. Decreased TV revenue and declining gate receipts would surely motivate NCAA decision makers to action, even against some institutional resistance.

As it turned out, we didn't have to wait that long. Prior to the 2015–16 season, with a nod to Davis's sunny side, the NCAA rules committee changed the shot clock to thirty seconds, extended the restricted area under the basket to four feet, and reduced the number of time-outs allowed. Scoring quickly increased.

The solution to gloom and doom in the major sports has always been pretty straightforward: sensible rule changes.

SHOULD ELITE COLLEGES EMPHASIZE ATHLETICS?

Basketball fans need not worry about Kentucky (2014) and Duke (2015) winning NCAA championships with several one-and-done players—that's what their programs are about and what their players want. Nor should they worry about the decline in college scoring —modest in scope and already responding to rule changes. Top-level college basketball is doing well.

I do wonder about something critics do not comment on (and probably approve): Harvard University won a first-round NCAA basketball game for the second consecutive year in 2014; their only postseason wins ever. They followed that with a 22–8 record in 2014–15, losing in the NCAA tournament to national powerhouse North Carolina by only two points. Something changed in Harvard's traditionally circumscribed interest in athletics. An academic powerhouse now prioritizes winning basketball.

Is that a good idea?

Less conspicuously, the same thing happened in Division III. Amherst College, the defending D-III national basketball champions, met its archrival, Williams College, in the semifinals of the 2014 national tournament (Williams won, then lost a squeaker in the finals). Amherst (21–8) returned to the NCAA tournament in 2015 for the fifth consecutive season, and advanced to the second round. Amherst and Williams are small (class size around 500) Massachusetts colleges, known (like Harvard) for their scholars and (historically) their de-emphasis of athletics.

I wrestled at Amherst in the mid-1970s. I went there for the academics (a place where the wrestling coach had a PhD in American history and was assistant dean of students), because I did not want (or perhaps did not warrant) the rigor of D-I athletics, and because of a single random meeting with the charismatic coach at a summer wrestling camp. That was typical of D-III athletics in New England, where no real recruiting took place.

Few if any Amherst students considered athletics the dominant part of their college experience, and the demands of athletic participation were relatively minor. Travel was limited, and some teams did not even have a bus. In those cases, athletes with cars drove teammates to away competitions. (The college reimbursed the drivers ten cents a mile.) I both captained and chauffeured the wrestling team. Five guys in a car, those road trips were good times.

The main athletic-related attention Amherst received came when ESPN asked to televise the 100th Amherst-Williams football game in 1985. Amherst coach Jim Ostendarp refused the offer for national exposure and a financial windfall. That's right, he refused. Darp, as he was called, explained that, "We're in the education business, not the entertainment business."

Fast forward twenty-plus years and my daughter captained her Amherst soccer team. The team was terrific—an overtime loss short of an NCAA Final Four—as the result of a new athletic culture. Every year, two or three all-state high school players came on board. Few players had secure positions. Some started as freshmen and were benched as juniors or seniors. Year-round weight training and conditioning was expected, and supervised by full time trainers. From the perspective of an ex-chauffeur, it looked like a scaled down Division I program.

In my day, Amherst had a great basketball player, Jim Rehnquist, who scored fifty points in a game (still Amherst's all-time record) and averaged twenty-eight points per game one season. Jim could shoot the lights out and was a smart player, but he was also a six-foot-three forward without extraordinary jumping ability or speed. Amherst and Williams now have guards who dunk, forwards who fly, and front lines that would tower over Jim. That's how they've both won D-III national titles. Jim might still find a spot on Amherst's current nationally competitive teams—great shooting remains crucial—but his teammates? No chance.

Soccer and basketball at Amherst are not idiosyncratic success stories. In the time between father and daughter, Amherst became an athletic powerhouse, with eleven national team championships (most recently, men's soccer, 2015) in five different sports, and eight top-five finishes for the D-III Director's Cup (given to the most successful school in the nation in athletics) since 2006. Williams has done even better, having won the Director's Cup eighteen times in the last twenty years. A dynasty that eclipses the Yankees' best runs! Who would have thought?

Increased attention to athletics goes beyond Amherst and Williams. Regional rivals Wesleyan, Middlebury, Bowdoin, Colby, Bates, and Tufts have also revved up their athletic programs. Ditto well-regarded D-III schools around the country, including Washington University (in St. Louis), Illinois Wesleyan, and Emory. This is probably an inevitable consequence of modern competitive society. Nobody in this day and age tolerates life as a patsy.

My daughter loved her collegiate athletic experience as much as I did mine. And I certainly thrilled in her exploits, including a hat trick in an NCAA postseason game. So what's the problem?

In addition to concerns about elite schools admitting athletes over more academically deserving students and implicitly deemphasizing their main mission (education), the pursuit of athletic glory raises another issue. We once had a distinction that made sense for everyone: the more gifted and serious athlete could aspire to higher level D-I; the less talented or intense athlete could play in the Ivy League or D-III. Not so much anymore. Today, even D-III schools pursue more gifted athletes, leaving the less talented with fewer options. Many of the varsity Amherst athletes from my day would now play intramurals. Intramurals are fine, but not the same thing as intercollegiate competition.

We continue to promote the student-athlete ideal but it turns out that it's no longer easy to provide optimal opportunities for all those interested. The student-athlete niche is shrinking, at the expense of the student-athlete who is more student and in favor of the student who is more athlete.

I enjoy when Amherst wins a big sporting event but with a nagging question in the back of my head: Is it worth it?

Problems with the NBA?

No sport is beyond criticism, and the NBA is no exception, yet complaints about the players, the competition, and the referees seem overstated.

THE NBA IS BETTER THAN EVER

The NBA has never been more competitive—nearly ten teams entered the 2015 postseason with some chance at a championship. Traditional have-nots like Golden State and Atlanta won their conferences with stellar play, and Golden State went on to win the title. The Los Angeles Clippers, with two all-stars, the 2014 Sixth Man of the Year Award winner and the league's leading rebounder faced the defending champion San Antonio Spurs in a first-round playoff series; two teams that good have never before met so early in the postseason.

There were four legitimate candidates for MVP in 2015. Stephen Curry broke the all-time record for three-point shots in a season and might be the greatest shooter ever (if it's not Kevin Durant or Kyle Korver). He beat out James Harden, who carried Houston to fifty-six wins. As superbly as they played, neither scored 55 and 57 points in a game (that would be Kyrie Irving); or 37 and 26 points in a quarter (Klay Thompson); or matched Russell Westbrook's one-man blitzkrieg; or equaled LeBron James's all-around play.

We can add twenty-five-year-old Kawhi Leonard, already a Finals MVP and twice the Defensive Player of the Year Award winner, to the wealth of talent. And Anthony Davis, possibly James's heir apparent.

Partly due to the great play, the league broke its all-time attendance record. In addition, a new TV contract kicks in soon, at nearly triple the current deal.

In summary, the NBA seems rife with great young talent, loaded with money, and attracting more fans (including internationally) than ever.

But many still complain that NBA players commonly travel, palm the ball, and shoot poorly, that current players (college and pro) run like gazelles and jump through the ceiling but lack the fundamental skills of the giants of old. Do today's stars excel because of the mediocrity of the entire group? Do modern players equal those of yesteryear?

That's impossible to know for sure without time-traveling NBA players back and forth. However, we do have objective criteria to assess one major criticism of the modern player—poor shooting. Comparisons of three-point-shot percentages involve shots of roughly the same distance. Free-throw percentage comparisons also eliminate defense as a variable.

The data suggest that NBA players shoot better than ever. NBA players averaged 35 percent from three-point distance in 2014–15, and again in the 2015–16 season, as compared to only 28 percent during the first year of the three-point shot (1979–80). The NBA did not reach 35 percent from the three-point arc until the league shortened the distance following the 1993–94 season.

Moreover, the mean value (out of context) does not fully capture the skills of today's shooters. Three-point attempts increased in 2015–16 for the fifth consecutive season, each time to a new record and now almost double the rate from the 1997–98 season (when the three-point line returned to its original distance). In the days when teams averaged only thirteen three-point attempts a game, the best shooters took most of them and typically when wide open. Nowadays, less-skilled shooters take more three-point shots, and many players shoot them when guarded, off the dribble, and with a quick release. In addition, with the recent emphasis on three-point shooting, teams defend the shot more aggressively.

Maintaining the same three-point shooting percentage as more players take more difficult shots against tighter defenses strongly suggests that current players shoot three-pointers better than at any time in NBA history.

Free-throw percentages provide additional evidence supporting modern shooting excellence, particularly the depth of great shooters. Five players shot 90 percent or more from the line in 2014–15. Only once in the first fifty years of the NBA (in 1990–91, the forty-fifth season) did that many players make 90 percent of their foul shots.

The tenth-ranked NBA player (Kevin Martin) shot 88.1 percent from the line. That would have led the league eleven times and come in second another six times over the first twenty years of the NBA.

The current foul-shooting excellence goes even deeper: twentieth-ranked Lou Williams (86.1 percent) would have finished in second place seven times from 1960 to 1970, in the top ten nine times in the 1970s, and in the top fifteen virtually every season until 2003.

The combination of the three-point shooting and foul-shooting data indicate that criticism of modern shooting skills does not pass analytic muster. We can probably extrapolate that to other criticisms of modern players that do not lend themselves to quantification.

Of course, today's players are not beyond criticism. But we should be wary of the siren song of nostalgia, of remembering olden NBA days as times when mythic men walked the earth and rarely missed a shot.

Oldsters commonly remember their youth in aggrandizing fashion out of proportion to reality. Thus, they frequently see the succeeding generation as failing to match up. In fact, speaking for many, my father once told me that my generation was (literally and figuratively) going to pot. Fond reminiscing about the old NBA should not dim the glory of today's game, its competitive balance, and overall excellence.

DID THE NBA REALLY FIX THE LAKERS-KING GAME?

Players and coaches are not the only ones in the basketball arena wrongly criticized. Ex-NBA referee Tim Donaghy accused the NBA of coercing referees to help the Brooklyn Nets defeat the less glamorous Toronto Raptors in their first-round 2014 playoff series. This echoed previous claims by Donaghy that the NBA manipulated games. The most notorious accusation concerned game six of the 2002 Western Conference Finals, when the two-time defending champion Los Angeles Lakers staved off elimination by defeating the Sacramento Kings. Donaghy alleged that two referees (understood to be Dick Bavetta and Bob Delaney) fixed the game.

Donaghy has been convicted of betting on games so he may not seem a reliable accuser, but many consider him an insider with privileged information. And he wasn't the only one who found something amiss in game six. Announcer Bill Walton (throughout the game), prominent sportswriters, and consumer advocate Ralph Nader all ripped the referees for poor calls favoring the Lakers. Many critics noted that the Lakers shot twenty-seven free throws in the fourth quarter, and the Kings only nine.

An NBA game could, of course, be fixed. That's why the NBA maintains an extensive security department. Their concern is largely about addicted, vengeful, or mentally ill players, referees, and even owners, perhaps in association with gamblers. History provides several examples of rogues rigging sporting events.

But Donaghy's allegations are more spectacular than that. He claims that the NBA *hierarchy* instigated the fix in 2002—that the referees received an NBA-approved message to manipulate game six in the perceived best interests of the league—and that the NBA persists in this noxious practice.

Game six in 2002 remains the most likely possibility of a game in which the NBA hierarchy participated in a fix. Was game six fixed? The alleged motive, of course, was money for the owners. This would derive from ensuring a seventh game, and even more so if the Lakers reached the Finals and boosted television ratings. The real payoff would come if nationally prominent teams routinely reached the Finals, translating into more lucrative television contracts.

The idea of monomaniacal money-hungry owners chasing down every loose buck at the risk of jail time appeals to conspiracy theorists, but does not comport with reality. Some owners are true sportsmen, others pursue winning for ego-boosting reasons, and these owners would not support schemes that ensure victories by other teams over theirs.

Moreover, owners derive NBA income from more than just TV contracts. Those owners primarily motivated by profit surely hold a more comprehensive financial strategy than simply propping up a few favored teams at all costs.

For example, championships provide a financial boon for the winners. Titles yield immediate economic benefits via increased attendance, merchandise sales, advertising revenue, and local television ratings and contracts. In fact, recent studies indicate that every championship generates lifelong fans, especially among youngsters —a cash cow that keeps on giving for decades.

Only a few NBA teams have national appeal, and a policy favoring them would obviously diminish the chances for all other teams.

Owners of the majority of teams, whether motivated by sporting interests, egotism, or the desire to boost local financial sources, would not tolerate a few-favored-teams policy. That's not to say that they're saints or even always law-abiding citizens; it's merely that fixing games for a few elite teams is not in their best interest.

That's why all the major sports leagues have adopted policies favoring competitive balance—the opposite of the few-favored-teams approach. These measures include impediments to free-agent movement (which is generally from small markets to large), such as compensating draft picks or other advantages given to the player's original team. The leagues also feature some combination of revenue sharing, salary caps, and luxury taxes. Player drafts proceed in inverse order of success. The NFL weights the schedule to help losing teams and make it harder for winning teams to repeat.

In 2011, the interests of competitive balance trumped the value of supporting prominent teams when the NBA nixed the Lakers' acquisition of Chris Paul from the New Orleans Hornets. With a backcourt of Paul and Kobe Bryant, the Lakers seemed poised for greatness. However, then-commissioner David Stern, reportedly encouraged by owners, vetoed the trade, going to unusual lengths to protect the relatively obscure Hornets (and competitive balance) at the expense of the glamorous Lakers and TV contracts.

The various competing interests, the persistent efforts to enhance competitive balance, and the nixed Paul trade argue strongly against the idea that favoring prominent teams is such a compelling interest that NBA owners would participate in perhaps the most odious of all behavior in sports.

Of course, even without a consensus of owners, an individual or small group of owners could try to fix a game (the historical "rogue model"). Yet fourteen years later there remains no significant evidence—no written evidence, no money trail, no last-minute changes in the betting line, no tapes, no confessions, no subsequent suspicious behavior, and so forth—that such a scheme manifested in game six between the Lakers and Kings.

In fact, game six was implicated only because the refereeing seemed so bad that many people thought there could be no other plausible explanation. As Nader wrote of the game, "Referees are human and make mistakes but there comes a point that goes beyond any random display of poor performance."

That point was not reached in game six. Nader and others underestimate the vast potential for randomness in sports. The close calls did favor the Lakers, but were due to happenstance and not plot.

Most of the disputed calls in favor of the Lakers could reasonably have gone either way. For example, Walton went apoplectic when Sacramento's Chris Webber was called for charging into the Lakers' Robert Horry. However, this was a standard charge-versus-block play. It occurs in every NBA game and is typically ambiguous; no matter what the referee rules, many observers complain.

Several disputed calls involved contact defending Laker Shaquille O'Neal in the post, something that plagued referees for Shaq's entire career. For example, on one Shaq shot, Scott Pollard seemed to have his arms nearly upright, but he clearly moved his lower body into Shaq. Was there enough contact to warrant a foul call? Walton and co-announcer Steve Jones disagreed.

The Kings' center Vlade Divac's sixth foul received ample criticism. This occurred when Horry fell to the floor retrieving a loose ball and Divac pounced on him. Referees often allow scrums like this to proceed until they can reasonably call a jump ball or grant a time-out. When Divac was called for a foul, Walton described the forlorn Kings' coach Rick Adelman as "beyond belief here." But Divac did not reach for the ball in the usual fashion and tie Horry up —he jumped on Horry and the contact helped knock the ball loose to another Kings player. At worst, this was another call that could have gone either way.

In the allegedly most egregious referee error, Kobe Bryant elbowed Mike Bibby in the face and no foul was called. But Bibby grabbed Bryant at the same time, perhaps even before Bryant's elbow hit. Bryant's contact was much more flagrant, but it might have been the second foul. More importantly, with twelve seconds left and the contact involving off-the-ball movement on an in-bounds play, the referee signaled to play on, to let the players decide the game, a common (and often praised) decision in that circumstance.

Game six had enough obviously bad calls to be considered a poorly officiated game. But the clearly bad calls went against both teams and were not the reason the officiating seemed biased. That perception came from the asymmetry of debatable calls, including the examples above, favoring the Lakers. If ten consecutive 50-50 calls favor one team, the officiating appears absurdly one-sided.

However, probability dictates that runs like this will occur. Ten 50-50 calls in a row benefitting the same team can be expected once in every 1,024 sequences of ten calls. There have been over 40,000 games played in NBA regular-season history, more in the postseason, and each game has numerous calls and non-calls. Over this large number of ten-call (and/or non-call) sequences, we can expect, as a matter of probability, perhaps 500 (500!) sequences of ten consecutive 50-50 decisions favoring one team. Even if each of the ten decisions had only a 25 percent chance of being called in one team's favor, we would still expect instances in NBA history of ten in a row going for that team.

In other words, lopsided officiating, even extremely lopsided officiating, occurs without ill intent. You should have specific incriminating evidence before ascribing poor officiating to ill intent, rather than to the laws of probability. Otherwise, the worst refereed games in the history of every sport will, by Nader's standard, be considered fixes.

The Kings were unlucky, but not cheated.

NBA REFEREES DESERVE HELP, NOT SCORN

Although the accusation of fixing game six in 2002 (and other games) lacks any evidence, Commissioner Adam Silver still identifies the NBA's biggest problem as the public perception that the league, through its referees, manipulates games in favor of glamorous teams. Silver, of course, dismisses the idea as ridiculous, but does not offer an explanation for the discordance between the perception and the reality. Nor does he offer solutions.

The perception likely derives from the speed of the players and some of the current rules, which commonly lead to impossibly difficult referee decisions. TV announcers often disagree about calls, even after watching replays. Inevitably, via statistical randomness, a series of 50-50 calls will favor one team, making referees appear biased or incompetent and fueling conspiracy theories (as we saw with regard to game six, 2002).

In response, the NBA should reduce referees' impact by making difficult calls both easier and less important. That's the best way to boost public confidence in them. The NBA focuses on instant replays as a solution, but these only address end-game calls. Early miscalls are also decisive when they sideline players at risk of eventually fouling out. In these instances, referees influence playing time and rotation, and induce passive play from foul-laden players.

For example, in game five of the 2014 Eastern Conference Finals, Lebron James played only twenty-four minutes because of persistent foul trouble. Three of his fouls were questionable, which meant that referee Ed Molloy essentially decided a playoff game. But the problem was not Molloy. The rule—six fouls and you're out—made his calls needlessly important.

The foul-out rule should be eliminated, following the lead of the old American Basketball Association. After the 1972–73 season, ABA teams shot free throws and kept possession of the ball with the seventh and successive fouls on a player. The additional penalty prevented incessant fouling—the number of fouls actually decreased. The significance of foul calls declined, as players neither fouled out nor were routinely benched for accumulating fouls. This single stroke reduced the impact of referees.

The NBA must also address specific problem areas. Several of the commonly missed calls that erode fan confidence in referees are simply too difficult to call accurately under current rules. The NBA should revise those rules, rather than abide fans yelling at referees for failing the impossible task of calling those plays.

For example, the charge-versus-block play commonly results in disputed calls. Several changes could help. First, move the "restricted" or "no charge" area (currently an arc with a four-foot radius measured from the center of the basket) out another two feet. The size of the restricted area is arbitrary, and has already been increased (following the 1997–98 season). Enlarging the restricted area decreases the incidence of charge/block calls.

In addition, the NBA should redefine the rule. Currently, a blocking foul is called on a drive to the basket when a defender moves into the path of an offensive player after the offensive player begins his normal upward shooting (or passing) motion. Changing the call-defining moment to a more precise and easily discernible action—picking up the dribble—would clarify these calls. Further consistency may be gained by instructing referees to resolve ambiguous situations by calling blocking fouls. Extending the restricted area and changing the rule as described would make the charge/block call both less common and easier to judge.

The pump-fake rule creates another difficult call—when defenders leave their feet in response to the fake and the shooter then leaps into the defender's downward path to create contact. The referee must decide if the defender came straight down (offensive foul) or whether he landed at an angle (defensive foul), and whether the offensive player moved in a "non-basketball manner" (offensive foul) or an unspecified length sideways (offensive foul). These are fine visual determinations of angles and other nuances. Not surprisingly, these calls commonly lead fans to question referee competence.

All players should have rights to the air above them and to land unimpeded (except on a stationary player), perfectly vertical or not. Any contact should be called a foul on the player who created the contact—consistent with standard foul-calling criteria. That rule would be easy for referees (and fans) to understand, and easier to see. There's no reason to reward an offensive player for purposefully creating contact.

Furthermore, let's eliminate offensive goaltending. Currently, players may not touch the ball in the imaginary cylinder above the rim. The referee stands well below the rim, often many feet away looking up at an angle, struggling to see if the ball is half an inch inside or outside the cylinder. The offensive goaltending rule serves no purpose—a ball in the cylinder is likely go in anyway—and subjects referees to second-guessing on a difficult call.

These are examples of plays that require snap judgments rife with fine distinctions from difficult angles. The rules set the referees up for failure. Yelling at NBA referees will always be part of rooting for one's team. But when the heat of the moment dissipates, let's remember that NBA referees are acknowledged as the best in the world. The problem is not referee incompetence or bias, it's that they have an impossible job.

While we're revising the NBA rulebook, let's not stop at helping referees; we can help everyone who watches the NBA by addressing its hacking problems. We need to use the plural—problems—because the issue goes beyond the "Hack-a-Shaq" strategy. But that's the more publicized of the NBA's hacking problems, so we'll start there.

The Houston Rockets and San Antonio Spurs turned games in the 2014–15 season against the Los Angeles Clippers into unwatchable bores with incessant, purposeful fouling of Clippers center, DeAndre Jordan, a notoriously poor foul shooter (41 percent lifetime success at the line). Jordan shot fifty-four free throws in the two games, making only twenty-two. Worse yet, the incidence of deliberate fouls more than doubled in the 2015–16 season.

We've seen the intentional-foul strategy before, utilized against Wilt Chamberlain, Shaquille O'Neal (the "Hack-a-Shaq"), and Dwight Howard, among others. It lies within the rules, but let's call it for what it is—a noxious loophole.

James Naismith and subsequent wise men defined fouls to dissuade defenders from preventing baskets through means deemed unworthy. They intended foul calls to punish fouling defenders, not reward them. They also aimed to make the game more enjoyable to play and watch.

"Hack-a-Jordan" turns all that on its head. "Hack-a-Jordan" is still not commonly used, but that's small solace to the 20,000 fans who waste big bucks at each of these depressing affairs. Nor does the scarcity ease our pain when the strategy ruins a playoff game.

But that's not the worst of it. The problem goes well beyond Jordan and the Los Angeles Clippers. The deliberate fouling of a bad free-throw shooter is only one example of intentional fouling. More commonly, defenders grab players near mid-court to prevent a breakaway. Or they deliberately wrap up a player about to make a layup or dunk. This occurs even more frequently in the playoffs, when NBA culture invokes a "no layup rule."

Over the long run, with the usual NBA foul-shooting success rate around 75 percent, intentional fouls around the basket turn 2 points into 1.5 (from two foul shots). A non-shooting intentional foul that prevents a fast break reduces 2 points to (on average) approximately

1.1 (the mean points scored per possession). Thus, in those situations we actually reward a defensive player for making a nonathletic, non-basketball play at the expense of another player who has outmaneuvered the defender through speed and/or skill.

The NBA addressed one loophole by enacting the "clear path" rule, which penalizes (with two foul shots and possession of the ball) breakaway-preventing fouls. Unfortunately, the rules committee focused on the "clear path" rather than the intent. This led them to gut their own rule with unnecessary nuances.[7] The current rule requires the play to begin in the backcourt (why?) and, worse yet, for the offensive player to be positioned beyond all defenders to invoke a clear-path call (why? why?). Otherwise, the referee calls a common non-shooting foul, which rewards the intentional-foul strategy.

The distinction (two shots and possession versus non-shooting foul) sometimes rests on a few inches. Action stops, referees check the videotape, and TV announcers argue about whether the fouling defender stood an inch ahead or an inch behind the would-be scorer, and sometimes about other details as well. This completely misses the point. regardless of player positioning, rewarding a foul makes no sense. It's completely contrary to the spirit of foul calls.

These fouls also detract from the pace and beauty of the game. Instead of watching Russell Westbrook, LeBron James, and others fly down the court and majestically dunk, we allow someone to prevent that by grabbing them—a play a fifty-year-old man could make.

Does anyone actually prefer that?

Some might argue that referees cannot judge intent. This argument fails. Almost all referee calls (or non-calls) have a subjective element—nothing new here. Referees see contact on virtually every play. They make calls only when they judge that the contact significantly affected the play. Sometimes they even make decisions based on context—how the game has proceeded in terms of physicality, previous calls, and game situations (late or early, close game or rout).

Moreover, almost all intentional fouls are obvious; like pornography, you know it when you see it. These would be among the easiest of all the judgments referees must make. They also lend themselves to some practical guidelines. Any foul on a player completely uninvolved in the play should be considered intentional. Grabbing a player around the torso or lowering a shoulder into him, whether at half-court or near the basket, can only have been intentional.

In contrast, unintentional fouls involve defenders moving their feet for better position, or making plays on the ball—fouling on the arms while trying to poke the ball loose or block a shot. In other words, playing defense as it's been taught.

If a defender cannot thwart a driving offensive player with standard basketball technique he should accept that as part of the game, no different from when an opponent sinks a long jump shot—not a big deal. Get the basket back at the other end; do better next time.

An exception might be made to allow a trailing team to intentionally foul a ballhandler in the last minute of a game. One could plausibly argue that this ploy has redeeming features; without it, more games would end at the forty-seventh minute. The strategy can keep a game exciting to the end.

But the "Hack-a-Jordan" and other intentional grabs lack any redeeming feature. The penalty for "Hack-a-Jordan" should be the same as for flagrant fouls and clear-path fouls: two foul shots plus possession of the ball. This would immediately end exploitation of the loophole.

As noted, that's the smaller part of the intentional-foul problem. The same penalty should apply to all intentional fouls. Rules should reward talent and successful play, not the opposite.

5

MYTHS AND MISUNDERSTANDINGS

The Narrow Thinking about Wins and Losses

Despite the obvious complexity of the game, including myriad nuanced player interactions and variations in player sizes, skills, and styles, basketball experts often spout alleged truisms regarding different aspects of play. Many of these reflect overly rigid thinking.

DO NBA TEAMS NEED A PASS-FIRST POINT GUARD TO WIN?

Russell Westbrook receives more criticism than any other NBA player near his stature. Critics take aim at his style of play at the point-guard position, in particular his propensity for shooting rather than passing. For example, TNT analyst Charles Barkley stated near the end of the 2014–15 season, "Westbrook is not a point guard." Co-analyst Kenny Smith and commentator Bill Simmons concurred. Hall of Fame Chicago Bulls writer Sam Smith asked skeptically, "Can the Thunder win with Westbrook?" Westbrook himself observed, "I have to do a better job of trusting my teammates more . . . trusting them regardless of what is going on, regardless of the time, score, and possession. Just find a way to trust them and let them make plays as well."

The criticisms imply that to win championships, NBA teams need point guards who hew to an ideal: a style exemplified by the unselfishness, court vision, and passing expertise of players like John Stockton, Jason Kidd, and Steve Nash.

Although these players demonstrated the huge benefits of great passing skills, the notion that a team must have a Stockton-type point guard to win a championship is easily debunked. Numerous NBA teams have won with shooting-oriented point guards. The list of scoring point guards (with variable passing skills) who have led teams to NBA championships includes Kyrie Irving, Steph Curry, Tony Parker, Jerry West (who played point guard in the 1971–72 season), Chauncey Billups, Gus Williams, Norm Nixon, and the Jo Jo White–Charlie Scott combination. In addition, Westbrook, Allen Iverson, Gary Payton, Paul Westphal, and Jason Terry led teams to conference titles.

Evaluations of point guards should consider skills in multiple areas, rather than how closely they follow one style of play. Some point guards are better passers than shooters and vice versa, or even best at defending (only Oscar Robertson excelled at everything). The players noted above, and others, all deserved high regard despite straying (to different extents) from the Stockton paradigm.

In Westbrook's case, both his strengths and weaknesses are pronounced. He has remarkable speed and overall athletic ability and fills up stat lines with copious points, rebounds, and assists. In fact, he contributes even more than these statistics measure. He corrals loose balls, deflects passes, fights through picks, and generates other cascading benefits from his boundless energy and competitive spirit.

On the other hand, he is not among the best or most willing passers in the league. He struggles with change of pace and situational awareness. This manifests in too many contested shots early in possessions, wild drives into traffic, turnovers, and low shooting percentages, particularly at the end of close games. His one-speed manic style too often marginalizes teammates, as Westbrook publicly acknowledged.

Although Westbrook, overall, ranks as an outstanding player, his talents do not excuse his flaws. The bulk of his career still lies ahead, along with the opportunity to improve.

Consider contrasting historical precedents. Allen Iverson was another incredibly athletic point guard with a high scoring average but too many wild forays, turnovers, poor decisions, and a low shooting percentage. Iverson won the MVP and was inducted into the Hall of Fame, which should temper criticism. But he won the MVP at age twenty-five and never really improved after that. Even when his speed diminished, he did not modify his game. After Iverson left

Philadelphia, he refused requests from other teams to adopt a more team-oriented approach. Thus, he bounced around four different teams his last two seasons and found himself out of the NBA at the too-early age of thirty-four. Iverson had a great career but never reached his full potential.

Lebron James took a different approach. James has always been a willing passer, but during his initial stay at Cleveland, like Iverson, he took contested long jumpers, other difficult shots, and too often drove recklessly into traffic. James then modified his style and his shooting percentage improved. He now follows the San Antonio Spurs' mantra "pass up good for great." He routinely turns down jump shots, sometimes open ones, to find even better opportunities. His drives to the basket are carefully chosen. He alters his pace, aggressiveness, and strategy based on matchups, opposing defenses, and game situations. And he does all that without sacrificing his scoring. James developed from an amazing athlete into a wiser and greater player.

Russell Westbrook need not emulate John Stockton, but he should take a close look at LeBron James.

DO NBA TEAMS NEED THREE-POINT SHOOTING TO WIN?

The NBA took a record number of three-point shots in the 2015–16 season, following the lead of the defending champion Golden State Warriors and the observation (based on historical success rates) that three-point tries yield more points per attempt than two-point tries. The need to emphasize shooting three-pointers for a team to achieve success in modern basketball had become incontrovertible truth in the minds of many fans and media members, similar to the demand for a pass-first point guard.[1] For example, popular ESPN Radio host Mike Greenberg observed, "The math makes the three-point shot almost unfairly valuable."

But contrary to what we hear on the airways and read in sports columns, the alleged superiority of the three-point shot did not translate into improved scoring efficiency (points per possession) as teams took more of them; across the league, the strategy did not pan out.

How can that be? It may seem counterintuitive, but the perceived efficiency of the three-point shot did not mean that teams would routinely benefit from shooting more threes. A concerted effort to take more three-pointers changes the conditions under which the shots are taken. No one can know beforehand the results of shooting more three-pointers in a new context, and how the law of unintended consequences might intervene.

For example, shooting more threes might result in a lower three-point shooting percentage. Less accurate players might shoot more of them, and better shooters might take difficult shots that they previously would have eschewed. Defenses against the shot might improve.[2]

In addition, personnel and strategic changes instituted to favor more three-point shooting might affect other aspects of the game. In fact, points per possession did not increase league-wide in recent years with more three-point-shot attempts. Quite the opposite: Points per possession in the last several seasons actually trailed that from nearly the entire decade of the two-point-shooting 1980s and the early '90s. At the halfway mark of the 2015–16 season—to virtually zero notice—points per possession decreased to nearly the lowest in twelve years.

The reasons: fewer foul shots and fewer offensive rebounds counterbalanced the benefit of more three-point shots (foul shots and offensive rebounds reached all-time lows in 2012–13 and 2015–16, respectively).

The decrease in offensive rebounds presumably resulted from utilizing smaller players at the power forward ("stretch fours") and occasionally center positions (to exploit their three-point-shooting abilities) and from moving players from their usual spots around the basket out to the three-point line. Fewer drives may also lead to fewer offensive rebounds that accrue when interior defenders leave good rebounding positions to cut off penetrators.

Foul shots are even more efficient shots than threes. They decreased owing to less play around the basket and because defenders strive to avoid fouling three-point shooters.

The 2014 finalists, Miami and San Antonio, ranked only fifteenth and sixteenth in the league, respectively, in three-point attempts. The 2015–16 Spurs ranked twenty-fifth in three-point attempts, yet still ranked third in offensive efficiency and won sixty-seven games—clearly, you can score points and win without shooting many threes. Time-travel Larry Bird and the 1985 Celtics (4.8 threes attempted per game) into the NBA today and they'd do just fine.

Thus, basic data do not demonstrate the benefit to offenses from emphasizing the three-point shot that many assume. However, something did change for the better: the aesthetics of the game. We don't see as much of behemoths banging bodies in the low post. Fewer players back down, slow dribble by slow dribble. And fewer players hold the ball, jab stepping, looking for a drive while everyone else stands around.

In contrast, the three-point-shot strategy emphasizes ball and player movement, speed and skill. Teams now commonly employ a "penetrate and dish back out" style. The penetration often comes from a pick-and-roll, sometimes from a pass to the low or mid post, with the dish to any of three or even four players spaced around the three-point line. Defenders then fly out at the three-point shooter. The ball often moves from one three-point shooter to another, from one side of the court to the other and sometimes back, with defenders frantically chasing before a shot materializes.

Some may prefer old-style size, strength, and banging to speed, skill, and movement. Not me. My preference: NBA players continue to fire away from three-point territory, even if the strategy does not work for many.

DO NBA TEAMS NEED A SUPERSTAR TO WIN?

The Atlanta Hawks won sixty games in 2014–15, the second-best record in the NBA. They got shockingly little respect for that.

Four Hawks made the All-Star team: three-time All-Star Al Horford, two-time All-Star Paul Millsap, the ascendant point guard Jeff Teague, and super-shooter Kyle Korver. They followed team-oriented principles espoused by iconic NBA thinkers such as Red Holzman ("hit the open man"), Phil Jackson (equal opportunity with the triangle offense) and Gregg Popovich ("pass up good shots for great"). The Hawks did not get much respect for that either.

Despite their talent, playing style, and success, virtually no one considered the Hawks title contenders. Their alleged flaw was not lack of a pass-first point guard or of three-point shooters. It was another bogus requirement: no superstars. Many NBA observers believe that classic team-centric teachings work only up to a point, and that you need hero ball to win in the playoffs.

That thinking does not derive from solid basketball analysis. Instead, it reflects our love of heroes, on display in everything from comic books to classic epic novels, and in our reaction to Westerns, military figures, athletes, adventurers, and politicians.

While the playoffs do differ from the regular season—playing rotations shorten, the pace slows, and teams have more time to prepare for each other—that does not render team basketball (without superstars) inadequate to the task. In fact, just recently (in 2014), the San Antonio Spurs won without a superstar. Following earlier examples set by the 1975–76 Boston Celtics, the 1977–78 Seattle Supersonics, and the 2003–4 Detroit Pistons, the Spurs won without a player earning first-team All-NBA honors or averaging twenty points per game.

They did have three likely eventual Hall of Famers—Tim Duncan, Manu Ginobili, and Tony Parker—but Duncan and Ginobili were obviously well past their prime and Parker also on the way downhill. Parker was the only Spur on the All-Star team (Duncan made it in 2015, but as a lifetime-achievement award) and only as a substitute. He led the Spurs with his lowest scoring average in four seasons —a modest 16.7 points per game—fewer than the leading scorer on the '76 Celtics, the '78 Supersonics, the '04 Pistons, and the same as Millsap on the '15 Hawks. Kawhi Leonard (zero All-Star appearances at the time) won the Finals MVP.

Many cite the Spurs as the epitome of a selfless, team-oriented, success story, easily defeating LeBron James and the star-studded Miami Heat in the 2014 NBA Finals. The Spurs also served as the model for the current Hawks, whose head coach Mike Budenholzer spent sixteen seasons as an assistant for Popovich before joining Atlanta.

The fallacy that teams need superstars also manifests in the final moments of close games. Prior to that, most teams strive for the classic team-oriented passing approach. But when games go down to the last few seconds, teams commonly clear out for their best player to create his own shot. This strategy allows the defense to set up and double-team the star almost wherever he goes on the court. Thus, he often ends up taking and missing long, off-balance, double-teamed jump shots—exactly what teams spend the first forty-seven minutes of the game trying to avoid.

This gets odder yet. On the few occasions when the star—often James—passes the ball to an open teammate who misses a potential game-winning shot, the star gets eviscerated for passing—for lacking superstar mettle.

One well-known example took place in the 2012 All-Star game. With a few seconds left and his team trailing by two points, James passed the ball (poorly in this instance, leading to an interception) rather than take on Kobe Bryant and the defenders behind him. Bryant immediately got in James's ear, criticizing his failure to play hero. Fans and media followed Bryant's lead.

Why is passing the ball to an open teammate considered desirable in the first forty-seven minutes of a game but not at the end? For the same reason so many of us praise teamwork during the regular season but diminish its importance when the playoffs begin: we love heroes.

The late sports commentator Stephen Jay Gould (*Triumph and Tragedy in Mudville*) captured the most basic aspect of sports hero worship: "the possibility for transcendence never dies. We live for that moment, the truly unpredictable performance that shatters all expectation." His melodramatic language fits the point: sports heroes provide thrills.

Michael Jordan scoring sixty-three against the Boston Celtics, Madison Bumgarner seemingly winning a World Series by himself, and similar feats, provide shock and awe. We rush home from work to get to the TV set or stadium, hoping to witness the transcendent and to bask in the reflected glory of Jordan and the few athletes of his caliber.

The greatest athletes also inspire. Kids dream of someday "be(ing) like Mike." Adults are more realistic about their own prospects but still revere the human spirit and capabilities revealed through epic deeds. Perhaps that subtly motivates us to do better at work or in the gym. Or aim for something grander.

But those parts of star-worship hold for the regular season and the first forty-seven minutes of games just as well. Another aspect manifests in the playoffs and the last seconds of games: we feel the need for superheroes most in critical situations.

Tom Wolfe (*The Right Stuff*) illuminated this phenomenon in his tale of America's early space program, when explaining why seven Mercury astronauts became national heroes even before they had gone into space. Wolfe likened them to the "single-combat warriors" who characterized the pre-Christian era going back to David and Goliath: "In single combat the mightiest soldier of one army would fight the mightiest soldier of the other army as a substitute for a pitched battle between the entire forces." Societies exalted these heroes-to-the-rescue.

At the time of the Mercury 7, the space race figured prominently in the Cold War. Early on, the Soviet Union jumped way ahead, fueling fears that the United States would be dominated in a forthcoming actual war. As Wolfe said of the first US spaceships: "ours blow up." In that context, the Mercury 7 became our Davids sent out against the Russian Goliaths.

Similarly, the Cold War–era Soviet Union used athletes as symbolic single-combat warriors, a theme popularized by *Rocky IV* (with Ivan Drago, the seemingly invincible Russian Goliath). Amateur wrestling provided a real-life example. When the American Dan Gable won a prestigious tournament in Tblisi, USSR (present-day Georgia), in 1972, the Soviets took this as an intolerable propaganda defeat: an American dominating a sport the Russians considered their own, and on their soil. The Soviet wrestling federation publicly announced a national initiative to find and train someone to defeat Gable at the 1972 Olympics. (Gable defeated the anointed Russian warrior in the Olympic finals at Munich in a match featured on ABC-TV.)

Sports heroes enrich our lives even when their feats do not have international implications. But hero worship should not distort analysis. It shouldn't stop anyone from passing the ball to the open man with the game on the line. The Atlanta Hawks did lose in the playoffs, but it was not because every championship team must have a single-combat warrior.

The Chicago Bulls' slump in January 2015 wasn't ascribed to the lack of a passing point guard, or lack of three-point shooting, or not having a superstar on the roster. Instead, providing yet another too-facile explanation for losing, Coach Tom Thibodeau ("Thibs"), as reported in the *Chicago Tribune* (January 12, 2015), berated his team for lack of effort, "We're going to have to bring a lot more intensity. And the only way you bring a lot more intensity is to work a lot harder. . . . There's no shortcuts. If you don't play with an edge you're in trouble. There's a serious price to pay. . . . We have to get that fight back in us."

Thibs's explanation of the Bulls' losses ignored several important injuries. It also ignored the effects of Derrick Rose missing several seasons; Jimmy Butler's shooting slump; Aaron Brooks's poor defense; Pau Gasol's slow feet; Nicola Mirotic's inexperience; Kirk Hinrich's age; and the difficult process of incorporating three new rotation players.

Thibs's comments did not surprise folks in Chicago. He frequently attributed defeats to poor effort. Most NBA coaches (along with media members and fans) share his view that basketball games measure character; the tougher guys usually win, and the losers need to get tougher. Coaches commonly ascribe losses to players not getting loose balls, not getting back on defense, not competing, not meeting the victor's effort, not fighting for their lives.

Few coaches speak about less talent. One refreshing exception is Doug Moe. Before his thirty-seven-win Denver Nuggets played the juggernaut Los Angeles Lakers in the 1987 playoffs, coach Moe stated, "We don't have a chance to win a single game." He turned out correct: the Lakers swept the Nuggets. Moe understood that talent matters—a lot.

But we often attribute victory to effort rather than talent. In fact, we're so fond of the gritty underdog upset—Seabiscuit outruns War Admiral, Rocky KOs Apollo Creed—that sometimes we distort reality to fit the theme.

The Bulls–New Jersey Nets playoff series in 2013 provides a classic example of a faux upset misattributed to superior character. The

Nets had the better regular-season record and home-court advantage. Las Vegas oddsmakers favored the Nets at 4–5 odds even before the Bulls lost two starters, Luol Deng and Hinrich, to illness and injury, respectively.

At that point, most pinned the Bulls' hopes solely on their usual (at that time) exemplary fighting spirit. Bulls beat writer Sam Smith explained, "Great contests are not necessarily won because you have more talent, but because you have more of the stuff of champions. . . . Perhaps that's the best thing the Bulls have going for them."[3] Butler added before game seven, "It's going to be a fight. The tougher team is going to get the win."[4]

The Bulls won game seven. Of course, the postgame analysis lauded their heart and hustle and shamed the Nets for lack of the same. It made for a great story, especially in Chicago.

In truth, the more talented team won the series. The Nets had the least skilled pair of starting forwards in the NBA—over-the-hill Gerald Wallace and non-scoring journeyman Reggie Evans (the two combined for 12.2 points per game). Injured guard Joe Johnson, their best player, could barely walk by game seven; on one leg, he shot two of fourteen. Even with their own injuries, by series end the Bulls had advantages at four of the five starting positions, a better bench, and a better coach. But no matter, the theme of the series had already been cast.

Bulls center Joakim Noah dominated his Nets counterpart Brook Lopez in game seven, even blocking five of his shots. The media, typecasting Noah as Seabiscuit, attributed his great performance to his toughness. That was only because Noah doesn't look like much, with narrow shoulders, an awkward gait, a hair bun, and the ugliest (side-spinning) shot in the league. In truth, Noah (before subsequent injuries) was actually one of the most athletic centers in the league: agile, with excellent lateral mobility, rapid second and third jumps, good hands, and coordination—an outstanding rebounder, passer, and defender. The next season he made first team All-NBA. Noah thumping the lumbering Lopez in the 2014 playoffs should have come as no surprise, just as the Bulls beating the Nets did not constitute an upset.

Returning to the Bulls' January 2015 slump: They rebounded

somewhat but played erratically throughout the rest of the season; according to Thibs-speak, winning when they tried hard and losing when they didn't. Their season ended with a disappointing 2015 playoff loss to the shorthanded Cleveland Cavaliers.

Then the Bulls fired Thibs.

It seemed odd that the Bulls would part with such a successful and highly regarded coach—Thibs won 65 percent of his regular season games over five seasons—but Thibs and his superiors, General Manager Gar Forman and Vice President of Operations John Paxson, did not get along. In particular, management disapproved of Thibs's wont to give starters heavy regular-season minutes in the interests of winning every game possible, but perhaps wearing the players out in the process.

Thibs's firing also derived from his refusal to change his approach to fit the potential offensive skills of his players.

Thibs made his reputation as perhaps the NBA's premier defensive coach, with some of his schemes now standard fare around the league. He utilized mutiple defense-oriented players (Noah, Omer Asik, Taj Gibson, and Hinrich) and, early on, relied heavily on the MVP Rose to create offense through his own considerable skills.[5] Then Rose suffered multiple injuries over several seasons. The Bulls did surprisingly well during that time (due to defensive excellence) but always succumbed in the playoffs to more injuries and difficulty scoring.

Optimism abounded in 2014. A healthy Rose, the newly signed center Gasol, and the developing Butler supplemented Noah, the returning Defensive Player of the Year. Thibs envisioned another strong defensive team with two seven-footers and added contributions from Rose and Gasol at the other end.

But the Bulls, troubled by recurrent offensive droughts, failed to meet expectations. Foremost, Noah receded playing alongside Gasol. With the offense running through Rose and Gasol, Noah played off the ball at power forward where his poor shooting allowed defenders to lay off him and help elsewhere. The Cleveland Cavaliers hid and rested players on Noah throughout the 2015 playoff series. Sometimes, defenders almost comically ignored him; the Bulls played nearly four-on-five at the offensive end.

Yet even with the season slipping away in the final game against Cleveland, and the Bulls going through yet another scoring drought, Thibs stuck with his old paradigm: defense first (Noah played thirty-five minutes, Hinrich twenty minutes; together they scored one basket) and the hope that Rose could carry the offense. But with Rose not the player of old, and Noah and Hinrich on the court, the Bulls could score only seventy-three points against a hobbled Cavs squad in game six. Season over, sooner than expected.

All that's in retrospect, of course, and perhaps it's not fair to expect Thibs to see it beforehand. But the more important question for the Bulls was whether Thibs would see it going forward.

Would he relegate the defensively skilled but scoring-challenged Noah to backup center (his natural position) behind Gasol? Would he replace Noah at power forward with scorer Mirotic, rather than Gibson, a superior defender? Would Thibs play sharpshooter Doug McDermott, whom he had marginalized because of defensive deficiencies?

The Bulls feared that Thibs would continue with his same defense-emphasized approach despite the disappointing season and regardless of his players' skills.[6] (As Einstein or Benjamin Franklin or perhaps someone else said, "The definition of insanity is doing the same thing over and over again and expecting different results.") So they fired him and hired the more open-minded and offense-oriented Fred Hoiberg.

Hoiberg began the 2015–16 season by replacing Noah in the starting lineup with Mirotic, giving McDermott more playing time, and stressing a faster pace. Most importantly, Hoiberg tinkered with various lineups and combinations, demonstrating interest in whatever works, rather than adhering to a fixed template—not a guarantee of success, but at least a different approach.

The Bulls started off well, winning twenty-two of their first thirty-four games. But even with a new coach, new rotations, and new strategy, one thing did not change: They only lost—as they explained it—when they didn't try hard enough.

After a fifteen-point loss to the Charlotte Hornets, Hoiberg said, "We didn't have any fight, no resolve, didn't try and go back at them. Just kind of accepted it tonight . . . you've got to fight." Butler concurred, "They just out-toughed us tonight." Rather than worry about strategy, rotations, or skills, Butler said that going forward the Bulls "need to compete. It's more important to go in tomorrow and compete, man up, roll that ball out and be dogs."

Then, after the Bulls blew a sixteen-point fourth-quarter lead at home to the Phoenix Suns, Gasol decried the lack of effort, "It's a mental thing, a mindset thing, a heart thing . . . a matter of wanting it." The *Chicago Tribune* headlined the game account of another loss with "Not Putting Forth the Right Effort."

The good start surprisingly turned into a second-half free fall and the Bulls missed the playoffs for the first time in seven seasons. Injuries were certainly a big reason: Noah's season ended after only twenty-nine games; Mirotic, Butler, and Rose all missed more than fifteen games and played subpar in others owing to lingering injury or illness.

The Bulls also had personnel problems. Mirotic and McDermott proved not yet ready for heavy minutes. The thirty-five-year-old Gasol slowed down defensively. Rose and all-star Butler played well individually, but did not complement each other in the backcourt. They all struggled in adopting the new offensive scheme, and Hoiberg made some rookie coaching errors.

But in his postseason analysis, Vice President Paxson downplayed injuries, strategy, player talent, and Hoiberg's inexperience in explaining the poor ending. Instead, he resorted to cliché: The Bulls disappointed because they had "a team that didn't have the collective fight and toughness to fight through adversity. And that's the biggest disappointment in all of this."[7]

I doubt that Doug Moe ("we don't have a chance to win") would buy that malarkey.

LeBron James's Odyssey

No player in the modern NBA has been as polarizing and harshly criticized as LeBron James. Haters deem him guilty of some crime or another for much of what he's done, from leaving Cleveland for Miami to various tweets, comments, and other on- and off-the-court actions. Much of that criticism is unwarranted.

THE DECISION

James received overwhelming criticism for leaving the Cleveland Cavaliers via free agency for the Miami Heat. Much of that derived from the mechanics and arrogance of the announcement, but there were three other more substantive criticisms. First, that joining Dwyane Wade and Chris Bosh suggested a lack of competitive chops. Second, that with steelier performances, James could win titles in Cleveland—that is, he had no reason to leave. Third, the superstar triumvirate meant easy championships in Miami that would not test James or require greatness from him. With the benefit of hindsight, we now know that these presumptions were all mistaken.

Many ex-NBA stars argued that great players should (and historically, did) strive to defeat each other, rather than join together. The latter, per their telling, circumvents the spirit of competition and speaks ill of those who partake. ESPN commentator Bill Simmons specified that "Michael Jordan would have wanted to kick Dwyane Wade's butt every spring, not play with him." Jordan publicly affirmed the point.

Simmons's comment was especially biting because of the invocation of Jordan, against whom James is commonly measured and whose achievements he aspires to equal. The criticism amounted to an attack on James's competitive spirit and character. Simmons and others implied that no matter how James played or whatever he won with the Heat, he'd remain short of true greatness.

However, in order for Jordan and other stars of yore to thump their chests and brag that in their day (that is, when giants walked the earth) star players did not join up, they had to willfully ignore their own histories.

Charles Barkley took a pay cut so that Scottie Pippen could join him and Hakeem Olajuwon as a super-trio (even if past their primes) in Houston. Things were not much different for Jordan, both as a youngster and a veteran. Coming out of high school, Jordan enrolled at dynastic North Carolina, teaming up with All-Americans James Worthy and Sam Perkins. Later on, as a Chicago Bull, he approved the acquisition of Dennis Rodman, subjugating his hatred of Rodman in the interests of creating a Hall of Fame triad (with Rodman and Pippen) and winning three more titles.[8]

In fact, basketball history provides numerous examples of great players teaming up. Bill Walton joined the UCLA dynasty. Every year, roughly ten McDonald's High School All-America players enroll at either Kentucky, Duke, or North Carolina; the rest play together at a short list of other elite basketball schools, sometimes as pre-arranged packages.

In the NBA, Wilt Chamberlain forced a trade to join Jerry West and Elgin Baylor with the Lakers. Tracy McGrady and Grant Hill signed with Orlando the same season. Kevin Garnett and Ray Allen sequentially influenced their way to a Big Three in Boston. Dr. J maneuvered himself to join George McGinnis and Doug Collins in Philadelphia. Moses Malone signed as a free agent to join Dr. J and Andrew Toney on the Sixers.

Each of these situations differed to some extent, but the same theme governed: Top players teamed up for a competitive edge. Modern players may have greater *ability* to team up,[9] but not necessarily greater intrinsic *inclination*.

If teaming up is more attractive to current NBA stars than those in the past, it's not because modern players lack true grit. Instead, it's because the sports world increasingly measures athletes by championship rings. We no longer appreciate the star player who competes valiantly but falls short. He's now often derided as a loser.

John Havlicek hugging Jerry West after yet another Lakers Finals defeat and whispering, "I love you," honoring West as a glorious hero now seems a relic of a bygone era. Back in the day, nobody considered Elgin Baylor, Oscar Robertson, and West losers (only Wilt was deemed a loser—a complicated story). Fast-forward several decades, and many deem Patrick Ewing, Karl Malone, and Barkley tainted by their lack of titles. The increased title fixation culminated in widespread fan and media derision of the ringless James at Cleveland.

This criticism encourages players like James to leave mediocre teams for those with title aspirations. That's human nature, not flawed character. The fault is ours, when we hold single players responsible for winning titles. Basketball is a team game; one player can only do so much, and only one of thirty teams wins the championship each season.

Of course, if James did have a viable opportunity to restore his reputation by winning a title at Cleveland (the second criticism), the mudslinging at him would have had less effect. He had, in fact, come close to winning there. But the issue for him as a free agent was not how the Cavaliers had done, but how they were likely to fare in the future. In truth, the franchise was in free fall.

Three aged starters—Shaquille O'Neal, Anthony Parker, and Antawn Jamison—had virtually nothing left. The fourth starter, Mo Williams, and reserve J. J. Hickson, disappointed in Cleveland and soon moved from team to team as journeymen. The third guard, Delonte West, left the NBA for personal reasons. Worse yet, the Cavs had no good means to obtain high-caliber replacements. They were over the salary cap for the near future, leaving them no hope of obtaining a top free agent. They had no draft picks that season, and no players coveted by other teams or young players likely to significantly improve.

Indeed, Cleveland lost twenty-six consecutive games, an NBA record for futility, the season after James left. No player in basketball history ever won a championship with a supporting cast as bad as that Cavaliers team. No one should have been expected to rejoin a team that weak, particularly someone routinely lambasted for lacking a championship ring.

The last prong of the criticism—that James would not be tested and could not prove himself Jordan-like in Miami—proved equally mistaken. The NBA had far too much talent for Miami to enjoy a cakewalk and James escape untested. Nobody should have imagined that Dirk Nowitzki and Jason Kidd, or Tim Duncan, Manu Ginobili, and Tony Parker, or Kevin Durant and Russell Westbrook, or Paul Pierce, Kevin Garnett, and Rajon Rondo would roll over for Miami. Moreover, the NBA salary cap limited the Heat; Pat Riley had to surround James, Wade, and Bosh with minimally paid, typically older, players.

Thus, Miami's postseasons were dogfights—the Heat lost two Finals series and had to win three seven-game series to win their two championships. The postseasons also provided appropriate tests of James's mettle. Wade, Bosh, and others helped, but at critical times Miami needed James to play sublimely for the Heat to win. He did just that.

For example, James played near-perfect games in must-win road contests in Indiana (40 points, 18 rebounds, 9 assists) and Boston (45 points, 15 rebounds) during the 2012 playoffs. In the 2013 Finals, trailing San Antonio by 10 points with seconds left in the third quarter of a win-or-go-home game six, James scored or assisted on the next 16 points, almost single-handedly bringing Miami back in the game, leading to an overtime victory. Then he carried Miami to a second championship, with 37 points and the game clincher in game seven. He left no doubt about his fighting spirit.

The irony of claiming that James's move to Miami evidenced his poor competitive spirit is that joining Miami actually enabled him to prove himself a warrior. Staying in Cleveland would have relegated James for the foreseeable future to early playoff exits (or worse) and increased ridicule as a loser. Further, Wade and Bosh's presence did not diminish James's accomplishments with Miami. To the contrary, they helped provide him with an opportunity to turn the narrative about him on its head.[10]

THE SECOND DECISION

James went back to Cleveland after his successful four-year run in Miami. That pleased most of the NBA world, which had been upset over him leaving in the first place. It also had a feel-good vibe: the prodigal son returning home. Of course, James leaving Miami angered Heat president Pat Riley—in an instant the Heat went from contender to also-ran, and Riley's ego does not abide anyone leaving his clutches without permission.

Still, one might have expected James to receive a hero's welcome from the fans when he returned to Miami as a member of the Cavaliers. After all, he led the Heat to four NBA Finals appearances, two championships, and played as hard for them as anyone could have wanted. Surely, you'd think, they appreciated that.

However, the Heat feared the worst, based on angry local reaction to the announcement of James's departure. Even Wade's public plea on James's behalf did not allay their concerns. After introducing James, the Heat's announcer immediately presented the next player so that any booing would dissipate quickly. Some animus still showed through.

Why were some Heat fans angry with James? Considering the four-year joyride James gave them, the public criticisms—that he didn't properly thank the fans, that he didn't make his decision quickly enough, and so on—seem inadequate explanations.

Kurt Vonnegut understood the basic dynamics. In his novel *Cat's Cradle*, he panned the superficiality of many relationships, noting that people often proudly claim a shared identity despite having nothing meaningful in common. He satirized these groups as "gran-falloons." For example, those who simply come from the same state: "We Hoosiers got to stick together. . . . Whenever I meet a young Hoosier, I tell them, 'You call me *Mom*.'" Or alumni: "Cornell! cried Crosby gladly. My God, I went to Cornell. . . . Three Cornellians—all in the same plane!"

Fan-player relationships are similarly shallow. They begin randomly when an athlete joins a team due to the vagaries of the draft, trades, or the financial (or other) rewards of free agency. Fans and players (on the teams the fans root for) share a goal of team success but the connection is more coincidental than a spiritual commonality that defines more meaningful relationships.

James came to Miami for the opportunity to win championships. He made no pretenses of any other link to the city of Miami or to Heat fans. Miami fans should have known that he might leave if and when the Heat declined, or for some other self-interested reason— the exit mirroring the entrance. Yet even though James delivered for Miami, many Miami fans turned on him when he left; the fans' bond to James was as limited as his bond to them.

Chicago Bulls' fans provide another example of superficial loyalties, though in the opposite direction. No player (other than teammate Bill Laimbeer) angered Chicago fans more than Dennis Rodman when he played for the Detroit Pistons. Rodman elbowed and hip-checked Jordan every chance he got, no matter how dangerous to Jordan, and he pushed a vulnerable Pippen from behind into the basket support, drawing blood.

Nevertheless, the Bulls and Jordan needed someone with Rodman's talents to win more titles, so they acquired him. Rodman rebounded and defended for the Bulls at an elite level, and Bulls fans (along with Jordan) turned quickly in his favor. The player they had hated with every sinew of their bodies became a hero.

James's return to Cleveland suggested an exception to the superficial fan-community-player relationship. His announcement letter was a paean to a spiritual bond with northeast Ohio ("It's where I walked. It's where I ran. It's where I cried. It's where I bled"), and his move to a losing team suggested priorities greater than championships ("I feel my calling here goes above basketball").

As noted, most people outside of Miami lauded James's rediscovery of his childhood connections, his evolution from someone consumed with winning to a more sophisticated person. Kudos to James and to the Heat fans who grasped his thinking. Those are the ones who got beyond knee-jerk home-team loyalty and applauded James during his introduction, acknowledging his efforts and accomplishments for the Heat.

They understood that James owed them his best on the court for as long as he played for the Heat. They did not demand the pretense of a long-standing bond.

LEBRON IN LOVE

James's friendship with Dwyane Wade survived his return to Cleveland. The following summer, James, Wade, and Chris Paul vacationed together in the Bahamas, and during the 2015–16 season, James flew to Miami on an off day to work out with Wade. They maintain steady communication.

Those superficialities only hint at the extent of their relationship. Wade's wife, actress Gabrielle Union, described a deep emotional bond between James and Wade and speculated whether they said, "I love you" to each other. Wade answered in an interview, "You know, yeah, we say *love* . . . We'll end a conversation with *love*. Or, *Love you, bro*. We have that kind of relationship."[11] No doubt, Bron and DWade really dig each other.

TNT commentators Charles Barkley and Kenny Smith did not comment publicly on the affirmation of love, but we know that they (and other ex-NBA players) deemed the in-season workout a crime. They broadened their previous "you can't join up with your rival" taboo (from when James joined Wade in Miami) to "you can't work out with him either," meaning "You can only want to destroy him, as we used to do."

Yet James and Wade broke no new ground here. The unwritten rule against fraternization was violated as far back as the early days of the NBA, and by one of the most respected and competitive athletes of any sport: Bill Russell, who palled around with his great rival, Wilt Chamberlain. The two met in Chamberlain's freshman year at the University of Kansas, when he drove to St. Louis, where as Russell described it, "He just introduced himself and we spent the day together and were friends ever since."

Early in their pro careers, they routinely stayed at each other's homes prior to games. They'd sometimes play with electric trains, and then have dinner. They made a point of spending Thanksgiving together. Russell said, "It was like this every year . . . at noon he would come to the hotel and pick me up and I would have Thanksgiving dinner with his family. . . . His mother would let me take a nap in his bed afterwards. And then we'd go to the game together."

The bromance later had its ups and downs, but Russell poignantly expressed his grief when Wilt passed away in 1999: "I feel unspeakably injured. I've lost a dear and exceptional friend. . . . I'm going to dearly miss my friend Wilton Norman Chamberlain."

What would Barkley and Smith say about the sleepovers the two historic rivals enjoyed? Actually, the better question is why they ignored Wilt and Russell altogether when they castigated James and Wade for befriending the enemy as if that had no NBA precedent. Russell and Wilt's friendship forms a pillar of NBA history, and Wilt's death spurred a public retelling; everyone affiliated with the NBA knows this story.

Barkley and Smith also suffered a curious case of amnesia when it came to their contemporaries Magic Johnson and Larry Bird. Fierce enemies early on, the relationship between Magic and Bird turned on its head when they did a Converse commercial together in 1985. Over lunch, it turned out that they actually liked each other, more and more as time went by. Bird was one of the first people Magic called to inform of his HIV diagnosis in 1991.

Magic didn't limit his affection among NBA stars to Bird. Johnson and Isaiah Thomas exchanged kisses prior to the opening taps at the 1988 Finals.[12]

Barkley's worst amnestic gap involved his own past. According to Suns players and others, at the 1993 Finals between his Phoenix Suns and Michael Jordan's Chicago Bulls, Barkley and Jordan—widely known as good friends—played golf and had dinner together on off days. Barkley never denied that until twenty years later when he implausibly—as Barkley and Jordan are famous, distinctive figures—attributed the misconception to mistaken identification.

There probably are more bromances today than in earlier NBA times, but it's not that mutated DNA, bad drinking water, or poor parenting made today's players soft. The players are essentially the same; the world around them changed. Long ago, for example, the Lakers played on the West Coast, the Celtics on the East Coast, and they mostly met in ultracompetitive circumstances that fueled enmity (even then, as noted, Celtic great John Havlicek said "I love you" to the heroic-in-defeat Lakers' Jerry West). Nowadays, NBA players often meet as kids on the AAU circuit or at all-star summer camps, or in high school on up age-group-national and all-star teams. In the NBA, they're often brought together by agents, commercials, other business and sporting interests, social media, and more. When people spend time together—like Chamberlain and Russell in the early days; later on, Magic and Isaiah, Magic and Bird, James and Wade—relationships develop, no surprises there.

And nothing is lost in the process. Havlicek loved West *before* game seven, and still went out on the court to kick the hell out of him. Bird and Magic continued to compete ruthlessly against each other. Magic flattened Thomas when he drove the lane in the 1988 Finals; Thomas responded with forty-three points in game six on a badly sprained ankle—one of the most competitive efforts anyone has ever seen.

As everyone who has ever had a brother knows, he's often the person you want to beat more than anyone else. Nevertheless, at the end of the game you tell him that you love him and you spend time together afterward.

Then you kick his butt again.

More Media Hysteria: The Chris Paul Affair

As it did with LeBron James's Decision, the media reacted (though on a lesser scale) histrionically to Los Angeles Clippers star Chris Paul's postgame criticism of a referee; like James with his decision, all Paul really wanted was to win. Lambasting referees is standard sporting fare, but this was no ordinary ref Paul had the temerity to disparage; in this case, the referee was female.

After a decisive loss to the Cleveland Cavaliers, Paul said of Lauren Holtkamp, "She gave me a (technical foul) and that's ridiculous. . . . If that's the case, then this (refereeing in the NBA) might not be for her." Immediately, social media lit up, deriding Paul for sexism. He also drew a rebuke from the NBA's Referee's Association, which "deplored the personal and unprofessional comments made by Chris Paul." It seemed like the full force of hypersensitive political correctness came to bear on Paul.

That's ridiculous. Paul has nothing to apologize for or defend. He criticized a referee—for good reason or not, no news there. He did not single her out for her gender; she's the one who gave him the questionable technical foul. He made clear, at least shortly afterwards, that "might not be for her" referred to her struggling (in his opinion) as a first-year NBA referee, irrespective of gender. The bogus brouhaha illuminated only those who took offense—their bias toward imagined slights and their yen for a fight.

And it obscured a real basketball issue. Paul's postgame comments reflected his in-game frustration. In a nationally televised game, the Clippers got drubbed, trailing by as many as thirty-two points in the third quarter. Paul shot four for fourteen, scoring just ten points. The referees assessed five technical fouls on his team. The Clippers, of course, claimed the technicals were unwarranted, but in the most favorable view of their response to a thrashing, they lost their poise and provided fodder for the referees to make the calls.

There may have been an underlying basis to the Clippers' behavior. This was more than a random midseason game. The Clippers held championship aspirations, and a road game against a solid opponent constituted a litmus test of their ability. They failed miserably.

The failure in a game like that may have particularly irked Paul
—a future Hall of Famer without a title on his resume (and we've
seen how fans and media treat stars without rings). He was nearly
thirty years old at the time. His window of opportunity to win a
championship is narrowing.

Paul surely knows the Clippers' limitations. The Clippers have
only three above-average players, and one of them has significant
limitations. DeAndre Jordan is a defense and rebounding specialist
who is sometimes removed at the end of games because of his woe-
ful foul shooting.

The Clippers' two outstanding all-around players—Paul and
Blake Griffin—do not dominate; neither rank among the NBA's
top half dozen players. The Clippers 33–18 record at the time may
have been a smokescreen that Paul saw through, and that may have
struck a nerve during and after the game.

In any case, the entire affair had to do with poor performance, not
gender.

Danny Ferry Deserves Praise, Not Exile

Like Chris Paul, Danny Ferry got skewered by sanctimonious political correctness; in Ferry's case, he was wrongly accused of racism.

As general manager of the Atlanta Hawks, Ferry made some racially tinged remarks about NBA player Luol Deng. Following public release of these remarks in mid-2014, Ferry took a coerced leave
of absence from his position with the Hawks. Subsequently, in June
2015, Ferry "resigned" (meaning: the Hawks fired him).

This was unfortunate. First, Ferry is no racist. Second, he constructed the 2014–15 Hawks team that won sixty games, a huge
twenty-two-game improvement over the previous season (see above,
"Do NBA Teams Need a Superstar to Win?"). Ferry should have been
given a raise and named NBA Executive of the Year. Instead, he got
almost no credit and was shooed away under a black cloud.

The same black cloud wrongly enveloped Hawks owner Bruce
Levenson. Several years ago, Levenson, in an e-mail, lamented the
poor attendance of white people at Atlanta Hawks games and pon-
dered what could be done to attract them. (The Hawks had just
finished nearly last in the NBA in attendance.) When this became

public knowledge (per Levenson's self-reporting) the backlash led him eventually to sell the team.

Thoughtful, race-sensitive ex-NBA players like Kareem Abdul Jabbar and Len Elmore deemed it all an overreaction. Kareem wrote that Levenson "is a businessman asking reasonable questions about how to put customers in seats," not a racist wishing black Americans away. Elmore concurred. Kareem noted that people should be allowed "minor insensitive gaffes if there is no obvious animosity or racist intent."

The same holds for Ferry. In a private conference call among Hawks executives, Ferry read from an external scouting report that free agent Deng "had a little Africa in him," meaning he's somewhat of a con man. Hawks minority owner Michael Gearon, Magic Johnson and others called for Ferry's head, and eventually got it.

For sure, Ferry should have omitted the derogatory stereotype. But this insensitive gaffe, by itself, did not make him a racist or warrant ruining his career. Ferry had no animosity or racist intent, and by Kareem's wise standards should have been forgiven.

Toronto Raptors general manager and Nigerian native Masai Ujiri cited Ferry's excellent reputation around the NBA and wrote, "If Ferry has made an honest, isolated error, we should forgive and move on." A subsequent review by an Atlanta law firm of 24,000 e-mails and interviews with nineteen witnesses did not uncover a single episode of racial animus or even insensitivity on Ferry's part.

Ferry expressed appropriate contrition and took sensitivity-training classes. He seems a good guy who had a thoughtless moment. But unlike Kareem, Elmore, and Ujiri, the Hawks' decision makers could not forgive. The shame falls on them, not Ferry.

Nowadays, virtually everything that anyone says or does may be captured on tape or film or a retrieved e-mail. Who among us would survive the scrutiny of a public persona? Who has never once done or said something that he later regretted? A single gaffe does not necessarily provide a window to one's soul.

Racism is vile and one might reasonably argue that every trace should be exposed and vilified. But the cause is not helped when we fail to distinguish between true racism and slipups devoid of animus. That failure dilutes the effect when we rail against the real deal.

Hopefully, a wiser NBA team will reverse this injustice and hire Ferry, a good guy and an unrecognized Executive of the Year Award winner.

Do Hot Hands Exist?

J. R. Smith went berserk in game one of the 2015 NBA Eastern Conference Finals. The Cleveland Cavaliers' guard amazed onlookers by scoring 17 points in 5 minutes, hitting six of seven shots (five of six three-pointers).

His game-altering outburst followed even more remarkable scoring streaks in basketball from earlier in the season. Florida State freshman guard Xavier Rathan-Mayes scored 30 points in the final 4 minutes and 38 seconds of an NCAA game against Miami. He scored 26 consecutive FSU points without missing a shot, hitting eight in a row, including six three-pointers. In an NBA game, the Golden State Warriors' Klay Thompson made thirteen consecutive shots, scoring 37 points in a single quarter. As if to show that was no fluke, Thompson followed that up with a 26-point quarter in another game.

These streaks brought back memories of Tracy McGrady closing a game with 13 points in 33 seconds, Isiah Thomas scoring 16 points in 94 seconds, and ex-Duke All-American Jon Scheyer scoring 21 points in 75 seconds in a high school game.

Man, those guys were hot. As any recreation-league player who has ever hit three jumpers in a row knows, they were "in the zone."

Actually, maybe not.

Researchers have exhaustively studied the purported "hot hand" in sports. They've evaluated the phenomenon in sophisticated ways in different athletic competitions. The results varied, but some prominent academicians vehemently deny that "hot hands" exist. As psychologist Daniel Kahneman (*Thinking Fast and Slow*) wrote, "The hot hand is a massive and widespread cognitive illusion."

In less esoteric terms, mathematician John Allen Paulos (*Innumeracy*) ascribed the perception of hot hands to "the result of minds intent on discovering meaning where there is only probability." The late professor Stephen Jay Gould (*Triumph and Tragedy in Mudville*) put it bluntly: "Everyone knows about hot hands. The only problem is that no such phenomenon exists."

These scholars explain eye-catching sports streaks as simply random sequences predicted by the laws of probability and illustrated by coin flipping. If you flip a coin enough times, at some point you'll get ten or even many more heads (or tails) in a row. That'll seem incredible, but the coin is behaving exactly as expected.[13]

Hot-hand naysayers deny any relationship between consecutive events. No matter how many shots in a row a shooter makes (or coins consecutively turn up heads), the expectation for the next shot (or coin flip) remains the same (the player's usual shooting percentage, or, for the coin flip, 50 percent for both heads and tails).

That may be overstated in basketball.

The totality of streak/hot-hand studies lies beyond the scope of this book, but we can look at the oft-quoted, pioneering work of Thomas Gilovich, Amos Tversky, and Robert Vallone to frame the issue.[14] They found no evidence of hot hands in either foul shots or field goals taken by NBA players. Making several consecutive shots did not lead to greater than usual success on subsequent shots.

Free-throw shooting, however, is the wrong place to seek hot hands. They are shot only one and two (on rare occasions, three) at a time, and sequential free throws may be separated by many minutes or even days. This negates the psychological or muscle-memory continuity that makes up the presumptive basis of a hot hand.

Field-goal shooting provides an area more suitable for finding a hot hand. Thus, the hot-hand phenomenon took a hit when Gilovich et al. found (as a representative example) that after sequences in which the Philadelphia Sixers' Andrew Toney, considered a streak shooter, hit three consecutive field goals, he made only 34 percent of his fourth shots (overall, Toney shot 46 percent from the field.)

However, tracking field goals illustrates a problem common to studying complex systems like sports: confounding variables. Ideally, Toney's fourth shot would have taken place under the exact same conditions as his first three. However, much changes when a player makes several shots in a row. To begin with, the player feels "in the zone," making him likely to take more difficult shots—the so-called "heat check" (Smith's streak in game one ended with a miss on a closely guarded three-point shot from well behind the three-point line). Defenders also put forth more effort when the player they are guarding scores. In fact, the entire defensive strategy may change: the defender may go over picks instead of under, double teams may be applied, substitutions made, defensive responsibilities altered, and so on.

You cannot adequately evaluate for a hot hand in basketball unless you can identify and control for all the counterresponses that consecutively made shots elicit. Perhaps Toney's 34 percent success rate with more difficult shots against tougher defenses did suggest a hot hand.

Hot hands are certainly less common than generally assumed. In fact, they're hard to prove. However, absence of proof is not proof of absence. Methodological problems vex these kinds of studies, fueling an ongoing debate.

Thus, J. R. Smith might really have been in the zone. He certainly looked it, and that's probably as much as we can know for sure.

The Larger Issue behind Derrick Rose's Alleged Softness

Chicago Bulls superstar Derrick Rose caused an uproar in the 2014–15 season by revealing that he sits out some games to minimize injury. Rose noted that he does not want to attend his son's future graduations "all sore." Charles Barkley and Shaquille O'Neal, among other critics, argued that playing with injuries is an occupational requirement justified by NBA salaries and athletic glory. O'Neal added that Rose seemed "soft."

The Rose brouhaha inverted the usual situation. Athletes typically brag about how tough or talented they are. Most people discount the talk; only performance matters. In this instance, however, critics focused on Rose's timid talk rather than on his exemplary on-court performances. Moreover, many observers previously suggested that Rose's aggressive play contributed to his injuries and recommended that he tone down his approach in the interests of his long-term health.

Following the exchange, Rose continued his physical play (seemingly at odds with his own sentiments), attacking the basket relentlessly. Unfortunately, in the next game, his characteristic aggressive performance ended prematurely with a pulled hamstring, perhaps giving voice to those advising more prudence in his play.

The Rose story should not have been limited to Rose—his courage or lack of it. Instead, Rose's comments suggested a larger sports problem: the inordinate risk of injury that commonly accompanies the pursuit of athletic glory.

This includes both orthopedic injuries and cognitive disorders. Rose surely knows of the crippling foot injuries suffered by Kevin McHale, Bill Walton, and Yao Ming, the knee injuries of Penny Hardaway and Brandon Roy, and the back pains of Larry Bird and Steve Nash. Orthopedic damage plagues football even more—many players end up with permanent physical limitations and chronic pain. And the cognitive disorders (pugilistic dementia in boxing and chronic traumatic encephalopathy in football) can be even more debilitating.

Growing awareness of these problems has resulted in declining participation in youth football. In fact, both Lebron James and President Obama stated that they would not allow their sons to play football. (Obama spoke hypothetically.)

Obama, however, added (about pro football) "there's a little bit of caveat emptor. These guys, they know what they are doing. They know what they're buying into." ESPN's Mark Schlereth, an ex-NFL player who required twenty-nine surgeries during his career, agreed: "I knew what I was signing up for.... I wouldn't trade any of it. Not one bit of the pain, swelling or overall discomfort that I still feel today."[15]

Not everyone agrees with allowing individuals to make their own risk assessments. For example, the American and British Medical Associations both called for the abolition of boxing. But this well-meaning suggestion suffers from applying the perspective of the privileged and successful to others less fortunate. James, wearing his sociologist's hat, spoke for the latter by distinguishing between his own youth football participation and his proscription for his sons: James needed a path out of poverty but his sons do not.

Riskier sports typically draw from lower socioeconomic classes. Some participants escape difficult circumstances via athletics. For instance, most boxers come from poor inner-city areas. Football participation is more heterogeneous but also may serve as a means out of a bad rut—illustrated by the book/movie/TV series *Friday Night Lights* about Odessa, Texas.

Banning and avoiding certain sports deprives too many of important opportunities. We can do better than that. We can make sports safer without losing anything in return. Instead of chiding Rose for emphasizing his personal health, let's use his concerns to inspire constructive action.

Some suggestions, across a range of sports:

Rose's orthopedic struggles would benefit from playing in fewer back-to-back games. The NBA could drop twelve of them and still keep a seventy-four-game schedule by increasing the length of the regular season one week (and reducing the preseason by the same). Fewer games back-to-back and overall (compensating for the longer postseason now played) will reduce wear-and-tear and overuse injuries.

Orthopedist James Andrews advises that youngsters not throw curveballs "until they can shave." This concept should also govern tackling in youth football. High schools already play seven-on-seven in noncontact passing leagues over the summer. If that works for high school players, younger players can play flag or touch football. This trend has already started: some seventh-graders now play touch football in football-crazed East Texas. Moreover, the Pop Warner national youth league limited full-speed head-on blocking and tackling drills during practices.

Thursday night NFL games should be eliminated. The health risk to players from the short turnaround time outweighs the contribution to the already bulging owners' coffers. Similarly, the NFL should stop thinking of increasing the regular season to eighteen games.

We should endorse the DEA's investigation into controlled-substance and other painkilling prescriptions in the NFL. These should be provided only by qualified personnel per the terms of the prescriptions, as guided by reasonable medical standards and subject to review by an independent head medical officer. Team physicians should be hired by the NFL, rather than by individual teams, to reduce conflicts of interest.

Soccer players also suffer head injuries, both via heading the ball and with head-to-head collisions that occur when they compete for a ball in the air. Prohibiting heading before high school competition would limit the risk to a three- or four-year span for the vast majority of soccer-playing youngsters.

Boxing remains brutal despite multiple rule changes (gloves, shortened fights, and more) that decreased injuries. Bouts should be further reduced to a maximum of ten rounds, a 17 percent reduction in blows that will not compromise the competition.

There are other sports to consider and room for disagreement on specific points. But broadly speaking, we should not accept the current level of injury in sports. Some incidence of injury is inevitable in physical competitions, but fans suffer when athletes cannot compete, and everyone loses when active athletes must concern themselves with whether they'll be able to attend their children's graduation ceremonies in the future.

Concussed Warriors Should Not Have Returned

The health risks that accompany playing basketball went on full display in the 2015 NBA playoffs.

Viewers gasped when Stephen Curry of the Golden State Warriors somersaulted out of control over the Houston Rockets' Trevor Ariza in game four of the 2015 Western Conference Finals, and hit the back of his head on the court. Curry lay immobile for several minutes before rising and walking with assistance to the locker room. Surprisingly, Curry returned to action in the second half.

After the game Warriors coach Steve Kerr explained that Curry had been evaluated by team doctors using the NBA's concussion protocol and was cleared to play. Kerr made it sound straightforward: big game, medical clearance, get out there and compete. In fact, Curry's return was unwise.

Concussions can be difficult to diagnose. One can suffer a concussion without losing consciousness, and symptoms may not develop for hours or even days after head trauma. The risk of exacerbating the injury with further contact is highest in the immediate aftermath. Accordingly, athletes who experience head trauma would best be served by at least overnight (and perhaps longer) observation to determine if symptoms of a concussion develop before allowed to return to competition. The NBA concussion protocol does not represent a scientific approach so much as a practical compromise between the realities of concussions (about which much remains unknown) and the exigencies of professional sports. More demanding protocols would mean that some non-concussed athletes would miss playing time.

Even assuming the NBA's approach is reasonable, it must be applied with and leavened by common sense. Curry had just experienced perhaps the worst fall in NBA history. It took him a long time to get up and he was obviously woozy when he did so. Under the circumstances, his return to the game is difficult to justify. The Warriors sent Curry out to play nearly twenty minutes of intense NBA basketball in the aftermath of a significant blow to the head.

The folly of that was illustrated by what happened the very next game to Klay Thompson, Curry's backcourt partner. Thompson received a knee in the side of his face; his head snapped visibly, and he had to be removed from the game. And yet, according to ESPN sideline reporter Doris Burke, the Warriors' doctor deemed the concussion protocol unnecessary. Thompson later seemed set to return to play, but had to go back to the locker room for sutures to his bleeding ear. The next day brought reports that after the game, Thompson exhibited symptoms of a concussion. The Warriors confirmed that Thompson did have a concussion.

In his postgame comments after game four, Kerr—one of the brightest coaches in the NBA—showed no awareness of the possibility of delayed symptoms. The official NBA concussion policy states "Every player and coach receives concussion education prior to the beginning of each season. Topics include information on the underlying mechanism of concussion, common *and uncommon* [emphasis mine] presentations of concussions." If that is the case, then Kerr should probably have known better.

In any event, the decision to return Curry to action was even worse than it seemed. Quite beyond the medical aspects, this decision made little sense in purely basketball terms. Putting Curry back in made it slightly more likely for the Warriors to win game four, but they were virtually certain to win the series regardless. The Warriors led three games to none; no NBA team in history has ever rallied from a 3–0 deficit, and only nine teams have overcome a 3–1 deficit to win a best-of-seven series. Only two of those teams won game seven on the road, as Houston would have had to do against Golden State.

Meanwhile, a more serious injury to Curry would have been devastating to Golden State's chances in the Finals. Thus, by returning Curry to the floor, the Warriors allowed a small potential benefit to trump the risk of a huge loss.

So what was coach Kerr thinking? Perhaps the recent Rockets–Los Angeles Clippers series weighed on his mind. In the preceding round, the Rockets became the ninth team in NBA history to overcome a 3–1 deficit. In a phenomenon cognitive psychologists call the "availability heuristic," recent events disproportionally influence decisions. For example, doctors more often mistakenly diagnose a rare disease if they have recently seen such a case.

Without the Rockets-Clippers series on his mind, the history of almost two hundred teams successfully protecting 3–1 leads might have led Kerr to be more conservative about returning Curry to game four. But that is only explanation, not justification. Curry should not have returned to play.

The problem obviously transcends this one series. Professional sports teams, aided and abetted by the physicians they employ, too often put concussed players at further risk. On several occasions in the 2015 NFL season, even after all the previous outcry about concussions, players stayed in games after receiving obvious blows to the head—with trainers, sideline doctors, and other personnel seemingly oblivious. It is increasingly apparent that these protocols are either inadequate or administered carelessly. Certainly coaches need to be well informed, and both they and physicians must prioritize protecting players' health. Brains are at stake.

Wrong Conclusions from NBA Finals

Curry and Thompson regained their wits and led the Golden State Warriors to the 2015 championship. The Finals stood out not only for their (and the Warriors) great play, but also for the several misconceptions it spawned among many viewers.

The most prominent misconception was that the champions provided a blueprint for how basketball ought to be played henceforth: with small ball and rampant three-point shooting.

For sure, they ended the Finals with six-foot-seven Draymond Green at center, and sharpshooters Curry and Thompson launched threes throughout. But the leap from there to broad statements about the way teams ought to play reflects fondness for simple explanations, new "truths," and overemphasis on the most recent games and series.

An earlier round against Memphis demonstrated the flimsiness of the purported paradigm shift in the NBA. The Warriors trailed Memphis two games to one and could easily have lost the series had Grizzlies star guard Mike Conley been at full health. In that event, the perceived future of the NBA would have turned completely around: A healthy Conley and a Memphis victory would have prompted the theme that you (still!) need big men and low-post offense (for example, Marc Gasol and Zach Randolph) and do not need to rely on the three-point shot.

Moreover, while the Warriors did go small at times, it was not their primary strategy throughout the year. Traditional big men Andrew Bogut, Marreese Speights, and Festus Ezeli averaged twenty-four, sixteen, and eleven minutes per game, respectively. Throughout their dominating regular season and until game four of the Finals, the Warriors mostly played a standard-sized lineup.

In fact, the Warriors went small in game four of the Finals only as a strategic response to Cleveland's effective defense. The Cavaliers double-teamed Curry, even beyond the three-point line, particularly when Golden State set picks for him. That was unusual enough; then they added an odder twist, purposely not rotating to the wide open Bogut, Ezeli, or Green when they received passes in the free-throw line area from the harassed Curry.

The Cavs challenged the three Warriors to make plays essentially unguarded: to take open foul-line jumpers or drive to the basket and score or make productive passes. For three games, the trio mostly failed. Bogut and Ezeli lacked the necessary skills, and the youngster Green, by his own admission, played nervously.

Warriors coach Steve Kerr responded by benching Bogut and

Ezeli and giving their minutes at center to the more dexterous David Lee and to Green. Importantly, Green shook off the jitters and began making plays commensurate with his ability. As Green made shots and productive drives, uncontested jumpers opened up for other Warriors (including MVP Andre Iguadola), and the team rolled from that point on.

Thus, the Warriors' small-ball success in the 2015 Finals should not be interpreted as defining the Warriors' best play, and certainly not as a polestar for how other teams should play. Instead, the Warriors provided an example of a smart coach with a talented, versatile roster adjusting his strategy to meet different challenges as they arose.[16]

The Warriors' success shooting threes was also commonly misconstrued, leading many to extol three-point shooting broadly, rather than make a narrower point about the Warriors' personnel. The Warriors' marksmanship provided only one sound conclusion: If you have two players who shoot 44 percent from beyond the three-point line—the greatest long-distance shooting backcourt in NBA history—you should shoot a lot of threes; you'll be hugely entertaining and very hard to beat.

But what about the NBA teams that don't have Curry and Thompson on the roster? Overall, as previously discussed, NBA players shot a record number of three-point shots in 2014–15. Yet points per possession actually decreased below the norm for the previous ten years, a fact that three-point shooting dogmatists typically ignore. The decline in offensive efficiency owed to unintended consequences of shooting more threes: a record low in offensive rebounds and a near-record low in foul shots per field-goal attempt (similar results obtained in the 2015–16 season).

The take-home point from the NBA database should be that if you have good three-point shooters you ought to use them, but if you don't, find another strategy.

The Finals provided more misconceptions that stemmed from our love of underdogs and particularly, successful underdogs. Curiously, this involved two players at the extremes of ability and reputation on the Cavaliers' roster: Matthew Dellavedova and LeBron James.

Media and fans credited Dellavedova with superb defense against Curry during the first three games, elevating the spunky guard's play to instant classic status. "Delle" did hustle, fight through picks, and stay reasonably close to Curry. But Delle-mania owed mostly to our love of the story: undrafted, little-known Australian backup stymies the MVP (David slays Goliath).

The initial Cavs success versus Curry derived from the team-based strategy described above rather than Delle shutting down Curry one-on-one. Nobody performs up to his usual statistical standards when relentlessly double-teamed so far from the basket. But when Kerr found an effective answer (small ball) to Cleveland's mega-focus on Curry, the court opened up, Curry thrived and everyone stopped referring to Delle as a Curry-killer. Actually, he never was in the first place.

LeBron James would seem the last athlete cast in the role of underdog and given the benefit of the doubt on that basis. Yet when Cleveland lost Kevin Love and Kyrie Irving to injury and faced the sixty-seven-win Warriors, that's what happened.

James played incredibly well, averaging 36 points, 9 assists, and 13 rebounds per game in the Finals. Beyond the statistics, he carried a shorthanded team with an overmatched point guard and a group of role-playing, generally undistinguished teammates to a 2–1 series lead. That fueled the likeable theme of a valiant warrior fighting an uphill battle virtually by himself against a superior team.

In that context, James's poor shooting (40 percent overall against Golden State, 31 percent on three-point shots) got explained away. Commentators typically characterized it as an unavoidable consequence of the injuries to Love and Irving. They noted that without the two star players, the Cavs needed James to take the preponderance of shots, even against a defense focused on him. Moreover, James had to shorten the game for his overmatched team by shooting late in the shot clock, often resulting in low-percentage shots. The latter may be true, but many analysts were so unconcerned with James's many misses they seemed to suggest that in the particular context, it was OK for him to misfire—that this was not a problem for the Cavs.

It was not OK, however, and not well explained by him having injured teammates. James just could not dominate Iguadola, and he simply shot poorly. He missed around the rim, he missed open jumpers, he missed a bunch of makeable 3s, and he missed them early in games before one could blame fatigue. Most importantly, he shot poorly the entire postseason (42 percent overall; 23 percent from the three-point line), including the thirteen games Irving played and the four games both Love and Irving played.

Bottom line: James suffered a prolonged postseason shooting slump and did not get called out for it. The "single hero[17] combating an entire team with the greatest postseason play ever" story appealed so much that contrary evidence got discounted.

The point here is not to diminish James. After all, he still dominated the Finals in historic fashion even while shooting poorly. The point is that many downplayed the weak part of his performance. As with Delle, the storyline was too good to give all the facts their proper due.

The same holds for much of the 2015 Finals.

Kobe Got It Right (Twice)

The Warriors' 2015 championship led into an active NBA offseason, highlighted by DeAndre Jordan's shenanigans (verbally committing to the Dallas Mavericks before reneging), all-star LaMarcus Aldridge signing with the already-competitive San Antonio Spurs, and thirty-seven-year-old Kobe Bryant eschewing retirement despite shooting a career-low 37 percent from the field.

When Bryant re-signed with the Los Angeles Lakers, he said that he hoped for a "rebirth." Many fans grimaced at this Panglossian dream, seeing Bryant mired in a steep late-career decline and risking ending up like Willie Mays in the 1973 World Series, when Mays had trouble catching routine fly balls.

Mays's World Series fiasco is often cited as a cautionary tale that warns against athletes playing too long. In truth, that striking image —arguably the finest outfielder ever, stumbling around in center field like a little leaguer—makes no significant point: not about Mays, and not for Bryant.

Superstars do not tarnish their reputations when they play poorly at the end of their careers. Nobody diminishes Mays for his awkward finale. Everyone remembers him flying around the bases, one of the greatest players ever, with 660 home runs, the Catch in the 1954 World Series, and other catches that might have been even greater than the Catch.

Nor do we place any import on Johnny Unitas struggling at the end in San Diego, Joe Namath in Los Angeles, O. J. Simpson in San Francisco, Mickey Mantle hitting .237, Derek Jeter's last season, Kareem Abdul-Jabbar averaging ten points a game, Shaquille O'Neal in Boston, Jason Kidd's Mays-like final ten games shooting 0–17 from the floor, or Rickey Henderson playing minor-league baseball with the San Diego Surf Dawgs at forty-seven years old. Those memories mean little and then fade.

The greatest players routinely play well past their prime[18] and for a reason entwined with their greatness: they have tremendous confidence in themselves. Johnny Unitas threw a pass from the seven-yard line in the waning moments of the 1958 NFL championship game because "when you know what you're doing, you're not intercepted." Joe Namath guaranteed victory against a hugely favored Baltimore Colts team in Super Bowl III. Muhammad Ali walked into the ring against Sonny Liston and against George Foreman as virtually the only person around confident of his chances.

Athletes like that cannot discard their bravado any more easily than a serial philanderer can join a monastery or an alcoholic give up drink. Thus, they often keep playing until they're essentially dragged away. In a sense, they have little choice. They are who they are.

That's for the better. When an athlete retires earlier he risks leaving something on the table. How many more yards could Jim Brown and Barry Sanders have gained?

In fact, many athletes made significant contributions during their declining years. Gordie Howe played eight seasons and scored 212 goals (in the NHL and WHA) after his last NHL All-Star appearance. Abdul-Jabbar and Kidd helped win championships as very elder statesmen. As a part-time player almost thirty-seven years old, Ray Allen hit the biggest shot of his life, perhaps anyone's life. Hank Aaron pushed his then-home-run record out to 755 with 22 home runs in his last two seasons.

When Bryant opted in for the 2015–16 season he expected a return to health, better teammates, meaningful games ahead, and a chance to supplement his legacy. That was not inconceivable; thus, it was a good decision. However, the rebirth did not come to fruition. No significant free agent joined the Lakers, touted youngsters Julius Randle and D'Angelo Russell struggled, and Bryant's skills continued to deteriorate.

So what? Nothing from the 2015–16 season will taint Kobe's five NBA championships, two Olympic gold medals, eighty-one points in a game, and his ice-cold killer persona.

Early returns from the season convinced Bryant that his tank was near empty. When that sank in, he announced plans to retire after the season, noting, "This is all I have left to give." It was now time to move on, no regrets, only an incredible career to remember.

Once again, Bryant got it right.

6 THE BEST AND THE BRIGHTEST

Would Wilt Dominate Today?

Bill Russell has eleven championship rings, but Wilt Chamberlain was basketball's near-mythic, Ruthian figure, scoring 100 points in a game and averaging 50.4 points per game for an entire season. Nevertheless, one might reasonably wonder if Wilt would dominate today. After all, NBA players as a group compare favorably to those Wilt competed against fifty years ago. Today's players are generally bigger, better trained, more fit (nobody smokes cigarettes at halftime anymore), jump higher (the dunk is no longer a great feat), and shoot better from distance. Globalization and better scouting improved the depth of talent. Analytics, video, and extensive scouting make current players more knowledgeable about the game and their opponents.

But Wilt dominated the average player. Improvements in overall NBA play might not affect someone leap years beyond the mean. In fact, by objective measures, the NBA has hardly matched Wilt's particular combination of size and athleticism, much less passed him by.[1] Wilt stood 7 feet 1, weighed from 250 to 300 pounds over the course of his career, and was a sensational athlete; in college, he approached the world record in both the high jump (over 6 feet 6 with old-style technique) and triple jump (over 50 feet), ran the 100-yard dash in 10.9 seconds, and shot-putted 56 feet. Later on, he dead-lifted 625 pounds. No current NBA player can match that combination of size, strength, speed, and leaping ability.

Shaquille O'Neal is the modern analog for Wilt. Shaq stands 7 feet 1, weighed over 300 pounds in his prime, and ran well in his younger days; his athleticism and skills rivaled Wilt's. Wilt may have jumped higher and been more agile; Shaq was slightly bigger and probably even stronger. One or the other might have had a slightly better drop step or bank shot, but overall, their physical gifts (when Shaq was in shape) and skill set seem similar—free-throw woes included.

Declaring the two roughly equal may seem unfair to Wilt, whose point and rebound averages dwarfed Shaq's. For example, Wilt scored the unfathomable 50.4 points per game in 1961–62, whereas Shaq topped out at 29.7. Doesn't that alone suggest Wilt's superiority?

No, because something odd went on in 1961–62. That single season produced the three highest scorers in NBA history up to that point. Further, the three players—Elgin Baylor (38.3 ppg), Walt Bellamy (31.6 ppg) and Wilt—all scored career highs surprisingly early in their careers (Bellamy as a rookie, Wilt in his third season, and Baylor in his fourth season). Each player then experienced yearly decreases in scoring.

Wilt, though still in his prime, was already down to Shaq-like numbers by 1965 (33.5 ppg) and 1966 (24.1 ppg); Baylor dropped to 27.1 ppg in 1964 (after which he injured his knee); and Bellamy fell to 19 ppg by 1966. This pattern—early career high followed by sharp descent—differs markedly from the usual career arc in which players improve on (or at least maintain) their early performance as their career unfolds. What was going on?

Chamberlain, Baylor, and Bellamy ushered in a new wave of athletes. They were far more athletic in the low post and driving to the basket than previous NBA players, and could not be handled by the customary passive one-on-one defense of the time. Films show the early Chamberlain posting up with ease and often receiving uncontested entry passes. Wilt would then hook, finger-roll, or even dunk against the overmatched lone defender.

Opposing coaches responded to the uber-athletes' scoring surge: defenses became more aggressive and sophisticated, and their scoring decreased. Wilt's 50.4 ppg, incredible as it was, must be seen in context: he dominated relatively primitive opposition and strategy, and in subsequent seasons his dominance decreased as defenses improved.

This sequence is common to competitive sports: Dominance occurs more easily in the infancy stage of a sport. As a sport evolves, training and strategic advances and an expanding pool of athletes (along with an occasional rule change, for example, widening the three-second lane in 1964) reduce the disparity of talents between the top and bottom. Better overall competition hinders individual domination.

Thus, for example, as the talent pool increased in Major League Baseball, the variation around the mean batting average of hitters continually decreased. Over time, both the lowest and highest batting averages moved closer to the mean. The decrease in the higher averages reflects some neutralization of the greatest hitters by improved pitching. Nobody has hit .400 in over seven decades.

Similarly, with the continued influx of African Americans and foreigners into the NBA (as well as improved scouting, coaching, and training) the overall play improved so much that nobody—not even Michael Jordan—has averaged more than 37.1 points per game since 1962–63. This says nothing about the quality of the top modern players. It speaks to improved competition blunting the ability of the best athletes to dominate.

Which brings us back to Wilt. Even though he played fifty years ago, it is hard to imagine anyone coming along with a better combination of size, strength, speed, agility, and leaping ability. Wilt would not have averaged 40 points per game in the modern NBA— not against sophisticated defenses and superior competition—but he would have been at least as good as Shaq, the dominant center of the modern era.

Which means that Wilt would still be great today.

Will the Great Phil Jackson Succeed with the Knicks?

The New York Knicks fared poorly in Phil Jackson's first two seasons as team president, losing 115 of 164 games and plummeting at the end, leaving little optimism for 2016–17. Jackson's first coaching hire, Derek Fisher, did not last the second season. All those losses surprised many of his fans, as Jackson brought a marvelous résumé to the job, including eleven championships as a coach. It also surprised Jackson—he had predicted immediate results.

To be fair, Jackson inherited a weak roster, but it shouldn't surprise if he never succeeds with the Knicks, and not simply because of the roster and an incompetent owner.

Many underemphasize the differences between coaching and running a team. Jackson had never been a general manager or team president. He had never evaluated coaches, made trades, negotiated contracts, navigated a salary cap, run a draft, or managed organizations.

We should not assume that his coaching genius[2] translates to genius in a different position. That's the big flaw in the thinking of his supporters and perhaps Jackson as well.

Genius is often surprisingly circumscribed, and not as transferable to different tasks as one might presume. This observation might be termed the Pauling principle, after the brilliant chemist Linus Pauling.

Pauling received the Nobel Prize in Chemistry in 1954. However, when he moved out of his field into clinical medicine, he floundered. In 1970, Pauling announced that mega-doses of vitamin C, much higher than the consensus recommended daily allowance, would not only prevent the common cold, but also reduce the incidence of, and treat, heart disease, cancer, arteriosclerosis, and other diseases, and also slow down aging.

The idea of any single entity having such profound diverse effects was (and remains) unprecedented, and seemingly quixotic. The gross misinterpretation of basic medical research by such a genius seemed puzzling, and Pauling's outré ideas were widely rejected by physicians and other scientists. Of course, Pauling claimed (and supporters still claim) that the medical community was ignorant, but forty-six years later, a vast amount of research has belied Pauling's hyperbolic assertions. Megadose vitamin C (and other megavitamins he touted) appears to have minimal to no benefit; certainly not the grandiose effects Pauling described.

The Pauling principle extends into the arts, politics, business, and more. A few examples: Mitt Romney's business genius did not translate into a wisely crafted presidential campaign. Presidential aspirant and neurosurgical whiz Ben Carson struggled whenever the topic strayed from separating conjoined Siamese twins. In contrast, Abraham Lincoln and Harry Truman were successful presidents but failed businessmen. Ulysses S. Grant was a military genius but another failed businessman and generally considered a weaker president. In the arts, Miquel Cervantes and Henry James (among others) were superb novelists, yet pedestrian playwrights. Edgar Allan Poe, a maestro of the short story, wrote two novels (one of which he never finished) to mixed reviews.

The Pauling principle also manifests in sports, including basketball. The business genius of James Dolan and Donald Sterling did not result in effective NBA ownerships (to say the least). College coaching stalwarts like Rick Pitino and John Calipari had sub-.500 records as pro coaches and returned to college. Perhaps the most relevant examples for Jackson are his ex-Knick teammates Willis Reed and Dave DeBusschere. The three of them had the same mentor, Red Holzman, and Reed and DeBusschere were also cerebral. Yet Reed and DeBusschere both had undistinguished careers as NBA executives.

Of course, the Pauling principle does not always apply—some people have moved from one position to another with great success. In fact, Bill Sharman, Larry Bird, and Danny Ainge achieved a basketball trifecta of sorts, with noted accomplishments as players, coaches, and general managers. Pat Riley is another example, with spectacular success as both a coach and an executive.

Jackson may yet replicate those successes. If you could select any ex-coach likely to be a successful team president, it probably would be Jackson. But you never really know: we have ample precedent of brilliant people who no longer seemed so brilliant once they moved out of their specific area of expertise.

THE TRIANGLE OFFENSE

The Pauling principle theorizes why Jackson *might* fail. Some observers cite a specific reason to suggest why he *will* fail with the Knicks: his insistence on using the triangle offense.

That might seem an odd critique, since the triangle succeeded for Jackson in Chicago and Los Angeles (and he attributed much of that success to the triangle), but those teams always had the best player on the floor and often the two best (from among Michael Jordan, Scottie Pippen, Kobe Bryant, and Shaquille O'Neal). Further, the triangle might be less successful with players with different skills than those on his previous teams. The triangle emphasizes certain skills (instinct, rapid decision making, moving without the ball) and de-emphasizes others (dribbling, pick and roll, and one-on-one abilities). Perhaps that contributed to the failures of several Jackson disciples when they used the triangle in coaching other teams.[3]

Jackson should be wary of the example set by ex-NBA coach Mike D'Antoni, who prioritized a system over his players' skills. D'Antoni coached the Phoenix Suns to the Western Conference Finals in 2005 and 2006 with an exciting and effective offense called "seven seconds or less" by writer Jack McCallum. D'Antoni fashioned a team of small speedsters who beat opponents up the court and took shots quickly.

The strategy worked in Phoenix, but not at subsequent coaching endeavors in New York and Los Angeles. The Knicks' failures could be ascribed to lack of talent, but the Lakers had big guns. With Bryant, Dwight Howard, and Pau Gasol on the 2012–13 roster, they expected to compete for the title.

However, Howard and Gasol struggled with D'Antoni's fast-paced offense. D'Antoni moved the seven-foot Gasol out to the perimeter to shoot more jumpers and took him out of the starting lineup for a while to improve team speed. The star-studded Lakers finished only 40–32 under D'Antoni and got swept in the first round of the playoffs (without an injured Bryant).

Howard then left as a free agent, unhappy with Bryant and with being marginalized (like Gasol) in the offense (D'Antoni candidly states that he doesn't like low-post play). Without Bryant for almost all of the next season, the Lakers fell to 27–55, management refused to extend D'Antoni's contract, and he resigned.

D'Antoni's outside-shooting, space-the-floor offense revolutionized the NBA but he contributed to his own demise in Los Angeles by implementing the strategy with an older, slower, poorer outside-shooting team; it was a mix ill-suited for "seven seconds or less."

Jackson should consider the contrasting example of flexible thinking shown by San Antonio coach Gregg Popovich. Almost everyone admires Pop—in part, for his humility. He does not present himself as anything other than ordinary. He never flashes or refers to his championship rings and always deflects credit for his success away from himself and onto his players.

Pop's humility does more than endear him. His perspective that players (more than coaches) win games enables him to take a secondary role. In particular, he has no qualms about choosing strategies tailored to his players' skills, rather than insisting that players adjust their play to fit his ideas.

Thus, his last championship team (2014) played differently than the first four (1999, 2003, 2005, and 2007). The '99 team walked the ball up the court, threw it into the post to twin towers Tim Duncan and David Robinson, and led the league in defense. The roster subsequently evolved, but the Spurs continued to win with a focus on Duncan and defense.

However, by 2013, as Duncan aged and with several younger, faster, better-shooting players in his arsenal, Pop adapted. He revved up the pace, spread the court, unleashed the three-point shot, and the Spurs became one of the top-scoring teams in the league, culminating in a near immaculate offensive destruction of Miami in the 2014 Finals.

The 2014–15 team continued with the new approach, but the resourceful Pop added a tweak: isolation plays to take advantage of Kawhi Leonard's immense athleticism. But by 2015–16, in part due to the off-season acquisition of big man LaMarcus Aldridge, the Spurs slowed down (near the bottom of the league in shots per game), took fewer three-point shots, and returned to leading the league in defense.

Jackson appears wedded to the triangle (for better or for worse), following the D'Antoni model rather than the Pop model. But it's too early for Knick fans to judge: the roster remains inadequate and according to Jackson (in *The Last Season*), "players need a couple years to grasp the triangle's complexities."

Hopefully, Jackson will acquire enough good players with the appropriate skills to put the triangle to the test. If the Knicks cannot obtain players with skills apt for the triangle, and a roster stable enough for the players to learn it, Jackson himself will be put to the test. Will he adapt like Pop? Or is Jackson's self-regard so tied up in the "brilliance" of the triangle that he'll go down clutching an ideology to his chest? His response to triangle critics after his second failed season suggests that possibility: "Who are these people? Do they have 11 championships?"

Will the triangle offense be the means by which the Zen master succumbs to the Pauling principle?

Is Krzyzewski the Greatest College Coach Ever?

Jackson, Popovich, Pat Riley, and Red Auerbach vie for the honor of greatest professional basketball coach ever. On the college side, Duke's Mike Krzyzewski surely belongs on the equivalent short list. In fact, following Duke's 2015 NCAA title, Dick Vitale and several ESPN colleagues proclaimed Coach K the greatest of all, including UCLA legend John Wooden.

Greater than Wooden? Vitale's preference for K required some explaining, given Wooden's vastly superior coaching record: ten wins in ten championship games over twelve years versus Krzyzewski's five wins and four defeats over thirty years.

We can quickly dismiss the first point Vitale made in favor of Krzyzewski over Wooden. He noted that the NCAA Tournament expanded from around twenty-four teams throughout most of UCLA's reign to sixty-eight currently, meaning that Duke had to win two more tournament games than UCLA each year—a fact of essentially zero significance. Increasing the field merely added patsies for championship-contending teams to trounce. Number one seeds have won all 124 games against number sixteen seeds in the expanded format. In the round of thirty-two, number one seeds have won 107 out of 124 games against teams seeded eight or lower. UCLA won their ten championship games by an average of 13.8 points. Wooden's Bruins would not have worried about additional preliminary games against far weaker teams that had no chance of defeating them.

Vitale then cited the greater pool of talent available today, emphasizing foreign players. But none of the Final Four teams in 2015 had a significant foreign player, and that was not an anomalous occurrence.

The current NCAA field as a whole does have a larger group of talented players than in the old days, but broader competition at the top hasn't followed. The 2015 Final Four included Duke, Kentucky, Michigan State, and Wisconsin. The most recent NCAA champions have been Duke (twice), Connecticut (three times), North Carolina (twice), Florida (twice), Louisville, Kentucky, Kansas, and Villanova —the championship essentially rotates among the elite few.

In addition, UCLA's Final Four games were mostly uncompetitive. The Bruins won eight of their ten championship games by double digits. A diffusely shared uptick in available talent does not close that huge gap.

Wooden may not remain the greatest coach forever, much as someone could surpass Michael Jordan (or Bill Russell) as the greatest player ever. There's no reason to believe any of them reached a putative maximum level of human ability. Thus, one can plausibly argue in favor of newer greats: Another coach might recruit better than Wooden (who barely recruited) or shine more at in-game strategy (Wooden mostly sat back and let his players play). Another player might be bigger, faster, stronger, and/or a better shooter than Jordan or Russell in their day.

However, Wooden, Jordan, and Russell set the performance bar so high that they essentially put to rest the question of "who accomplished the most?" It's virtually impossible for anyone to surpass ten of ten NCAA titles, six of six NBA Finals (with six Finals MVPs and without ever needing a seventh game), and eleven NBA titles in thirteen years, respectively.

An argument for superiority over those three faces an uphill climb, and requires clear-cut explanation of why the allegedly better coach or player accomplished less.

Vitale's meager arguments do not scale that hill.

Are Stephen Curry and the Warriors Really That Great?

The most compelling take-home point from the 2015 NBA Finals should have been the greatness of Stephen Curry and the Golden State Warriors.

Then, remarkably, they got even better. In 2015–16, Curry had the greatest shooting season ever, joining Steve Nash as the second full-time player in NBA history to shoot at least 50 percent from the field, 45 percent from the three-point line, and 90 percent from the foul line (Curry's season ranks over Nash's as Curry scored many more points). He won his second MVP, the only unanimous choice ever. That spurred Golden State's all-time record seventy-three victories.

THE OLD GUYS WEIGH IN

But not everyone felt the love. NBA legend Oscar Robertson diminished Curry's deeds, claiming that modern coaches do not understand defense, that Curry shot so well only "because of what's going on in basketball today," and that if Curry played back in the Big O's day, he'd have been stymied by all the double-teams and three-quarter court defenses that Oscar claimed to have faced.

Ex–Chicago Bulls star Scottie Pippen added that he'd have held Curry to under twenty points per game. And fellow Hall of Famer Charles Barkley spoke for many by stressing how much benefit Curry and others receive from the ban on hand checking ("They might as well be playing touch football out there now").

Barkley also claimed that the 1996 seventy-two-game-winning Bulls would have romped over Golden State: "Can you imagine Michael Jordan, Scottie Pippen, Dennis Rodman, three of the most athletic players in the history of basketball . . . [against] that little Warriors team?"[4] Pippen claimed the Bulls would have swept the Warriors; his old teammate Toni Kukoc magnanimously opined that the Warriors might win one game.

Aside from self-aggrandizement, these claims suffer from questionable recollections: In truth, Oscar never faced relentless double-teaming and three-quarter court pressure, and by 1996, the slowed-down thirty-five-year-old Rodman no longer qualified as an all-time great athlete.

They also rely on selective memory, cherry-picking. The comments about hand checking make a valid point—offensive players clearly benefit from the ban—but they were offered as if basketball is an otherwise static system in which the hand-check ban was the only change made over the last twenty years.

In fact, basketball is a complicated system, and many changes took place as the game evolved from Oscar's 1960s rendition to Barkley and Pippen's 1990s to the current game.

The old-timers ignored at least three major changes that made scoring *more* difficult for Curry and his peers. First, the NBA lifted the ban on zone defenses (with the exception of the defensive three-second rule). Few NBA teams use a formal zone, but probably all of them now use zone principles, overloading the ball side.

Thus, when Curry receives the ball out on the wing, he typically faces not only his defender, but two and sometimes three others lurking behind. Oscar, and later on, Jordan, Pippen, and Barkley did not face this sort of suffocating team defense—it was illegal in their day.

Steve Kerr, a player on the '96 Bulls and the current Warriors coach, noted, "If you actually put the two teams in a hypothetical game [under '96 rules] . . . [the Warriors] would be called for a million illegal defenses when we overloaded the strong side."

Second, Curry and the Warriors face better opposition than players and teams from the 1960s and even the 1990s faced. As previously discussed, if we picture athletic performance as a bell curve, the bulk of the curve (that is, most of the players) moves slowly over time in a favorable direction. This occurs as a result of improved training, broader demographics, greater understanding of the sport, and other factors.

It can even be demonstrated quantitatively. While the average height of an NBA player has barely changed since 1962 (6 feet 6 then, 6 feet 7 since 1980), the mean weight has slowly increased (205 pounds in 1962, 213 pounds in 1996, 220 pounds in 2015). The additional weight certainly represents more muscle, owing to improved and greater weight training, and attention to nutrition.

Moreover, the increased prevalence of foreign players in the NBA (23 in 1991, 100 in 2015) means that a large number of inferior players who made rosters in the 1990s have been replaced by superior talent.[5] More extensive scouting also means that we now identify talented American players who previously escaped attention. There's also quantitative evidence that shooting has improved (discussed in chapter 4, "Answering Basketball's Critics").

Finally, the advent of sabermetrics, video, and improved scouting has allowed teams to scrutinize opposing-player tendencies and success rates and foster superior defensive strategies. For example, Michael Lewis ("The No-Stats All-Star" *New York Times Magazine*, February 13, 2009) described how Shane Battier used film-derived statistics to great advantage as a defender, with a "gift for encouraging (players) into their zones of lowest efficiency." Film study and statistical evaluation have blossomed recently; by now, every defender knows everything he needs to know about Curry's proclivities, strengths, and weaknesses.

How does all this—the ban on hand checking versus the several other factors—play out in total? It's impossible to know for sure, of course, but if you gave credence to the sure-of-themselves stars of old, you'd think that scoring efficiency (measured by points per possession) shot up as soon as the NBA banned hand checking. It turns out, nothing of the sort happened. In fact, points per possession in the NBA declined from 1995–96 (1.076) to 2015–16 (1.064). One statistic does not tell the whole story, but this suggests that, if anything, the combination of changes in the NBA over the last twenty years made scoring a bit harder, and Steph Curry's accomplishments even more amazing.

False and selective memories help some of our old heroes feel better about themselves, but only if they ignore the data.

AN UNBIASED OPINION

How does Curry compare with Oscar and Jordan? He's smaller, not as strong, and not as good defensively or on the boards; Curry can't be ranked as an equal. On the other hand, his shooting superiority, particularly from distance, makes up some of that ground. And it's worth noting that Curry's no one-trick pony: he passes beautifully with either hand, off the dribble and at distance, and he led the league in steals.

It's also worth noting that Curry's three-point marksmanship is, if anything, underrated. Yes, underrated: Curry broke his own all-time record with 402 three-point shots made in 2016, eclipsing his closest competitor in NBA history, teammate Klay Thompson (276), by Ruthian dimensions—the equivalent of hitting 103 home runs in a Major League Baseball season.

Furthermore, Curry is unique in that he shot so accurately (45 percent from beyond the three-point arc) despite attempting by far the most threes (886) in NBA history. For example, he shot better than the four players closest to him in three-point attempts for a season—George McCloud (678, 38 percent made), James Harden (657, 36 percent), Ray Allen (653, 41 percent), and Thompson (650, 42.5 percent). If these players try (or had tried) to catch Curry in three-point shots made in a season by shooting 200-plus more threes, they would likely have (or have had) to take more contested shots than usual and their success rate would decrease.

Curry can shoot so many threes with great marksmanship for several reasons. First, he has unprecedented range: For example, he shot 48 percent on forty shots from beyond thirty feet in 2016 (the rest of the NBA averaged 7 percent). Almost no one else takes three-point shots (other than last-second heaves) from anywhere other than right at the three-point line.

Second, and more importantly, no one in NBA history has been able to generate open threes like Curry: shooting while at full speed in transition, off the dribble going in either direction, stepping back, and sometimes stepping back after three or four dribbles between his legs in both directions or behind his back. And he shoots with a lightning fast release, so he gets shots off even while closely guarded.

The failure to defend those kinds of skills is not due to coaching stupidity. It's because Curry approaches the limit of human ability in this specific area; he's gone boldly where no one has gone before.

As for the daunting task of comparing the 1996 Bulls and 2016 Warriors, teams that played twenty years apart under different rules without any common opponents: The Warriors' loss in the Finals to Cleveland might seem to settle the matter in favor of the Bulls. However, that's not quite fair. With Curry still recovering from a sprained knee, additional injuries to Andrew Bogut and Andre Iguadola, and Draymond Green's one-game suspension, Golden State was not the same team that won seventy-three regular season games.

Nevertheless, it would be hard to choose against Jordan, a guy who won six titles in six Finals appearances, and scored thirty-eight points with a 103-degree fever in a Finals game against Utah before having to be helped off the court. For as great and historic as Curry and the Warriors truly are, and as silly as the Oscar et al. sniping is, Jordan would probably find a way to win.

That's said with zero disrespect for Curry and the Warriors.

Ernie Vandeweghe Did the Impossible

Former New York Knicks player Ernie Vandeweghe passed away on November 8, 2014, at eighty-six years old. His obituaries routinely reviewed a long list of accomplishments by both Ernie and his notable lineage.

However, they missed his most difficult and unique feat.

Ernie began the family reign with an All-American basketball career at Colgate. He also played soccer at Colgate and received an invitation to the 1948 US Olympic Soccer Team trials. After graduation in 1949, Vandeweghe played in the NBA for six seasons; in 1952–53 he averaged 12 points per game and ranked sixth in the league in field-goal percentage.

Ernie's son Kiki became the most famous Vandeweghe, scoring 29.4 points per game in 1983–84 with the Denver Nuggets and making two NBA All-Star teams. Kiki also set a national age-group record in the butterfly as a youth swimmer.

Ernie had three other children, each of whom excelled at sports: Tauna won the US national championship in the backstroke and reached the semifinals of the 1976 Olympics. Heather captained a US national water polo team. Son Bruk medaled in beach volleyball at the 1994 Goodwill Games and subsequently played professional volleyball.

The third generation continued the excellence. Tauna's daughter CoCo won a junior national tennis title in 2008 and has ranked in the top fifty on the women's professional tour. Another daughter, Honnie, achieved All-American age-group status in water polo. Tauna's son Beau played with the beach volleyball junior national team and made all-tournament at the 2008 Junior Olympics.

In summary: three generations, both male and female stars, eight individuals with national or world-class ability at six different sports —pretty impressive.

Yet Ernie accomplished even more off the court. When he retired from the NBA he began a long career as a physician. Initially, he served as a doctor for NATO. Then he returned to private practice in Los Angeles, became a professor of pediatrics at UCLA and the Los Angeles Lakers' team physician. He also chaired the President's Council on Physical Fitness and Sports and served on an Olympics sports commission.

That leads to the most unusual and unremarked aspect of Vandeweghe's life. Other athletes have also gone on to greater things. (For example, quarterback Frank Ryan earned a PhD in mathematics.) But Vandeweghe did not earn his medical degree after retirement from the NBA or even during off-seasons. Vandeweghe attended medical school *during* his NBA seasons and graduated in the usual time frame — no part-time or deferred schooling for Ernie.

I went to medical school, so I know this: You can keep a hobby from time to time but you cannot play professional sports and study medicine at the same time. That seems impossible, especially at the elite places Vandeweghe attended (Columbia Medical School with an internship at Bellevue Hospital). After a day spent dissecting cadavers or plating petri dishes or reviewing pathophysiology, medical students go home exhausted and need to rest up for more of the same the next day.

After the first two years of rigorous academic study they move on to in-hospital duty, which in Vandeweghe's day meant eighty-or-more-hour workweeks, sometimes staying overnight in the hospital (for thirty-six-hour shifts) every other night for sustained periods of time. Even granting that Vandeweghe missed some NBA road games (he topped out at sixty-one games played in a season) and changed into uniform in airplane bathrooms, I cannot fathom finding the energy or time to play NBA basketball while taking a full load of medical school courses, passing difficult exams, and then assuming patient-care responsibilities.

Going from a twelve- to thirty-six-hour hospital shift to play in an NBA game and then returning to the hospital at 6:00 a.m. for another long rigorous day, and to repeat the same day after day: Ernie Vandeweghe did the impossible.

Almost the Best: The Agony of Near Victory

In game six of the 2013 NBA Finals, the San Antonio Spurs, ahead of the Miami Heat three games to two, took a 94–89 lead with twenty-eight seconds left. League officials and security personnel began preparations for the postgame San Antonio victory celebration. Then, an improbable sequence ensued, which included Miami-friendly caroms, a missed foul shot, an untimely fall, and a terrific game-tying Ray Allen three-point shot.

The Heat won in overtime, and again in game seven, earning the

NBA title. Months later, Spurs coach Gregg Popovich related that he still thought about game six "every day" and remained "as sad as you possibly can be." Similarly, star player Tim Duncan noted "the series would always haunt me." Even subsequently winning the 2014 NBA title did not completely heal those wounds.

There's a loser in every series, but nobody mourns like that when they are trounced; it is the particular burden of those who come so close to fulfilling their dreams, yet still fail.

The Spurs were not the first to have what seemed like certain victory slip away. For example, in 1962, Frank Selvy missed a wide-open fifteen-foot jumper that would have won the Los Angeles Lakers an NBA title; they subsequently lost. In 1969, a similar shot by Don Nelson hit the back rim, bounced higher than the top of the backboard, and dropped in, bringing the Boston Celtics another title over the Lakers. Over forty years later, Lakers star Jerry West spoke of the continued agony from these (and other) near misses.

Baseball has a similar history. Bill Mazeroski's epic home run in the 1960 World Series reduced Mickey Mantle to tears, unable to process how the Yankees lost while outscoring the Pirates 55–27 and outhitting them 91–60. "Just then," Mantle said, "except for someone close to me dying, I felt as bad as I had ever felt in my life."

The Yankees would suffer again. Twice they went into the ninth inning of potential series-ending games—game seven of the 2001 World Series and game four of the 2004 ALCS—with a lead and the peerless Mariano Rivera on the mound. Both times, they lost the game and the series.

Yet even losing ninth-inning leads with Rivera on the mound did not equal, for misery's sake, what the Boston Red Sox did in game six of the 1986 World Series. They were ahead 5–3 with two outs in the bottom of the tenth inning and nobody on base—one out away from the franchise's first championship in sixty-eight years. They got two-strike counts on both Ray Knight and Mookie Wilson—one strike away—and still lost the game and series.

Misery does not require the World Series or NBA Finals to be at stake; near misses of less lofty dreams can also be crippling. In J. P. Kinsella's book *Shoeless Joe* (the basis for the movie *Field of Dreams*), Moonlight Graham was one of the characters who converged upon the Iowa baseball field in search of fulfilling his own particular dream. Graham's dream was to play Major League Baseball. The real Moonlight, upon whom the fictional character was based, did play two innings in right field on June 29, 1905.

However, he never got to hit, so his dream went unfulfilled (the usual childhood baseball dream involves batting)—as Graham said in *Shoeless Joe* "I never got to bat in the Major Leagues. I would have liked to have had that chance. Just once."

Of course, few people ever get a major-league at bat, so that failure was not unusual. Kinsella highlighted Graham's zero-at-bat career for its poignant near miss: he was called up, he got in uniform, he walked on the field, he played in the field, he was on deck when the game ended, but no at bat. How close can you get?

Yet by the criteria of an official at bat, Graham was not the ultimate case of coming close yet still failing. At least thirteen position players had a single career plate appearance in Major League Baseball, but by virtue of drawing a base on balls (nine players) or being hit by a pitch (four players) were not credited with an at bat. As these players got in the batter's box, they got even closer than Graham; their dreams seem even more tantalizingly unfulfilled.

The most famous of the thirteen are the three-foot-seven Eddie Gaedel, who drew a walk, and poor Adam Greenberg. On July 9, 2005, Greenberg had his first plate appearance in Major League Baseball. Unfortunately, the first pitch to Greenberg hit him in the head and he had to be helped off the field. Post-concussive symptoms seemed to end his career without an at bat. Seven years later, however, aware of Greenberg's angst over his unfulfilled dream, the Miami Marlins gave him a one-day contract for one at bat. Although Greenberg whiffed on three pitches, he called the experience "magical." A dream finally fulfilled.

A zero-at-bat career didn't always lead to the despairing unfulfilled life of the fictional Moonlight Graham, who traveled hundreds of miles, decades later, still seeking one big-league at bat. Or to the Marlins' public relations gimmick that eased Adam Greenberg's pain.

Bob Berman played in two games for the Washington Senators in 1918. In his first game, he only pinch-ran. In the second, he caught the bottom of the ninth inning, but did not hit and never played again, another seemingly failed zero-at-bat career. But almost forty years later, as a teacher in the New York City school system, Berman spoke proudly to my father about his major-league career: for in the one inning he caught, the pitcher was Walter Johnson, one of the greatest pitchers ever.

Who needs an at bat after you've caught Walter Johnson?

III. FOOTBALL

7 NFL VIOLENCE

Is Playing in the NFL Worth Dying For?

Chicago Bears safety Chris Conte offered what seemed like an odd view of NFL on-field violence, "I'd rather have the experience of playing in the NFL and die 10 to 15 years earlier than not play in the NFL and have a long life."[1] The comment came in the context of an injury-filled 2014 season. Conte missed four full games and failed to finish seven others as a result of two concussions and various shoulder, eye, and back ailments. It also came amid widespread discussion about the link between head trauma, concussions, and eventual debilitating brain disease.

Twenty-four-year-old San Francisco 49ers linebacker Chris Borland expressed the opposite sentiments when he announced his retirement after only one NFL season. Borland said, "I just want to do what's best for my health. . . . I'm concerned that if you wait till you have symptoms, it's too late. . . . I just want to live a long healthy life, and I don't want to have any neurological diseases or die younger than I would otherwise."[2]

Though Conte's comments shocked some, he really did not break new ground. As far back as the *Iliad*, Achilles chose a short, glorious life over an unspectacular longer life. Later on, Hollywood chimed in, with Julia Roberts noting (in *Steel Magnolias*), "I would rather have thirty minutes of wonderful than a lifetime of nothing special."

The theme also has historical roots in the sporting world. In 1896, A. E. Housman wrote the poem "To an Athlete Dying Young."

The time you won your town the race
We chaired you through the market-place

Man and boy stood cheering by,
And home we brought you shoulder-high . . .
Smart [emphasis mine] lad, to slip betimes away
From fields where glory does not stay,
And early though the laurel grows
It withers quicker than the rose
Eyes the shady night has shut
Cannot see the record cut,
And silence sounds no worse than cheers
After earth has stopped the ears . . .

It turns out, however, that the hullaballoo surrounding Conte's comment missed the unglamorous reality: NFL players need not worry about an early death. A study conducted by the National Institute for Occupational Safety and Health indicated that NFL players as a group, despite their considerable injuries, have lived *longer* than the general population.

Yet Conte did not evoke an entirely false drama. Soldiers, policemen, firefighters, mountain climbers, perhaps boxers, and more, engage in high-risk behaviors that threaten their lives. In addition, a few football players—for example, those who committed suicide presumably as a result of football-induced neurologic damage—do succumb to an early death. And football players commonly suffer impaired health down the line, if not a shorter life.

Are these activities worth the risk of a shorter or impaired life? Robert Browning extolled later life:

Grow old along with me!
The best is yet to be,
The last of life, for which the first was made . . .

It might seem folly to risk Browning's fine old age for immediate gratification (even more so in sports than in public service positions), but graceful aging does not come guaranteed. Those who play it safe risk coming up completely empty, devoid of glory and still ending up with a short life or a bad ending (for example, in a nursing home with Alzheimer's disease). We shouldn't discount Conte's statement as patently ridiculous. Homer (demonstrated by Achilles's choice) and Houseman agreed, in principle, with him.

The length and quality of the later life makes all the difference. Thus, for any individual, the answer to "Is it worth it?" seems as unknowable as the future. Which probably explains why the topic remained alluring from as far back as Achilles to as recently as Chris Conte.

Costas Misfires on NFL's "Gun Problem"

Sportscaster Bob Costas added a new wrinkle to the concerns about on-field head trauma in the NFL, connecting it to off-field violence and gun use.

After a series of shameful episodes involving NFL players, Costas noted that when out-of-control player Greg Hardy threw a woman onto a couch, she landed on a variety of shotguns and assault weapons. Concerned that a person like Hardy owned such weapons, and with other NFL gun-related incidents in mind (for example, Jovan Belcher's murder/suicide, Dave Duerson's and Junior Seau's suicides, Aaron Hernandez's murder charge, and more), Costas suggested that the league consider guns as an urgent problem related to player culture and to the downstream effects of on-field head trauma.

We usually don't discuss contentious gun-control issues on the sports page, but a possible link between NFL play, head trauma, subsequent behavioral problems, and reckless gun use merits consideration.

Let's examine the evidence behind the entire head trauma story.

It begins with contact suffered in the course of playing the game. Both direct and countercoup (when the brain bounces off the skull opposite the initial contact site) impact may damage the frontal lobe. This area does not fully develop in males until the midtwenties. Thus, a potential double whammy for many football players: repetitive trauma to an immature part of the brain. Worse yet, that's the part that regulates impulse control.

Pathologists commonly find unusual tangles of tau protein in the brains of NFL players at autopsies. The tau protein is widely believed to form the link between head trauma and the impaired cognition and other clinical features characteristic of a neurologic syndrome called chronic traumatic encephalopathy (CTE).

Narcotics (for football-related pain) and anabolic steroids may exacerbate the impaired decision-making ability and diminished impulse control attributed to frontal lobe damage.

This all allegedly comes together in the NFL as a toxic mix that fuels off-field violence: macho, sometimes self-entitled athletes, immature frontal lobes bouncing off hard skulls, CTE, narcotic and/or steroid use—all leading to impaired judgment and impulse control. NFL players commonly own guns, and those affected by CTE would seem more prone to irresponsible gun use. The story makes sense: violence on the field begets violence off the field, including reckless gun use.

But making sense does not make the story firmly established. In fact, both the science and the epidemiology behind CTE remain unproven. To begin with, though most scientists believe that tau-protein tangles cause neurologic disease, this has not been proven. Theoretically, the tangles could be innocent bystanders or a marker for some other causative factor.

Nor do we know the prevalence of tau tangles in NFL players, as the available autopsy results suffer from selection bias. They have been performed mostly in players who exhibited disturbed behavior. We do not know the prevalence, for the purpose of comparison, of tau tangles or other structural neurologic damage in football players without cognitive or behavioral problems, or the prevalence of cognitive and behavioral problems in NFL players.

Comparisons of NFL players to the general public do not isolate NFL play as a variable that might end up contributing to cognitive disease and/or violent behavior. We must compare NFL players to a similar cohort that differs mainly by not playing in the NFL in order to establish that playing football contributes to cognitive dysfunction, off-field violence, irresponsible gun use, or any other symptom or problem. This has not been done.

NFL play requires mental and physical aggression. People selected in part for those traits would seem more likely prone to violence whether they played football or not (another selection bias). That would explain at least some off-field violence without implicating NFL-induced brain trauma.

Moreover, gun ownership and even use by NFL players does not establish that guns form a necessary part of the putative toxic mix. Out-of-control players might find other means of wreaking violence if they had no access to guns.

Thus, the supporting evidence for the entire story remains less established than many assume. One can and should remain concerned about the effects of on-field head trauma without leaping to specific concerns about an NFL gun-control problem. That part of the story requires much more supportive evidence before the NFL would be justified in wading into such a volatile area.

8 NFL RULES AND MISRULES

Why Are NFL Coaches Scared of the Two-Point Conversion Attempt?

The controversy over Dez Bryant's amazing "no-catch" in Green Bay's 26–21 2015 postseason victory over Dallas obscured a bone-headed decision made earlier by Packers coach Mike McCarthy.

Quarterback Aaron Rodgers threw a touchdown pass to Davante Adams late in the third quarter, narrowing the Cowboys' lead to 21–19. Inexplicably, McCarthy chose to kick an extra point rather than attempt a two-point conversion. A successful two-point conversion would have tied the game. Failure would have left the Packers down two points instead of one (with the extra-point kick)—a distinction of minimal significance. Had the game ended at 21–20, or had both teams subsequently scored equally (also leading to a one-point Cowboy win), the failure to go for two points would have made McCarthy the goat. As it happened, Rodgers's fourth-quarter touchdown pass saved the Packers and his coach.

We should give McCarthy a bit of a break. His errant thinking occurred in the context of widespread underutilization of the two-point conversion by NFL coaches. They attempted only fifty-nine the entire 2014 season.

Two-point attempts succeed around 48 percent of the time, and that includes aborted kick attempts (which are counted as two-point attempts, usually failed). Thus, over the long run, *intended* two-point attempts—which succeed around half the time—provide the same number of points (essentially one point per possession) as the point-after-touchdown kick.

Moreover, teams could probably achieve better than 50 percent success with two-point conversions by running more often, as the success rate with runs on two-point tries has significantly exceeded that with passes.

In any case, specific game situations arise for which mathematics clearly favor a two-point attempt. Coaches keep charts that identify these situations, but the scarcity of two-point attempts indicates that they remain scared of these plays. One example occurs when a team that trails by fourteen points scores a touchdown. This situation calls for a two-point attempt, yet teams routinely kick extra points instead.

Similar coaching conservatism pertains to fourth-down situations: mathematical analysis by professor David Romer of the University of California at Berkeley reveals that NFL coaches punt too often, rather than try for first downs.[1]

Numbers alone should not mandate these decisions. Specific situational characteristics and intangibles should also be considered. But this is the information age, the age of data explosion in baseball and, increasingly, in other sports. Why are football coaches so reluctant to incorporate these important data into their decisions?[2]

We know of one outside-the-box thinker: North Carolina high school coach Kevin Kelly, who almost never punts (and routinely calls for onside kicks). Bill Belichick is another. From 2000 to 2009, the New England Patriots coach eschewed punting on 100 fourth-and-one or fourth-and-two situations. The Patriots succeeded on 78 percent (86 percent of their last 58 attempts). However, they failed on a notable fourth-and-two attempt on their own twenty-eight-yard line against Indianapolis in 2009.

Other NFL coaches had religiously followed the original punting strategy for these situations developed more than eighty years before. Not surprisingly, the common practice shaped public opinion about New England's failed fourth-down play: fans and media railed on Belichick, even though the math supported his call. Surely, other coaches took notice of the rampant criticism.

NFL games would be even more interesting and smarter played if coaches were less bound by convention, less risk averse, and less concerned about criticism.

181

The NFL Needs Seven-Point Touchdowns

Pusillanimous coaches, with their inertia and fear (loss aversion) of two-point conversion attempts, led the NFL to move the line of scrimmage for the point-after-touchdown kick (PAT) from the two-yard line to the fifteen-yard line for the 2015 season. Unfortunately, this constituted an ineffective solution to a lesser problem.

The PAT bored everyone because it became virtually automatic (over 99 percent success in 2014). The NFL recognized this in 1994 (PAT league average: 98.8 percent) when it introduced the far more exciting two-point conversion option. Unfortunately, as noted, timid NFL coaches rarely attempted two-point conversions despite mathematical support for broader use.

The NFL hoped that the new rule would prompt more two-point conversion tries (which remain from the two-yard line). However, still-cowardly coaches attempted two-point conversions after only eight percent of touchdowns in the 2015 season. The longer PATs succeeded as predicted (based on NFL field-goal success rates from about thirty-three yards) with a conversion rate of 94 percent. At this rate of success, the PAT still bores us—essentially a bathroom or refreshment break.

The new rule did not go far enough. If the NFL prefers two-point conversions (as it should), why bother toying with the PAT distance to entice coaches to "go for two"? Eliminating the PAT and leaving the preferred two-point attempt as the sole option would have made more sense. And no reason to stop there: we can further enliven football by introducing a one-point conversion option from the one-yard line.

By merely moving the PAT line of scrimmage, the NFL ignored the greater problem that developed as kicking prowess improved: kickers and field goals assumed an outsized role in the game. The ratio of touchdowns to field goals declined about 45 percent from the early 1960s (before Pete Gogolak introduced soccer-style kicking to the NFL) to today. Despite kicking from longer distances, kickers made 85 percent of their field-goal attempts in 2015 (compared to 53 percent in 1964), including 65 percent of attempts from beyond fifty yards. They do better from long distances (that their straight-on style predecessors didn't even attempt) than most previous kickers did at shorter distances.

Thus, the value of core football skills (running, passing, blocking, and tackling) and touchdowns decreased as compared to a single skill (kicking) and field goals. Further, kicking moved from the skill set of the all-around player to the exclusive province of non-field-playing specialists.

The NFL already expressed its concern with the unanticipated field-goal-kicking success when it moved the goal posts to the back of the end zone following the 1973 season (even though the field goal success rate then was only 63 percent). That failed to curtail the continually increasing impact of kickers, and the future bodes more of the same: with continued improvement by kickers, the NFL may soon see "scoring drives" of one or two first downs followed by fifty-five- to sixty-yard field goals.

One way to blunt the increasing impact of field goals is to reward touchdowns with seven points.

When valued at seven points, a touchdown followed by a two-point conversion equals three field goals. That's a better balance for those who prefer games decided (as in earlier days) more by those who run and pass, and block and tackle.

Furthermore, with greater value given to a touchdown and with the potential for a nine-point drive, coaches will more often try for a first down on fourth-and-short situations. These are more exciting plays than punts and field goals.

Imagine football with one- and two-point conversion attempts rather than automatic PATs. Imagine more fourth-down runs and passes. No bathroom breaks there.

Unfortunately, the NFL showed no imagination when it merely kicked the PAT problem down the field.

Why We Don't Know What a Catch Is

After changing the PAT yard line, the NFL moved on to reassess another staple of the game, creating a committee to study the rule defining a completed pass. You'd think that after more than one hundred years of play we'd know what it means to catch a football, but the NFL has had at least three widely noted plays in which a seemingly obvious reception was ruled incomplete.

In 2010, Detroit Lions wide receiver Calvin Johnson leaped high to grab a long pass in the corner of the end zone, spun around and came down with control of the ball (for an apparent game-winning touchdown), but subsequent contact with the ground knocked the ball out of his outstretched hand. Johnson possessed the ball for several seconds but the referee called the pass incomplete because the NFL rule reads "If a player goes to the ground in the act of catching a pass (with or without contact by an opponent), he must maintain control of the ball after he touches the ground."

Similarly, in a 2015 playoff game between the Dallas Cowboys and the Green Bay Packers, late in the fourth quarter with Dallas trailing 26–21, Cowboy wide receiver Dez Bryant leaped high near the goal line and brought the ball down securely with both hands, only to bobble it when he subsequently stretched his arm (and the ball) out to the goal line and the ball made contact with the ground. The referee ruled an incompletion for the same reason that governed Johnson's play.

Then, in the 2015–16 regular season, with the New York Giants playing the still undefeated New England Patriots, receiver Odell Beckham Jr. caught what appeared to be a decisive touchdown pass late in the game, bringing the ball down to his chest, landing on both feet and in the process of taking a step when cornerback Malcolm Butler knocked the ball loose. The referee called the pass incomplete because "the receiver had not yet become a runner." The rule states that a receiver must "establish himself as a runner to complete a catch" (the rule once demanded the even vaguer "make a football move").

These plays fulfilled common sense characteristics of a catch—the receiver fully controlled the ball, and for long enough. Ruling them incompletions made no sense. The realization that the relevant rules violated common sense prompted the NFL to form the "catch committee."

What should the committee do?

First, recognize the thinking error that spawned the current rules—they violate Occam's razor. William of Occam was a fourteenth-century logician who proposed the "law of parsimony." It followed a previous suggestion by philosopher John Punch that "entities must not be multiplied beyond necessity"; it's more easily understood as "simpler explanations are generally better than more complex ones." Occam's razor does not govern all situations, but it's a good way to begin an analysis, and in this instance it pinpoints the problem with the current catch rules.

There's a simple "explanation" for a catch: A receiver controls the ball for long enough, that is, more than an instant, at least until both feet hit the ground. Once he comes down to earth with possession of the ball, he's caught it, end of story. We all know that when we see it—no controversy there and no reason to add more complexity to solve a problem that does not exist.

The NFL's extra nuances merely introduced uncertainty where it didn't exist before. For example, "The receiver must make a football move to complete a reception." Why? What does that contribute? And what's a football move? The receiver must "establish himself as a runner to complete a catch." Why? What does that contribute? And what does it even mean?

More broadly, we should not concern ourselves with what happens *after* a player makes an easily recognizable catch. The aftermath ought to be governed by the usual rules and not used to define what happened before it.

The NFL should get rid of all the nuances it unnecessarily added in defining a catch. Very simply, as noted, if a receiver controls the ball when he returns to the ground, it's a catch. If a defender subsequently pokes the ball out or, in selected instances, the receiver loses the ball due to contact with the ground,[3] the play should be deemed a reception and a fumble. If the reception is in the end zone, it's a touchdown, no matter what happens afterwards.

By these criteria, all three "incompletions" cited above would have properly been ruled catches. There'd have been no ambiguity, and the rulings would have comported with the common wisdom.

9

NFL STARS (UNFORTUNATELY) IN THE COURTROOM

The Real Problem behind Adrian Peterson Smoking Pot

Minnesota Vikings running back Adrian Peterson pleaded no contest (November, 2014) to a misdemeanor reckless assault charge based on having beaten his then four-year-old son with a branch, leaving the toddler with bruises, welts, and cuts. However, according to *Sports Illustrated* (January 11, 2016), Peterson still attributes his legal problem, subsequent NFL suspension, and public criticism to a "misperception," a cultural divide. He believes he was wronged.

I have zero sympathy for Peterson and his defense of the child beating. Reasonable people practice tolerance of other cultures, but cultural differences do not justify all behavior. "The way we've always done it" does not constitute a reasoned argument in the face of common sense and modern thinking.

On the other hand, like everyone else, Peterson deserved fair and rational treatment from the legal system. He almost did not get that —an overlooked but important part of the entire proceedings.

After Peterson's indictment and bail proceedings, prosecutor Brett Ligon filed a motion asking to jail Peterson for violating the terms of his bond. The prosecutor's office wrote, apparently with a straight face, "The state argues that the defendant has smoked marijuana while on bond." Marijuana remains an illegal drug in Texas, so by the letter of the law, Peterson violated his bond provisions.

The jail request (like Peterson's defense) violated decency and common sense. Courts typically deny bail when the accused presents a flight risk or a danger to society. If the state did not previously consider Peterson a flight risk or a danger to society, why worry now? What about marijuana—increasingly legalized and used by many high-functioning people including some prosecutors — concerned Mr. Ligon to the extent of asking for incarceration? The worst part may be that some legal analysts predicted that Ligon's motion would be granted (fortunately, it wasn't).

I wish there had been a counter-motion for prosecutorial misconduct, if only to send a message. We should worry when those in power abuse it in pursuit of personal vendettas or self-aggrandizement or from the intoxicating effects of having power. Or when, in the most favorable interpretation of Mr. Ligon's conduct, they lack the nuance and wisdom to apply their power other than by rote.

That's more worrisome than someone smoking a joint in his own home, whether the smoker is out on bail or not, and even if he's famous.

Only Tom Brady Can Exonerate Himself

Tom Brady's suspension for his alleged involvement in Deflate-gate was overturned and then restored in sequential legal proceedings. The final judgment (Brady refrained from further appeal) did not suggest his guilt: the legal system evaluated NFL commissioner Roger Goodell's adherence to established policies and procedures rather than the merits of his decision. In fact, Brady continues to profess innocence, and his many supporters cite the absence of direct evidence against him.

However, Brady's reputation took a hit outside of New England, and he has mostly himself to blame: his behavior in response to the investigation remains unexplained and incriminating.

Most impartial readers found that the Wells Report provided clear-cut evidence (from interviews, phone and electronic communications, and scientific study) that New England Patriots locker room attendant Jim McNally (in conjunction with equipment assistant John Jastremski) deflated footballs used by the Patriots in the AFL Championship Game to less than the allowed lower limit of 12.5 psi.

Wells also concluded that it was "more probable than not that Tom Brady was at least generally aware of the inappropriate activities." However, Wells provided no direct evidence against Brady. While Brady expressed a preference for softer footballs and he surely knew that McNally and Jastremski were deflating footballs, none of the text messages or other communications demonstrated that Brady was "generally aware" that they deflated footballs to less than 12.5 psi. Wells simply presumed that the underlings McNally and Jastremski would not have broken the rules without boss Brady's approval.

That's worth considering, but the messy realities of life and erratic human behavior allow for other reasonable possibilities. Brady could have been aware of "activities" (deflating footballs), without being aware of "inappropriate" activities (deflating to less than 12.5 psi). McNally and Jastremski could have initially followed Brady's preference for softer footballs within the rules, and then run amok without Brady's knowledge.

Perhaps, for example, Brady complained about the footballs after a game without a specific agenda in mind. Or even without a specific complaint about the pressure: maybe he grumbled about the grip. It's within the realm of human behavior for McNally and/or Jastremski to have heard that and decided (even later) on their own to provide Brady and their team with softer footballs. One can also imagine other scenarios in which Brady remained not "generally aware" of the decision to go below 12.5 psi.

Are those scenarios more likely than Brady directing or (in some fashion or other) knowing about the excessively deflated footballs? Maybe not: most people might agree that low-level employees would not risk their own necks without approval from above. However, there's a lot of ambiguity there, enough that suspending Brady on presumptive grounds alone would have been quite shaky.

Then Brady shot himself in the foot.

If he had told the investigators, "Yes, I know Jim McNally, and I told him and Jastremski that I like footballs at 12.5 psi but I had no idea that they deflated the footballs below that," and turned over his phone and electronic material (which, if he spoke truthfully, would provide no incriminating evidence), there'd have been no case against him.

Instead, Brady lied about knowing McNally and his responsibilities, and other related matters. He obstructed the investigation by refusing to turn over documents and electronic information (including texts and e-mails). He destroyed his cell phone. That should not be taken lightly: jurors and investigators may draw compelling inferences of guilt from such conduct (for example, flight from a crime scene).

Brady could have made amends after the report was issued. He could have offered a mea culpa, stating that he had lied and obstructed because (insert plausible reason) but that he had done nothing else wrong. Plausible explanations (other than attempting to hide his guilt) would have made Brady's behavior non-incriminating.

But he still hasn't come forth with any good explanation for his conduct. Could Brady have been concerned about releasing embarrassing extraneous material to the investigators? No, because Wells reported that "those requests [for texts, e-mails and phone records] were limited to the subject matter of our investigation . . . and we offered to allow Brady's counsel to screen and control the production so that it would be limited strictly to responsive materials." Brady never rebutted that part of the report. That leaves his refusal to turn over the requested material and his several lies as evidence of guilt.

Brady's behavior smacked of a cover-up. That suggested an antecedent crime, as the alternative—a cover-up without a crime—defies reality. Even if the latter somehow was the case, the cover-up per se would have been a misdeed deserving of a penalty. Thus, Brady took a sack, and it wasn't the fault of a biased investigator or commissioner. He put himself in an indefensible position.

10

HEROES FROM LONG AGO

Why Unitas Won and the Seahawks Lost

The slant pass called by Seattle offensive coordinator Darrell Bevell from the one-yard line with twenty-six seconds left cost the Seahawks the 2015 Super Bowl.

The Baltimore Colts faced a similar situation in the 1958 NFL championship against the New York Giants, often called the "Greatest Game Ever Played." In overtime, the Colts drove down to the Giants seven-yard line. On second-and-goal, quarterback Johnny Unitas audibled from a running play to a sideline pass. He completed the pass to tight end Jim Mutscheller for a six-yard gain down to the one-yard line. On the next play, fullback Alan Ameche scored a championship-winning touchdown on a plunge up the middle.

The pass seemed to many an unnecessary risk. When challenged about it after the game, Unitas's response came to define him and lived on in football lore: "When you know what you're doing, you're not intercepted."

He explained, "The strong-side linebacker took an inside position on Mutscheller. . . . The defensive back was well into the end zone and had to worry about Lenny Moore coming out of the backfield. Really, they were the only two defenders in the picture. . . . People said it was a gamble, but they couldn't see what I was seeing. . . . If Mutscheller wasn't open, I'd have thrown it away. . . ."

The last part was especially important. With Mutscheller on a sideline route, Unitas had time to observe the coverage and opt to throw the ball out of bounds if he saw any risk of interception.

One could argue with Colts coach Weeb Ewbanks eschewing an easy fourteen-yard field goal, but Unitas clearly knew what he was doing with his play calling. He chose a play he had reason to believe would succeed, with trivial risk of interception.

Fifty-six years later, Bevell also called for a pass. Fans and media pounced on that as an egregious error—ignoring star runner Marshawn Lynch! However, over the last five years in the NFL, passes from the one-yard line have succeeded roughly as often and with as few turnovers as runs. Lynch probably tipped the odds in favor of the run for Seattle (presuming that his modest record in goal-line runs reflects the small sample size involved) but nowhere near the point of making a Lynch run a no-brainer.

The rush to judgment about passing per se obscured Bevell's actual big error: his *particular* pass play, which differed in important ways from Unitas's sideline pass. Bevell's play called for a line-drive pass with a risk of deflection at the line of scrimmage or ricochet off the receiver's hands or shoulder pads into the air, in an area of the field where a bevy of Patriots stood well situated to intercept. In addition, the Seahawks' quick-hitting slant required virtually a reflexive throw, with almost no time for quarterback Russell Wilson to ponder throwing the ball away (for example, if defender Malcolm Butler was near enough for a terrific close on the ball).

Unitas chose the safest pass possible; Bevell chose a much riskier pass. And that made all the difference.

Homer Jones Was Better Than Frank Gifford

Frank Gifford deserved all the high praise he received upon his death on August 9, 2015, at eighty-four years old: he was a Hall of Fame football player, respected announcer and ambassador for the game, humble, and well liked.

I saw Gifford play as a wide receiver in his last few years and knew of his previous success as a great all-around running back. He remains the New York Giants' leading career touchdown scorer fifty years after his retirement. But I do not consider him the Giants greatest offensive player ever, nor their greatest runner/receiver of the 1950s and 1960s. The latter would be the little-remembered wide receiver Homer Jones, who holds an even greater (and largely unknown) NFL record: a career average of 22.3 yards per catch, the best in NFL history. No one went deep better than Homer Jones.

The Giants drafted Jones in 1963 in the twentieth round, the 278th overall pick, out of Texas Southern University. He had been known in college more for track and field than football, having run a 9.3-second 100-yard dash and once beating Bob Hayes, the World's Fastest Human, in a 220-yard race. At 6 feet 2 and 220 pounds—huge for a receiver in those days—Jones presented an unprecedented package of size and speed.

At the 1967 Pro Bowl game, officials arranged a match race at halftime between Jones and the Olympic gold winner Hayes (then on the Dallas Cowboys)—100 yards in full uniform, carrying a football. But Hayes backed out, admitting in his autobiography that he considered that he might lose and damage his reputation.

Jones was no Henry Carr or Tommie Smith—track stars who failed as NFL receivers. He averaged 27.3 yards per catch in 1965 and made the Pro Bowl and first or second team All-Pro in 1967 and 1968. Nothing stirred Giants' crowds in those days more than bombs to Jones, or his end-around runs. Jones added to the excitement by inventing the spike to punctuate his touchdowns. He became a childhood sports hero of mine.

Jones would have accomplished even more with a different quarterback. Fran Tarkenton, although a legitimate Hall of Famer, had a weak arm. Not uncommonly, Jones would be seen yards behind his closest defender, waiting or even backtracking for a fluttering Tarkenton long ball.

On the other hand, Gifford had a longer career, with Jones limited by injury to only six full seasons. Gifford could run, catch, and pass, played defensive back, and also kicked early in his career. He made the Pro Bowl eight times and at three different positions. Gifford won an MVP and made the Hall of Fame. Objectively, Gifford trumped Jones.

A kind naysayer might ascribe my preference for Jones to emotion, to the lasting impact of childhood sports heroes. As one example of this impact, Bob Costas carried a Mickey Mantle baseball card in his wallet through adulthood. Similarly, at a Mantle book signing I attended in the early 1990s, the line went out the door and down several city blocks. Almost all the attendees were men of Costas's vintage, each looking like he too had a 1950s Topps card in his pocket.

At ninety-three years old, my father reveled in reading (and *rereading*) biographies of Joe DiMaggio, Stan Musial, and Hank Greenberg. Sports fans often enhance their treasured memories. My father, like Professor Gould ("DiMaggio . . . cheated death" with The Streak), believed that no player ever matched DiMaggio. Dad (another serious-minded professor) often uttered the standard DiMaggio-phile hyperbole that "he never threw to the wrong base," "never was thrown out on the bases," and "never had to make a difficult catch because he always got right under the ball." Perhaps we bask in the reflected glory of the giants of our youth; the greater we think they were, the better we feel.

Maybe that's what I'm doing with Jones—but not wholly. I never thought of him as an all-time great like Mantle or DiMaggio or, later on, Jerry Rice. However, for several years he ranked among the top receivers in the game. Unfortunately, he did not get his proper due; his prime period was brief, and he never played on a winning team.

In 1966 the Giants went 1–12–1; most Giant fans tried to forget the almost two decades of bad teams between the 1963 Eastern Conference champions and Lawrence Taylor. Certainly, pro football fans across the country do not find their heroes in players on weak teams that never got postseason exposure. But at least one impressionable young mind in New York thrilled to Jones's heroics. And childhood sports-idol bonding tends toward enduring, even to ninety-three years old.

Whether or not Jones ranks as the Giants greatest offensive player ever, he should not be forgotten. The NFL career record for yards per catch is a big deal, not a false or exaggerated memory. Homer shined at catching the bomb, the greatest play in football.

Costas has his Mantle baseball card; I keep a replica Homer Jones football helmet from 1966.

11 OVERRATED

The NFL's Draft Impact Is Mostly Hype

The NFL's draft process has become an industrial complex that maintains the rapt attention of seemingly everyone interested in pro football.

Sports Illustrated devoted sixty-eight pages to predraft analysis in 2015. An estimated 200,000 people attended the 2015 draft in Chicago. The city rerouted downtown traffic and provided 900,000 prime square feet in its central park for a massive NFL fan festival. ESPN televised the three-day affair, and attracted over seven million viewers for round one alone. And just prior to the 2016 draft, Chicago mayor Rahm Emanuel promised an even "bigger, grander, and better experienced" extravaganza.

The massive hoopla stands out of proportion to the typical modest effect of the draft on team performance, particularly in the short run.

That effect is limited by the imprecision of player selection, which really consists (with rare exception) of not much more than educated guesses. For example, despite all the videotape, scouting expertise, psychological and physiologic probing available—basically, total body colonoscopies of all the prospects—NFL general managers still commonly err at the most important position (quarterback).

They passed on Tom Brady 198 times, on Joe Montana 81 times, on Drew Brees 32 times, and on Dan Marino (drafted after quarterbacks Todd Blackledge, Tony Eason, and Ken O'Brien) 26 times. Tony Romo went undrafted. More recently, Russell Wilson went 75th in the 2012 draft. And NFL fans know the list of quarterbacks selected early, even in recent drafts, who disappointed.

Drafting imprecision goes well beyond dramatic errors selecting quarterbacks. For example, only two of the top twenty picks from the 2012 and 2013 drafts (one through ten in each) made the 2015 Pro Bowl. In contrast, players selected as low as 31st, 47th, 48th, and 173rd in those drafts were honored.

Other sports also struggle with accurately assessing prospects. NBA general managers selected Michael Olowokandi, Andrea Bargnani, Anthony Bennett, and Kwami Brown as top overall picks, along with a slew of other first-round busts. In baseball, twenty-four general managers passed on Mike Trout.

This is not a knock on the drafting folks. Even with all the computer modeling, statistics, technology, and expertise available in the modern world, complex systems often resist fine understanding. For example, the *Chicago Sun-Times* once compared a monkey (named "Adam Monk") and a team of financial experts in predicting the stock market. Mr. Monk retired undefeated after several years' competition. Long range weather predicting provides another example where experts armed with sophisticated equipment routinely err.

Drafting imprecision is not even the worst part for fans who hope that a draft will reverse a team's bad fortunes. The effect of a single season's draft would be limited even if player assessment improved.

The draft is conducted in reverse order of teams' records in the previous season. The last-place team picks first in every round (barring trades), giving it an advantage toward choosing better players. But the net advantage these "first-chosen" players provide (relative to the players selected by other teams) is smaller than it might seem.

We can clarify that by contrasting the draft picks of the first- and last-place teams. The last-place team makes the first choice in the draft; the first-place team makes the last pick in the draft's last round. In between those extremes, all the other picks of these two teams are consecutive—the last pick in one round (by the first-place team) and the first pick in the next round (by the last-place team)—forming couplets, for example, 32nd/33rd; 64th/65th; 96th/97th, and so on.

If each couplet consists of players with similar ability (meaning that we give no advantage to the first-place team selecting first in each couplet) then the entire difference between the two groups of draftees comes down to one player: the first pick of the draft (relative to the last player chosen in the draft).

That's usually (though not always) a fine player. However, short of a Hall of Fame quarterback, no one player transforms a team. Even a Hall of Fame quarterback does not turn the Tampa Bay Buccaneers into the New England Patriots. And that one player represents the biggest predictable difference between any two teams in the talent they acquire.

If the players selected just barely dent the competitive balance, why all the hoopla about the draft? Because it benefits everyone involved. The NFL and the host city love the publicity. Pro football personnel, sports publications, expert draft analysts, and more, all enjoy the hype. For some, the draft is the yearly culmination of their professional raison d'etre. Thus, all interests line up in terms of focusing more attention on the draft, whether warranted or not.

Fans benefit too. The simplest aspect probably involves a basic emotion: "Hope springs eternal in the human breast" (Alexander Pope, *An Essay on Man*). We heard "wait 'til next year" from Brooklyn Dodgers fans and "wait 'til next century" from Chicago Cubs fans.

Every year, no matter how bad their team, fans can always hope that the new draftees will make all the difference. That rarely happens, but fans don't know that for sure until the next season evolves. By then, the run-up to the next draft (and new hope) has already started.

That said, we can acknowledge the reality of the draft without spoiling the party. Hope buoys our spirits, and if it comes with a great time (which the draft provides for many)—terrific. No harm in thinking that if this year's draft picks don't help much . . . there's always next year.

Tebow's Failed Comeback

Tim Tebow's return to NFL competition with the Philadelphia Eagles in the 2015 preseason rekindled the polarized debate about his qualifications, with his passionate fans at odds with NFL analysts and executives.

Tebow's Denver Broncos won seven out of the eleven games that he started in the 2011 season, and followed that with a playoff victory over the Pittsburgh Steelers. In the ensuing offseason, Denver traded Tebow to the New York Jets, where he served as a little-used backup quarterback for one season. The Jets released him, he failed to make the New England Patriots, and he dropped out of football —unwanted—for two years. Perhaps no quarterback in NFL history has been as quickly discarded after a successful season as Tebow. His many supporters find that unfathomable. They hoped that Eagles coach Chip Kelley would correct that egregious error by keeping Tebow on the roster.

However, NFL talent evaluators interpret Tebow's 2011 season differently from his fans. Even though Denver won games, talent evaluators saw only red flags in Tebow's performance.

For one thing, he played terribly in Denver's five losses (including a postseason rout by New England). As a result, Denver averaged only fourteen points per game in those games and had little chance to win. In addition, several Denver victories required touchdowns from an interception return, a punt return, or a long touchdown run from scrimmage; also, there was an improbably long field goal following an inexplicable blunder by the opposition.[1] Tebow gets no credit for those important plays.

Tebow did perform superbly in several fourth quarters—five of the seven wins were come from behind—leading some to promote him as a clutch player who could play poorly throughout most games but reliably win at the end. In contrast, football experts view his unexpected late-game heroics as flukey. They consider his larger body of (poor) work as the better measure of his abilities and predictor of his future performance.

This echoes the thinking about clutch hitting in baseball, which does not appear to be a real entity. As discussed in chapter 3 ("Clutch Hitters and 'Owning' Pitchers"), almost all hitters perform in clutch situations similar to how they do in other at bats (statistical randomness explains the few exceptions), without tapping additional character or skills held in reserve for these moments. Superior hitters outdo lesser hitters in important situations, sometimes generating reputations as clutch hitters, but they do so by performing at their usual high level.

Similarly, quarterbacks such as Johnny Unitas and John Elway became known for engineering many late-game comeback victories, but accomplished that because they were great quarterbacks. The historical ranking of the most fourth-quarter comeback wins per quarterback essentially iterates the Hall of Fame roster.

In fact, there is no precedent in NFL history for the ability to routinely turn three quarters of bad play into Hall of Fame closing skills. Thus, Tebow's come-from-behind wins in 2011 did not strike NFL front offices as sustainable phenomena.

Tebow passed poorly in his first NFL go-round, but worked on his throwing mechanics with ex–baseball pitcher Tom House. His motion improved, but House could not help Tebow with a bigger problem: his difficulty finding secondary receivers.

NFL defenses keep getting more complex and increasingly able to take away a quarterback's first receiving option. Successful quarterbacks often shine more in their ability to find open secondary receivers than with unusual arm strength. That's where Tebow, like other failed NFL scramblers before him (Bobby Douglass, Vince Young, and Terrelle Pryor), struggles. In the preseason games with Philadelphia, he continued to hold the ball too long, leave the pocket too quickly, and commit to the run when outside the pocket. Tebow ran well but still could not reliably pass the ball downfield, similar to his performance several years ago.

NFL quarterbacks now routinely throw for 300-plus yards and several touchdowns a game even against good defenses. In that context, playing a quarterback who runs well but passes poorly is like bringing a knife to a gunfight. And few, if any, NFL executives believe that Tebow can turn himself, on demand, into a fourth-quarter gunslinger.

Not surprisingly, the Eagles, like several teams before them, released Tebow. No one picked him up. To the consternation of his fans, the ex–Heisman Trophy winner is back in the broadcast booth.

EPILOGUE: ALI, THE MYTH AND THE HERO

Muhammad Ali's passing on June 3, 2016, evoked an outpouring of love befitting perhaps the best known and most admired man in the world. Ali entered public awareness as a prizefighter, but by the time of his death he had reached mythic proportions as a man, even more for his life outside the ring than in it. Many posthumous accounts detailed the reasons Ali earned global reverence.

However, to present Ali in all his glory, these accounts often viewed the early Ali with blinders, censoring out what many do not want to admit. That's unfortunate. We all love heroes and great feats —they inspire and elate—but whitewashing the story only diminishes the man. Ali doesn't need mythologizing: the full account, acknowledging complex truths, still portrays a hero.

The Ali of the 1960s, with his braggadocio, self-exaltation, relentless taunting of opponents in and out of the ring, and often meanspirited disdain for others all cut against the grain of white America's ideal of the selfless, humble sports hero. He was like some kind of anti–Lou Gehrig, and for that many reviled him. Many likewise abhorred his embrace of the Nation of Islam, and the racially charged, heterodox theology of its founder W. D. Fard. But as he matured, Ali evolved. He came to embrace the inclusive and peaceful aspects of his faith, which he continued to hold close for the rest of his life.

The recount of Ali as a pure boxer is more straightforward, highlighted by the sorts of things that make sports so alluring. First, a rags-to-riches story: an indigent Louisville boy becoming champion of the world. Second, incredible athletic skills. Third, a unique and endearing style. Ali defied conventional wisdom by dropping his hands and responding to punches with slight head movements rather than ducking or deflecting blows. Writer Garry Wills (*New York Review of Books*, October 1975) noted that his head movements kept his vision unblocked, his eyes always on his opponent. Ali not only had the fastest hands and feet but "the best eyes" in boxing—all of it a joy to behold.

Most of all, we laud Ali's courage. The silver lining in boxing's brutality is that it allows a look into the hearts of the combatants. Sometimes we see things fathers tell their sons about for generations.

Ali fought bravely against the fearsome Sonny Liston; he suffered numerous blows from George Foreman; he fought on against Ken Norton after his jaw broke. Yet none of those efforts equaled for epic grit what both Ali and Joe Frazier displayed in their third bout, the Thrilla in Manila.

Longtime boxing reporter Ed Schuyler said that he never saw a fight where two boxers took more of a beating. Ali called it "the closest thing to death." His former doctor and cornerman Ferdie Pacheco described it as a "slow murder."

Both fighters answered the bell, punishing round after punishing round. Their mutually sadistic battle ended only when Frazier's trainer, Eddie Futch, over the protest of his essentially blinded fighter, threw in the towel after the fourteenth round.

Following the bout, according to Pacheco, "It took about 24 hours for Ali's brain to recuperate, for his thought processes to become complete." Not surprising, as Frazier hit Ali 440 times and later noted, "Man, I hit him with punches that would bring down the walls of a city."

Ali, of course, eventually developed trauma-induced Parkinson's syndrome, rendering him physically disabled and, sadly ironic for the Louisville Lip, barely able to speak. He received countless blows throughout his career, but surely the damage in Manila, the worst pounding he ever took, contributed much to his decline.

Did Ali ever regret staying the distance? Did he ever stop to think that, if only he called it quits after the eighth or ninth or even twelfth round, he might have led a more normal and longer post-boxing life? He certainly never said that. Champions don't think that way.

Sport is most compelling when athletes appear to transcend the limits of human capability, and particularly when they overcome great obstacles. The pantheon of such performances includes Ali and Frazier mutually testing the limits of athletic courage, endurance, and tolerance of pain.

Futch consoled the defeated Frazier by assuring him that "no one will ever forget what you did here today." Still less will anyone forget what the victorious Ali did.

What price can be put on the achievement that assures immortality? If Ali had quit against Frazier, he might have been able to light the Olympic Torch in 1996 with a steadier hand. But he probably would not have been asked to light the torch in the first place.

ACKNOWLEDGMENTS

I'm grateful to the many people who helped with this book.

My wife, Linda, scheduled our wedding date around the 1985 NBA Finals and abided my sports addiction ever since. Can't ask for more than that. Looking forward to at least thirty-one more years together.

Our children, Robert, Jackie, and Richard, are beautiful people. Robert served as my primary reader and put every word and idea under illuminating scrutiny. Awesome job, Rob.

My mom, Shula, watched almost every match I wrestled, and supported everything I've ever done. Thanks, Mom.

My brother, Alan, edited and provided (since our childhood) sound, creative arguments that honed or inspired much of what I've written. This book doesn't happen without him.

My sister, Marilyn, turned out to be the best athlete in the family, and a good writer too.

Arnie Berns and Bob Cohen greatly improved various parts of the manuscript. John Middleton's support also helped a lot. Thanks to them and to other great friends.

Professor Matthew Schulkind provided important scholarly advice in several areas. Thanks for educating my daughter, and me as well.

Sam Chi, editor of RealClearSports.com, provided unwavering support, good cheer, and fine advice. All sports fans should check out RealClearSports every day.

My agent, Chip MacGregor, saw potential in an early version of the book, encouraged it, and found it a fine home. I'd recommend Chip to any writer.

Stephen Hull and colleagues at ForeEdge added the finishing touches, beautifully done.

NOTES

1. MYTHS

1 Similarly, Cal Ripken would have helped the Orioles more if he missed a few games when he was banged up, and played better upon return, than he did by playing in 2,632 consecutive games.

2 Zero has always been an oddity even outside of sports, given much greater attention than other numbers. It has theological implications that actually frightened people for millennia (discussed in Charles Seife's *Zero: The Biography of a Dangerous Idea*). Thus, zero did not enter basic arithmetic until the seventh century (in India). And since medieval scholars considered zero evil, it took another 500-plus years for common sense to overcome fear and zero to enter Western mathematics.

3 For a truly great zero streak, consider Bob Gibson's accomplishment: the St. Louis Cardinal's star pitcher was never removed from the mound in the middle of an inning for 479 consecutive innings beginning at the end of the 1967 season, going through the entire 1968 season, and continuing until July 1969—three outs, every inning. Cardinals manager Red Schoendienst could have slept while Gibson pitched.

4 A batter must attempt to avoid being hit by a pitch. In 1968, home plate umpire Harry Wendelstedt did not call a hit-by-pitch with the bases loaded and pitcher Don Drysdale chasing the consecutive-scoreless-innings record, ruling that batter Dick Dietz failed to attempt to avoid the pitch. Drysdale got out of the inning without allowing a run, and went on to set the record.

5 Triandos, a three-time All-Star catcher for the Baltimore Orioles in the late 1950s, ran like a tortoise—remembered in the TV show *The Wire* as "a big, slow guy." Going into the final game of the 1958 season Gus had reached first base safely over 600 times in his career without attempting a stolen base. With the Orioles down 6–3 in the ninth inning, he singled. In the last half inning of the season, with the Orioles 16½ games out of first place, Gus stole second. He reached first base safely around 500 more times after that without attempting another steal. For Gus, a single stolen base (even a ridiculous one) sufficed.

6 Nor did the failures of Short and Bunning alter the practice. About two weeks later, Bob Gibson threw a complete-game victory in game seven

of the World Series on two days' rest. Koufax threw shutouts to win game seven of the 1965 World Series and to clinch the 1966 pennant, both on two days' rest. More than twenty starters have pitched on two days' rest, often successfully, during the last fifteen postseasons.

7 The losing streak began when the Reds' Chico Ruiz made a bone-headed attempt to steal home with future Hall of Fame slugger Frank Robinson at bat. Ruiz succeeded (the only steal of home in his career), scoring the only run of the game, and becoming known in Philadelphia as "Chico F#!@-ing Ruiz." Teammate Pete Rose called it "the dumbest play I've ever seen." Oddly, just two days before, the Phillies lost a game when the Los Angeles Dodgers' Willie Davis stole home in the bottom of the sixteenth inning. The Phillies must be the only team in baseball history to lose two games down the stretch of a pennant race on steals of home.

8 Casey Stengel said of the young Mantle, "He has more speed than any slugger and more slug than any speedster—and nobody has ever had more of both of 'em together."

9 Alan M. Nathan, "Mantle's Griffith Stadium Home Run Revisited," University of Illinois, accessed 8/20/2016, http://baseball.physics.illinois.edu/mantle565.htm.

10 "ESPN Home Run Tracker," ESPN Stats and Information Group, accessed 8/20/2016, http://hittrackeronline.com/.

11 For example, Mantle conceivably could have hit fewer grounders and more fly balls than other players in double-play situations. However, I cannot find data or contemporary reports to support that, and Mantle's fly ball/ground ball ratio would have to have been quite unusual to explain the scarcity of his double-play balls.

12 Carter stole a backcourt pass, drove to the basket and then jumped completely over Weis to dunk. Weis bent his head a bit and Carter pushed down on it with his free hand, but Carter's torso went directly over Weis's head; never seen before, never since, at least not in a game.

I always wondered what made Carter think he could jump entirely over Weis (and without risking injury). What prompts someone to decide he can leap tall buildings in a single bound? Years later, Carter (*Sports Illustrated*, February 23, 2015) answered the question, "I never thought I could jump over a man who was 6'4", much less 7'2". I get home a month later and tried to re-create that situation and jump over a 6'4" guy and couldn't do it. It was just the moon and stars were lined up. . . . Every time I see it to this day, I shake my head and say, How?"

Weis explained it: "I learned people can fly."

13 "Babe Ruth's Longest Home Run," *St. Petersburg Northeast Journal*, posted by adminNEJ, March 7, 2014, http://northeastjournal.org/babe -ruths-longest-home-run/.

2. MISUNDERSTANDINGS

1 If the Cubs and the Red Sox, both built to a large extent by Theo Epstein, meet in the World Series, Epstein could be considered the executive of the year in both leagues.

2 The genre of "good field–no hit" middle infielders at the bottom of the lineup basically ended. No longer does someone like Gene Michael, shortstop for the New York Yankees in the 1960s, get 3,000 plate appearances with a .229 lifetime batting average and only fifteen home runs. Nowadays, there'd be a long line of prospects with better bats to replace Michael.

3 Films of some of baseball's historic greats, including Babe Ruth and Mickey Mantle, frequently show long, loopy swings and even shuffling feet that are no longer tolerated (they succeeded because pitching ability and technique were similarly nascent).

4 For example, the 1963 Los Angeles Dodgers, led by Hall of Famers Sandy Koufax and Don Drysdale, allowed only four runs as they swept the Yankees in the World Series. Even that didn't match the 1966 Baltimore Orioles, who defeated the Dodgers in four straight while allowing only two runs, none in the last thirty-three innings.

5 We shouldn't go so far as to say that randomness always rules. For example, the Yankees won three consecutive World Series from 1998 to 2000, winning twelve games and losing only one. Perhaps with enough World Series played, some team would do that well based on randomness, but it's certainly no surprise that it was those Yankees who actually did it.

6 Ray Bradbury's "A Sound of Thunder" illustrated the point. In that story, the inadvertent death of a butterfly caused multiple alterations in the world.

7 The vagaries of a short series also humbled some of the greatest hitters ever. In the 1962 World Series, Willie Mays and Mickey Mantle combined to hit .189 with no home runs in 53 at bats. Consider an all-time team with an outfield of Mays, Ty Cobb, and Joe DiMaggio, an infield of Mike Schmidt, Honus Wagner, Jackie Robinson, and Stan Musial, Roy Campanella behind the plate, Barry Bonds as DH, and Frank Robinson on the bench. Collectively, this esteemed group batted .249 in the postseason with a modest thirty-nine home runs in more than 1,100 at bats.

3. ANALYTICS

1 Examples of the law of unintended consequences include the decrease in walks that followed more emphasis on on-base percentage (see chapter 1, "Baseball's Exaggerated Demise") and the failure of more three-point shooting to increase offensive efficiency (discussed in chapter 5, "Do NBA Teams Need Three-Point Shooting to Win?").

2 Mitchel Lichtman, "The FanGraphs UZR Primer," FanGraphs.com, May 19, 2010, http://www.fangraphs.com/blogs/the-fangraphs-uzr-primer /#12.

3 For example, with regard to the 2015 MPV award, FanGraphs and Baseball-Reference (to a lesser extent) ranked Josh Donaldson as a better defender than Trout; Baseball Prospectus and Win Shares had Trout as the superior defender.

4 It also does not really help general managers accurately evaluate players, since defensive ability diminishes so quickly that, per Lichtman "almost any player who has been a combined average defender over the last three years is likely (now) a below-average defender due to aging." Thus, by the time you accumulate enough data to yield a less random assessment, you are no longer measuring the same player.

5 For example, Mantle provided one of the most instinctive, athletic, and unsung baserunning feats in baseball history in the 1960 World Series. In the top of the ninth inning of game seven, with one out and the Yankees down by one run, Mantle on first and Gil McDougald on third, Yogi Berra hit a one-hopper to Pirate first baseman Rocky Nelson. Nelson caught the ball by first base and quickly stepped on the bag. Mantle, with a significant lead off the base, did not head to second as runners on first base routinely do on groundballs. When Nelson stepped on first, Mantle instinctively realized the force play was off and that the usual sprint to second would be a season-ending losing move (a rundown out or McDougald thrown out at home). Instead, Mantle held his ground for a moment and eyed Nelson, who stood squarely between Mantle and first base. Mantle then deked Nelson with a clever and subtle head-and-shoulder fake toward second base. With Nelson drawn slightly out of position and off-balance from the fake, Mantle dove headfirst away from the first-sacker and safely hooked the home plate side of first base. The distraction allowed McDougald to score the tying run.

Without Mantle's brilliance in the top of the ninth, the game would have ended then, and there would have been no Bill Mazeroski epic walk-off World Series–ending home run in the bottom.

6 Henderson was almost certainly the greatest leadoff hitter ever, but ac-

cording to sabermetricians, that earns him no special compensation over players who batted elsewhere in the lineup. Sabermetricians find the batting order mostly unimportant, owing to its looping nature.

7 It also evoked fond childhood memories of Maury Wills leading off first base, the entire world seeming to stop, and a raucous Dodger Stadium crowd chanting "Go! Go! Go!"

8 Of course, there are exceptions to general rules; the greatest players, or even just one player—for example, Henderson as a base runner— may differ from the pack. Tango found no "Hendy effect" specifically for Henderson, but the sample size was too small to be conclusive.

Sabermetricians, including Bill James (*The Bill James Gold Mine 2009*), also claim that an outstanding batter on deck (like an outstanding runner on first base) does not help the batter at the plate.

As an exception to that rule, Roger Maris did not receive a single intentional walk in his seven seasons with the Yankees when Mickey Mantle batted behind him   including his record sixty-one-home-run season in 1961. In comparison, Maris received eleven intentional walks in thirty-nine games Mantle missed in 1962, plus a few instances when he was removed for a late-inning defensive replacement.

Maris clearly benefitted from being pitched to with men on second and/or third and first base open. But that was the smaller benefit Maris reaped from having Mantle on deck: from 1961 to 1963, with a substantial sample size, Maris batted approximately seventy points higher and hit home runs at almost twice the rate with Mantle behind him as compared to when other players followed him in the lineup.

9 Comparing players who pitched for the same team over a substantial period of time essentially eliminates defense and ballpark configuration as pitcher-to-pitcher variables.

10 Jeter batted .310 in his career with an .817 OPS, and .301/.810 with RISP; Ortiz is currently .289/931 overall and .296/942 with RISP; Jackson was .262/.846 and .263/.856.

11 To support the *Moneyball* story, Lewis lauded players who contributed only modestly (for example, Scott Hatteberg and Chad Bradford) or not at all (for example, Jeremy Brown and Brant Colamarino) to the A's success and glorified unconventional hypotheses (not drafting high school players and de-emphasizing defense) that subsequently were discredited.

12 Teams managed by Tony LaRussa are the only major exceptions.

13 Maddon also quickly displayed his delightful way with words, which has Chicago fans constantly wondering what he'll say, in addition to what he'll do. For example, in his introductory news conference, he called his

hiring "A one-in-a-107-year opportunity." Later on, he described the gap between his young team and the veteran St. Louis Cardinals, "We need more experience. We need a little more salt and pepper. A little oregano."

14 A common statistical tool used in sabermetrics in which multiple independent variables are individually weighted and combined in a formula that assesses a single dependent variable, or outcome. Baseball examples include the linear-weights formula for overall offensive contribution and WAR formulas for player value.

15 Nate Silver received enormous publicity for correctly predicting the outcome of all fifty states in the 2012 presidential election. Silver used the RealClearPolitics.com average poll results of each state as a basis (the "back of an envelope") and then made a number of adjustments, using computer models for different factors. As it turned out, the polls predicted forty-nine of the fifty states correctly, missing Florida (by predicting Romney) by about one percentage point. Silver correctly predicted Obama (50.1 percent of the vote) to win Florida, giving him the clean sweep. Thus, Silver, with his sophisticated knowledge and advanced methodology beat anyone who simply cited the poll results by virtue of winning one coin flip.

4. ANSWERING BASKETBALL'S CRITICS

1 "Allonzo Trier Is in the Game," *New York Times Magazine*, March 19, 2009.

2 Roman Stubbs, "Allonzo Trier Is a Complicated Case Study of Free Agency in Elite High School Basketball," *Washington Post*, August 8, 2014.

3 The year in college also helps the NBA assess these players and avoid big drafting errors.

4 "Ask Sam/Sam Smith Opens His Mail Bag," Bulls.com, April 3, 2015, http://www.nba.com/bulls/news/ask-sam-sam-smith-opens-his-mailbag-4.03.2015/.

5 NCAA, University of Memphis Public Infractions Report, August 20, 2009. http://usatoday30.usatoday.com/sports/college/mensbasketball/2009-08-20-ncaa-memphis-report.pdf.

6 Luke Winn, "The Deep Blue D: Is Kentucky's Defense the Best of the Modern Era?" SI.com, February 6, 2015. http://www.si.com/college-basketball/2015/02/06/kentucky-wildcats-defense-john-calipari-rick-pitino.

7 The NFL did the same with unnecessary additions to the rule defining a completed pass—discussed in chapter 8, "Why We Don't Know What a Catch Is."

5. MYTHS AND MISUNDERSTANDINGS

1 As one example of this rigid thinking, several commentators lambasted Los Angeles Lakers coach Byron Scott because the Lakers took few three-pointers in the 2014 preseason. At the time of the criticism, the Lakers ranked last in the NBA in three-point shooting percentage with a pathetic 26.9 percent. Shooting more threes would have resulted mainly in more missed shots.

2 As it turns out, the league-wide three-point success rate has been relatively stable for twenty years.

3 Sam Smith, "Bulls Heading to Miami with 99–93 Win over Nets," Bulls.com, May 5, 2013, http://blogs.bulls.com/2013/05/bulls-heading -to-miami-with-99-93-win-over-nets-in-game-7/.

4 Nick Friedell, "Joakim Noah: 'We're Going to Win,'" ESPN.com, May 3, 2013, http://www.espn.com/nba/story/_/id/9238120/2013-nba-playoffs -joakim-noah-says-chicago-bulls-win-game-7-brooklyn-nets.

5 Thibs's Bulls recalled Larry Brown's 2000–2001 Philadelphia 76ers. Brown, another defensive maven, surrounded superstar scorer Allen Iverson with offensively challenged but superb defenders. The Sixers' offense came from their defense (turnovers and fast breaks) and Iverson's individual brilliance. The offense wasn't great, but when the defense excelled, the offense merely needed to be good enough. The Sixers made the NBA Finals.

6 Thibs's fealty to his system recalled Mike D'Antoni's narrow thinking. See chapter 6, "Will the Great Phil Jackson Succeed with the Knicks?"

7 Sam Smith, "Bulls Executives Address Team's Present and Future," Bulls.com, April 14, 2015, http://www1.nba.com/bulls/news/samsmith /bulls-execs-address-present-future.

8 Jordan signed a long-term contract early in his career. During that time, the Bulls won multiple NBA titles, so Jordan was never in the position of being a free agent on a losing team, that is, where his self-aggrandizing talk about never leaving would have been put to an actual test.

9 Current players have more freedom to move around because Oscar Robertson and colleagues fought for free agency—for freedom of choice, no-strings attached. If James could not join Miami, other similarly talented teams (who would become "undeserved" favorites with James) would also be taboo, amounting to a significant restriction of choice.

   NBA players remain only partially free. The NBA draft, the mandatory two-year rookie contract, salary caps, and other rules restrict player movement. These restrictions are all at the expense of players and to the benefit of wealthy owners. We ought to ease those restrictions, following the arc of history toward expanding individual freedom, not reinforcing those restrictions via public shaming.

10 James succeeded in changing his personal narrative, but the popular proscription against star players joining forces remains in force, and as narrow-minded as ever.

For example, Carmelo Anthony caught flak for just considering joining the Heat when he became a free agent following the 2013–14 season. Barkley stayed true to his myopia, stating that Anthony joining the Miami Heat via free agency would be a "travesty" (even though it meant Bosh would not be re-signed) and another "hijacking" of the NBA by the Heat.

11 Pablo S. Torre, "The Friendship That Divides the NBA," ESPN.com, May 20, 2016, espn.go.com/nba/story/_/id/15617204.

12 The Johnson and Thomas relationship dated to their early days in the NBA. When Johnson became the goat of the 1984 Finals — "Tragic Johnson" — Thomas stayed at his home and helped Magic out of his doldrums.

13 As discussed, this explains the refereeing in the infamous Lakers versus Kings 2002 playoff game.

14 Thomas Gilovich, Robert Vallone, and Amos Tversky "The Hot Hand in Basketball: On the Misperception of Random Sequences," *Cognitive Psychology* 17 (1985): 295–314, http://www.cs.colorado.edu/~mozer/Teaching/syllabi/7782/readings/gilovich%20vallone%20tversky.pdf.

15 Marc Schlereth, "Schlereth: It Was All Worth It," ESPN.com, January 26, 2004, http://www.espn.com/nfl/playoffs03/news/story?id=1718301&src=mobile.

16 In 2015–16 the Warriors returned to their standard big-man lineup with Bogut and Ezeli getting most of the minutes at center. Their small-ball "Death Lineup" played great but was mostly used just to close games.

17 See "Do NBA Teams Need a Superstar to Win?" earlier in this chapter.

18 A few exceptions: Jim Brown with an incipient movie career; Sandy Koufax, with an injured arm; the eccentric Barry Sanders.

6. THE BEST AND THE BRIGHTEST

1 The same holds, as discussed in part 1, for Babe Ruth, Mickey Mantle, and modern-day baseball.

2 Contrary to what his few critics argue, Jackson's great coaching success was not due solely to superstar players. His calm wisdom and leadership skills enabled unheralded players like Steve Kerr, John Paxson, Robert Horry, and Derek Fisher to hit huge shots and play significant, overachieving roles.

One example of Jackson's ability to inspire lesser players came in game six of the 1992 NBA Finals against Portland. With the Bulls losing by fifteen points at the end of the third quarter, Jackson sat Jordan down. He sent out Bobby Hanson, Stacy King, B. J. Armstrong, and Scott Williams, along with Pippen. That unassuming group scored on seven consecutive possessions and narrowed the deficit to three points before Jackson reinserted Jordan, and the Bulls prevailed. No one else would have rested Jordan that long at that point of the game and season. No one else would have relied on that group at such an important time.

3 Notably, when the Los Angeles Lakers hired Jackson disciple Luke Walton as head coach after the 2015–16 season, Walton announced that he would not use the triangle in L.A., "I don't think the triangle's the most appropriate style of offense for the players they have in place."

4 Neil Best, "Golden State Warriors' Wins Pursuit Aided by New NBA Rules, says Charles Barkley," Newsday.com, March 8, 2016, http://www .newsday.com/sports/basketball/golden-state-warriors wins-pursuit -aided-by-new-nba-rules-says-charles-barkley-1.11551229.

5 As noted (chapter 4, "Kobe's Wrong. US Basketball Is Just Fine"), the quality of the very best foreign players seems to have hit a wall or even declined, but every foreign player on an NBA roster means that a less talented player—who would have played against Oscar—did not make the team.

7. NFL VIOLENCE

1 ESPN.com News, "Chris Conte: NFL Worth Early Death," ESPN.com, December 17, 2014, http://www.espn.com/chicago/nfl/story/_/id /12040968/chris-conte-chicago-bears-says-playing-nfl-worth-long-term -health-risk.

2 Mark Fainaru-Wada and Steve Fainaru, "SFs Borland Quits Over Safety Issues," ESPN.com, May 17, 2015, http://www.espn.com/espn/otl/story /_/id/12496480/san-francisco-49ers-linebacker-chris-borland-retires -head-injury-concerns.

It is too soon to know if other NFL players will follow his lead or if his decision will trickle down to the youth level, but two polls surely grabbed the NFL's attention. First, in a Bloomberg Politics poll, 50 percent of respondents indicated that they would not want a son playing competitive football. Second, in a Robert Morris University poll, 49 percent of respondents supported a ban on tackle football until high school, and 47 percent recommended against contact football at any time.

8. NFL RULES AND MISRULES

1 David Romer, "Do Firms Maximize? Evidence from Professional Football," University of California at Berkeley, July 2005, accessed August 20, 2016, http://eml.berkeley.edu/~dromer/papers/PAPER_NFL_JULY05 _FORWEB_CORRECTED.pdf.

2 Psychologists call this form of cowardly thinking "loss aversion": when the undue fear of losing what one already possesses (in this case, a certain point from the point-after-touchdown kick) trumps the rational pursuit of greater gain.

3 The ground cannot cause a fumble when a runner's knee touches the ground before further contact with the ground knocks the ball loose. In that event, the runner is considered tackled, and the play over, when the knee touches. In the case of a diving catch where the receiver's torso or outstretched arm hits the ground first, then he should be required to maintain possession of the ball to complete the catch, consistent with controlling the ball "long enough," that is, until return to ground.

11. OVERRATED

1 Chicago Bears running back Marion Barber unnecessarily ran out of bounds near the end of the game, stopping the clock and enabling Denver's Matt Prater to subsequently tie the score with a fifty-nine-yard field goal with three seconds remaining.

SELECTED BIBLIOGRAPHY

Barra, Allen. *Clearing the Bases: The Greatest Baseball Debates of the Last Century*. New York: Thomas Dunne Books, 2002.

———. *Mickey and Willie: Mantle and Mays, the Parallel Lives of Baseball's Golden Age*. New York: Crown Archetype, 2013.

Baumer, Benjamin, and Andrew Zimbalist. *The Sabermetric Revolution: Assessing the Growth of Analytics in Baseball*. Philadelphia: University of Pennsylvania Press, 2014.

Bowden, Mark. *The Best Game Ever*. New York: Atlantic Monthly Press, 2008.

Carroll, Will. *Saving the Pitcher: A Revolutionary Analysis of Pitching Injuries and How to Prevent Them*. Chicago: Ivan R. Dee, 2004.

Cherry, Robert. *Wilt: Larger Than Life*. Chicago: Triumph Books, 2004.

Donaghy, Tim. *Personal Foul: A First-Person Account of the Scandal That Rocked the NBA*. Sarasota, FL: Four Daughters LLC, 2010.

Faulkner, David. *The Last Hero: The Life of Mickey Mantle*. New York: Simon & Schuster, 1995.

Gibson, Bob, and Reggie Jackson, with Lonnie Wheeler. *Sixty Feet, Six Inches*. New York: Anchor Books, 2011.

Goldman, Steve, ed. *Extra Innings*. New York: Basic Books, 2012.

Gould, Stephen Jay. *Full House: The Spread of Excellence From Plato to Darwin*. New York: Three Rivers Press, 1996.

———. *Triumph and Tragedy in Mudville*. New York: Workman, 2005.

Gray, Scott. *The Mind of Bill James: How a Complete Outsider Changed Baseball*. New York: Doubleday, 2006.

Hirsch, Sheldon, and Alan Hirsch. *The Beauty of Short Hops: How Chance and Circumstance Confound the Moneyball Approach to Baseball*. Jefferson, NC: McFarland & Company, 2011.

Jackson, Phil. *The Last Season: A Team in Search of Its Soul*. New York: Penguin Press, 2004.

James, Bill. *The New Bill James Historical Baseball Abstract*. New York: The Free Press, 2001.

———. *The Bill James Gold Mine 2009*. Chicago: ACTA Sports, 2009.

———. *Solid Fool's Gold: Detours on the Way to Conventional Wisdom*. Chicago: ACTA Sports, 2011.

———. *Fools Rush Inn: More Detours on the Way to Conventional Wisdom.* Chicago: ACTA Sports, 2014.

Kahneman, Daniel. *Thinking, Fast and Slow.* New York: Farrar, Straus and Giroux, 2011.

Kaplan, Jim. *The Greatest Game Ever Pitched.* Chicago: Triumph Books, 2011.

Keri, Jonah, ed. *Baseball Between the Numbers.* New York: Basic Books, 2006.

———. *The Extra 2%: How Wall Street Strategies Took a Major League Baseball Team from Worst to First.* New York: Ballantine Books, 2011.

Kram, Mark. *Ghosts of Manila: The Fateful Blood Feud Between Muhammad Ali and Joe Frazier.* New York: Harper Collins, 2011.

Leavy, Jane. *The Last Boy: Mickey Mantle and the End of America's Childhood.* New York: HarperCollins, 2010.

Lewis, Michael. *Moneyball: The Art of Winning an Unfair Game.* New York: W. W. Norton, 2003.

McCallum, Jack. *:07 Seconds or Less: My Season on the Bench with the Runnin' and Gunnin' Phoenix Suns.* New York: Touchstone, 2006.

Moskovitz, Tobias J., and L. Jon Wertheim. *Scorecasting: The Hidden Influences Behind How Sports Are Played and Games Are Won.* New York: Crown Archetype, 2011.

Paulos, John Allen. *Inumeracy.* New York: Holt McDougal, 2001.

———. *A Mathematician Reads the Newspaper.* New York: Anchor Books, 1995.

Pierce, Gregory F. Augustine, ed. *How Bill James Changed Our View of Baseball.* Chicago: ACTA Sports, 2007.

Reisler, Jim. *The Best Game Ever: Pirates vs. Yankees, October 13, 1960.* New York: Carroll & Graf Publishers, 2007.

Remick, David. *King of the World.* New York: Random House, 1998.

Ross, John P. *The 1964 Phillies: The Story of Baseball's Most Memorable Collapse.* Jefferson, NC: McFarland & Company, 2005

Ruth, Babe, as told to Bob Considine. *The Babe Ruth Story.* New York: Scholastic Book Services, 1948.

Sherman, Ed. *Babe Ruth's Called Shot.* Guilford, CT: Lyons Press, 2014.

Tango, Tom M., Mitchel G. Lichtman, and Andrew E. Dolphin. *The Book: Playing the Percentages in Baseball.* Washington, DC: Potomac Books, 2007.

Tetlock, Philip E., and Dan Gardner. *Superforecasting: The Art and Science of Prediction.* New York: Crown Publishers, 2015.

Thorn, John, and Pete Palmer. *The Hidden Game of Baseball: A*

Revolutionary Approach to Baseball and Its Statistics. New York: Doubleday, 2005.

WEBSITE RESOURCES

The following websites provided most of the statistics cited in this book:

www.baseball-reference.com

www.basketball-reference.com

www.fangraphs.com

www.pro-football-reference.com

INDEX

Worthy, James, 130
wrestling, 124

Yastrzemski, Carl, 61
yips, the, 7
Yost, Ned, 70–74

Young, Vince, 198
Yount, Robin, 61

zero focus, 6–9, 170–72, 205nn2–3
Zimbalist, Andrew, 50–51
Zoubek, George, 88